From
MANGLE
to
MICROWAVE
The Mechanization of Household Work

To my mother,
Dinah Hardyment,
with love

CHRISTINA HARDYMENT

Polity Press

Copyright © Christina Hardyment 1988

First published 1988 by Polity Press
in association with Basil Blackwell
First published in paperback 1990

Editorial Office:
Polity Press, 65 Bridge St
Cambridge CB2 1UR, UK

Basil Blackwell Ltd
108 Cowley Road, Oxford OX4 1JF, UK

Basil Blackwell, Inc.
3 Cambridge Center
Cambridge, Massachusetts 02142, USA

British Library Cataloguing in Publication Data
A CIP catalogue record for this book is available from the British Library.

ISBN 0–7456–0206 1
ISBN 0–7456–0207–X (pbk)

Library of Congress Cataloging in Publication Data
Hardyment, Christina.
From mangle to microwave: the mechanization of household work/
Christina Hardyment.
    p. cm.
    Bibliography: p.
    Includes index.
    1. Household appliances—History—19th century. 2. Household
appliances—History—20th century. 3. Household appliances,
Electric—History—19th century. 4. Household appliances, Electric—
History—20th century. 5. Housewives—History—19th century.
6. Housewives—History—20th century. I. Title.
TX298.H37   1988
643′.6′09034–dc19   8727582
ISBN 0–7456–0206–1
ISBN 0–7456–0207–X (pbk)

Typeset in 10½ on 12 Palatino
by Cambrian Typesetters, Frimley, Surrey
Printed in Great Britain by
Page Bros Ltd, Norwich

Contents

Preface   vii

Acknowledgements   xi

1   Homes without Machines   1

2   Of Pig-iron and Parlourmaids   21

3   The Mechanical Tailor   41

4   Laundry Work   55

5   House-cleaning   77

6   The Bathroom   91

7   From Roasting-spit to Trained Lightning   113

8   Essential Kitchen Technology   137

9   Kitchen Gadgetry   157

10 The Domestic Mystique   177

Notes   200

Bibliography   203

Index   211

Man never is, but always to be blest. If with one part of his brain he invents a labour-saving appliance, the other lobes immediately create as much new labour as the apparatus saves.

Englishwoman's Domestic Magazine, 1867

Miles are walked in exchange for a feeling of perpetual defeat.

Ann Oakley, *Sociology of Housework*, 1974

There will be no true liberation of women until we get rid of the assumption that it will always be women who do housework and look after children – and mostly in their own homes.

Ellen Malos, *The Politics of Housework*, 1980

Home-making is house-keeping plus. The plus is the art, the individual variation, the creative work. The house-keeping is the science, the universal likenesses, the necessary activities which must be carried out in order that one may have more time and energy for the rest.

Lilian Gilbreth, *The Home-Maker and Her Job*, 1927

Preface

This book is full of idiosyncracies. It is the culmination of a personal obsession with old domestic machinery – sewing-machines in particular. I did the research for it when setting up house and looking after babies in the 1970s, a time when the problems and practices of domestic management were weighing me down heavily. Instead of running our house efficiently, I poked around back-street junk shops and wasted long hours derusting and oiling antiquated gadgets. There was clearly a deluded escapism in all this: perhaps I unconsciously expected them magically to perform all the housework overnight, just as the elves did for the shoemaker.

By the time we had accumulated nearly forty ancient sewing-machines, many of them treadles, seven carpet-cleaners, a motley collection of small kitchen appliances and four children, there was a school of thought that felt one desk and a (modern) typewriter would take up a lot less room and provide just as effective a distraction. So the book was not originally written as an argument – I set out to give a detailed descriptive history of the mechanization of the household in Britain and the United States (the two countries' development in this sphere are almost inseparably connected) from the time of the Great Exhibition in London in 1851 up to the middle of the twentieth century. I wanted to know exactly how washing-machines worked and how long the old machines took to wash; who invented the corkscrew and why; what it was that women really did, minute by minute, in those grimy smoke-stained kitchens that novels and films still hark back to with sentimental nostalgia. I still do not know all the details, and I am aware that this is in many ways a highly eclectic collection of facts – I have only touched the tip of the iceberg. But as far as I know, no one has ever assembled so many of the extremely scattered references that relate to the invention, design, development and cost of domestic appliances. It is meant as a sketch – with enough vivid detail to bring to life the importance of the machines that we all now take so much for granted, and also a useful guide for more systematic research.

I took 1851 as my starting-point because the generously illustrated catalogue of the 'Great Exhibition of Arts and Manufactories' in London's Crystal Palace was a convenient summary of the achievements thus far. Most of my information came from the grass roots – manufacturers' catalogues, trade journals, magazines and household manuals. I have to admit to a loss of interest in the machines around the time of the Second World War. Flimsy, imperfect, over-styled, they no longer seemed much worth admiring. They were intended to be replaced; they were no longer the staunch allies of the household that the massive cast-iron Bradford mangle or the everlasting Aga cooker were designed to be. To my mind today's fussy Magimix food processor cannot compare with a Spong Tinned Meat-Mincer, nor an ingeniously hi-tech Hoovermatic with the solid thrum of a Thor washer. My mother-in-law's 1937 Thor has seen out two of my own tinny Italian jobs. Now I don't have one at all – I use a reliable launderette with a service wash. So the machines that I describe in the most detail are the ones that appeal to the lover of nostalgia, the man or woman whose head turns when a veteran car goes by, and who bids with enthusiasm at auctions for an old coffee-grinder or marmalade-slicer.

But although this book is largely a celebration of the innovatory inventions – some lunatic, many inspired – which transformed domestic labour between 1851 and 1951, it proved impossible to ignore the message driven home by studying the development of domestic technology. Some massive opportunities have been missed in our efforts to relieve domestic drudgery over the last hundred years. For drudgery it apparently remains – experts have calculated that many women work as long or longer hours in the home than their great-great-grandmothers did. Why?

First it began to strike me that the machines we use are not necessarily the most desirable ones available. Because our economy is now based on the home as a major consumer, there is a vested interest among manufacturers to make domestic appliances short-lived, in-efficient objects, bought by households on a one-to-one basis. In 1922, an enthusiast for the new domestic machines estimated that a washing-machine would last twenty years. Today, for all the improvements in its washing and spinning action, its lifespan is around seven years. Since this pattern extends to cookers, vacuum cleaners and many of the smaller machines that save time in the house, there is a profligate waste of mineral resources and energy nation-wide.

This pattern is not simply a matter of conspiracy by get-rich-quick manufacturers. It is the logical outcome of the mistaken belief that machines could replace the servants, children and dependent relatives who were once part of the domestic economy of the family. The responsibility for carrying out household chores now lies more heavily than it ever did in the lap of the housewife, instead of being shared between members of a family, friends and the community. It is also only in the last fifty years that over 50 per cent of housewives are using what the Rolling Stones called 'little helpers' in the shape of tranquillizers and anti-depressants to help them through their 'busy day'.

There once were, and still could be, different ways of arranging things. Throughout the book, I have examined alternatives to the one-house, one-machine pattern that afflicts modern domestic management, and in my concluding chapter I argue that today very few machines are actually needed in the home: what we need are more professional agencies servicing it from the outside.

The plan of the book then, is to give a preliminary sketch of the practical management of pre-mechanical domestic life, contrasting the worlds of the rich and the poor. The next chapter looks at the allied technologies which had to be developed before domestic appliances could be mass-produced, and examines other influences on the timing of their widespread adoption – above all, the introduction of the small electric motor, and the disappearance of the servant class. Successive chapters concentrate on the details of technical advances in the various areas of household management that have been most affected by machines: sewing, laundry, cleaning, bathing and cooking. Inevitably, the emphasis at this point is on the well-equipped homes of the prosperous middle and upper classes – it was there that the new frontier of domestic machinery made its greatest impact. Not until the construction of the 'homes for heroes' built after the First World War did appliances become part of the daily life of Mr and Mrs Average.

Interestingly, it becomes clear that in terms of liberating women from domesticity rather than merely saving them time and effort, the most successful domestic appliance has been the sewing-machine. In the beginning, it alleviated the labour of sewing enormously; ultimately, by making mass production of garments possible, it has removed the task from the home completely. An examination of the history of the mechanization of laundry work and cleaning in this light suggests that there was no reason why these major tasks could not have followed the same route out of the home. Bathrooms, I concede, are conveniences no home should be without, although we may be the poorer for the lost camaraderie of the public tubs of the ancient world and the Middle Ages. The kitchen is a problematic and disputed area because food is so important psychologically, but there are undoubtedly options more imaginative than the treadmill of fortnightly menus which Shirley Conran's *Superwoman* offers to the 'jaded cook'.

Finally I have given an overview of the 'improvements' in household appliances since the Second World War, and considered them in relation to current understandings of the vitally important concept of home-making. What lies behind the apparently compulsive female urge to spend incredibly long hours on unnecessary housework? Is it atavistic nest-building or filling up empty hours? Ultimately, the evidence is that the problem of the woman who is still 'chained to the sink' is not one of technology but of psychology. The critical distinction between the role of the housewife and the matter of housework, to which Ann Oakley drew attention in her seminal study, *The Sociology of Housework*, has still not been clearly enough appreciated. Until it is, the chances are that the majority of women in affluent western societies will continue to run poor seconds to men in the career stakes – not because they are deliberately oppressed or discriminated against, but because they are profoundly handicapped by their own psychological make-up from seizing the technological means to liberate themselves.

Acknowledgements

The groundwork of the research for this book was the collection of trade periodicals and domestic magazines held by the British Library Newspaper Library at Colindale, and the collection of domestic appliances at the London Science Museum. The staffs of both these institutions were unfailingly helpful and patient, particularly Frank Alflatt of the Science Museum. I would also like to thank the staff of the Cambridge University Library, the London Library, the Science Museum Library, the Museum of Rural Life at Reading. The late Mr Barnett of Reading University kindly made available his outstandingly fine collection of sewing-machines. The National Trust was kind enough to direct me to the most suitable of its many historic properties, and these and folk museums and historical societies in Britain and America have all added most usefully to the still very incomplete history of the mechanization of domestic life.

My second debt is to the present-day manufacturers of domestic appliances who have had the historical sense to keep examples and records of their early history, and who generously made these available to me: Hoover, Bex-Bissell, Parkinson-Cowan, Morphy-Richards, Smith and Wellstood, Aga, Belling, Frigidaire, Electrolux, Birdseye; Doulton and Co., Spong, Enterprise, Hotpoint, Ewbank, Siemens, Goblin, Singer, Jones, Armitage-Shanks and Twyfords.

Thirdly, although none of my friends had the technical knowledge to add to this book, I must thank Elizabeth Crawford for her constant interest, Nicola and Chris Beauman for reviving my flagging spirits, Peter Bowie for the rigorous logic that indirectly provoked the conclusion. Most of all I am indebted to my husband Tom Griffith for his support, advice and constant encouragement.

The author and publishers are grateful to the following for their kind permission to reproduce illustrations: Ann Ronan Picture Library (p. 144); The BBC Hulton Picture Library (pp. 131, 181); Bissell

Appliances Ltd (p. 79); The British Library (pp. 61, 68, 100, 124, 137, 148, 167, 169); The British Library © The Condé Nast Publications Limited (p. 153); The British Library and Frigidaire Consolidated Limited (p. 141); The British Library and *Ladies' Home Journal* (p. 174); The British Library and Siemens (p. 85); *Country Life* (p. 5); Culver Pictures (p. 3); David Mellor Design Limited, Sloane Square, London (p. 156); Gerald Duckworth & Co. Ltd. (p. 136); John Jaques & Son Limited (p. 184); The Maids, Oxford (p. 196); The Mansell Collection (p. 96); Mary Evans Picture Library (pp. 10, 13, 26, 29, 44, 112, 152); Museum of the City of New York (pp. 9, 16, 40); The National Trust (pp. 2, 115); The New-York Historical Society, New York City (pp. 73, 118); Penguin Books Limited © Frederick Warne & Co., 1905, p. 5, (photograph The National Trust) (p. 54); A Private Collection (pp. 105, 173); State Historical Society of Wisconsin (p. 35); The Tate Gallery, London (p. xiv); Trustees of the Science Museum, London (pp. 24, 43, 72, 95, 107, 125, 164); The Wimbledon Sewing Machine Company Limited (p. 49); Paula Youens and The Women's Press Limited (p. 176). All other photographs were kindly supplied by the author.

Primitive conditions lasted well into the twentieth century: poor light, stone floors, heavy pans and tedious tasks such as plucking and drawing poultry
(F. W. Elwell, *Beverley Arms Kitchen*, 1919)

1

Homes without Machines

To a woman the home is life militant, to a man it is life in repose.
Anon, A Further Notion or Two about Domestic Bliss, 1870

Traditionally, a home should supply its members with comfort: shelter, warmth and nourishment. What was involved in keeping the family well-fed, warm and clean in 1851?

When there were virtually no machines in the home, most families spent at least twice as long making themselves less than half as comfortable as they are today. A few – the very rich who could afford to keep a large staff of servants – spent rather less time on house management and in some ways lived even more luxuriously than their modern counterparts. Consequently, the contrast between different classes in domestic life used to be extremely wide. Squalid Liverpool cellar dwellings, crawling with rats and dripping with water, and fever-ridden Chicago tenements had nothing remotely in common with the gracious English country manors or the brownstone mansions of New York.

Today we can sketch a Mr and Mrs Average who are familiar to everybody. They have two children, a car, a three-bedroomed house with a bathroom, a gas or electric cooker, vacuum cleaner, washing-machine and sewing-machine and to some extent these attributes govern their way of life. A redundant shipbuilder qualifying for welfare payments could possess some or all of them, so too could a wealthy stockbroker, and neither would see any incongruity in their both doing so. There might be differences in the quality of their possessions, but they are no longer the startling ones that marked the gulf between Disraeli's 'two nations – the Rich and the Poor'. No one now buys used tea-leaves from prosperous back doors to resell to the needy.

Another crucial fact about the pattern of domestic arrangements in the last 200 years is that the Industrial Revolution has turned the home from a productive unit into a consuming maw, and from a nest and refuge to a 'physical service station', a battery of bought conveniences from which individuals recharge themselves with food and sleep. Before 1851 it was a place where bread was baked, beer brewed, clothes made. Today it is more like a shop window.

To give a full account of each aspect of home-making in the mid-nineteenth century would fill a book longer than this one; to be brief about everything would not give a powerful enough impression of the work involved. So I have spotlighted some of the major tasks in order to emphasize how labour-intensive domestic life used to be.

Kitchen Tasks

Without shops as we know them, the kitchen required expert management. Non-perishable foods had to be bought in bulk at the

A view of the nineteenth-century kitchens at Cragside, Northumbria

**Ice harvested by steam-cutters on the St Lawrence river,
North America, was exported all over the world**

appropriate season, and then stored carefully. Anne Cobbett 'kept a
quantity of rice more than three years by spreading a well-aired linen
sheet in a box and folding it over the rice'. The sheet was lifted out onto
the floor once every two or three months and the rice spread about on it
for a day or two. This 'had the effect of keeping away the weevil'. Tea,
coffee, sugar, cocoa, mustard, pepper and spices 'will last many years',
she assured readers of her *English Housekeeper* (1835). A larder was
necessary for more perishable stuffs, and large houses had several,
including one specifically for game. Meat, said Anne Cobbett, 'should
be examined every day . . . Scrape off the outside if there is the least
appearance of mould on mutton, beef or venison, and flour the scraped
parts. By well peppering meat you will keep away flies, or the joint may
be saved by being wrapped in a cloth and buried overnight in a hole
dug in fresh earth'.

Compared with our casual tossing of a joint into the controlled
temperature of a refrigerator, such vigilance was time-consuming in the
extreme and unlikely to prevent severe tainting of the meat. The
preserving properties of ice were understood very early on, however –
in 1626 Francis Bacon died of a chill caught while gathering snow to
stuff into the body cavity of a chicken and so keep it fresh. In the United
States many farmers looked on ice as a winter harvest, cutting it first
with horse-drawn, later steam-powered saws, and by the middle of the

nineteenth century ice was big business. Mr Tudor of Boston was exporting 160,000 tons a year by 1850, sending it by sailing-clippers as far afield as Calcutta. He conceived the brilliant plan, sadly never executed, of capturing, grappling and towing an entire iceberg into Boston harbour. Besides the great ice-depots of Portland, Maine, almost every town had its local companies to provide what was felt to be a necessity of life in the long hot summers. The American Wenham Lake Ice Company sent ice to Britain, as did Scandinavia. In a cold winter, ice could be collected locally – the shallow inland waters of the British fens, Norfolk and Suffolk, produced a regular supply of ice, transported across the Broads in huge pitch-blackened wherries. Ice was delivered to the home by an iceman, driving a sawdust-lined cart, and then kept in an insulated chest. This could be improvised from a barrel packed with sacks and sawdust, or be one of the purpose-built veneered cabinets displayed at the Great Exhibition. Great country houses had their own ice-houses in the grounds, often elegantly disguised as pagoda or temple. Many of these were mechanical triumphs in their own right – at Ashridge in Hertfordshire a pulley system raised or lowered the ice and three sets of doors conserved the low temperatures inside.

Keeping food fresh was difficult. Most of it arrived in much cruder form than we are used to today. Whole carcasses might have to be dismembered, potted and salted. The killing of the family pig was an affair of general interest, and nothing was wasted – black puddings were made up from the blood, sausages from the intestines. Butter was bought by the firkin (56lbs) and then patted into table-sized portions with beautifully carved butter-pats. Sugar came in huge cones, was chopped into lumps with great tong-like shears called sugar-nippers, and then ground into powder with a pestle in a mortar. Vegetables and fruit could only be bought in season, so bottling and preserving were important skills in a well-run kitchen. Wine and beer was often home-brewed, bread home-baked and milk processed in the dairy to provide milk, butter and cheese.

All these highly labour-intensive tasks were performed in extremely primitive surroundings. Stone-flagged floors, bare wooden tables and slate larder shelves had to be scrubbed frequently. Wood ash was used to scour the iron, copper and brass kitchen utensils. The kitchen sink was a shallow stone rectangle: cold, rough and a popular playground for slugs. Water had to be pumped into it, or brought in from an outside wall. A wooden bowl was used to protect china and glass, and if a draining-board existed it too was of wood. It required careful preparation – several coats of linseed oil rubbed into it each night for two weeks gave it a good water-repellent surface. When in time dirt and slime accumulated, it had to be scoured off and re-treated.

**The exterior of the Temple of the Winds Ice-House,
West Wycombe**

The actual cooking of the food was still carried out on the wide open hearth of medieval times in many parts of the country, but more modern houses had simple iron ranges fitted to the chimney-breast. Fires were still open, and the old equipment of spit, chimney crane and idle-back was retained. Sometimes a turnspit was used, to economize on the cook's time. Some were powered by a dog, or even a small child,

Crude cooking arrangement and dog turnspit in an ale-house kitchen

working a treadmill; others, such as that in Brighton Pavilion, featured an elaborate battery of connecting rods and cog-wheels geared to a chimney fan turned by the fire's own heat. Although the quality of the roast meat achieved by such methods was often excellent, the labour of attending to the fire and cleaning the blackened pans and smoke-begrimed kitchen afterwards kept a kitchen-maid busy all day.

Labour-intensive cooking methods were only part of the problem. Eating habits among the rich outdid anything we know today. Breakfast alone was a substantial culinary challenge – it was also seen as vitally important. 'The moral and physical welfare of mankind depends largely on its breakfast,' wrote Mrs Beeton in her definitive work on household management in 1861:

> There are over two hundred ways of cooking eggs, to say nothing of grilled chops, steaks, cutlets, kidneys, fish and mushrooms, anchovy and sardine toast, sausage rolls, sausages broiled or fried, meat patties, rissoles, croquettes and croutes, fish omelettes, fish cakes, fish soused and kedgeree, pressed beef, galantine of beef, potato chips, potatoes fried in a variety of ways, and a host of other inexpensive and easily prepared dishes.[1]

Luncheon was a light meal by Victorian standards, but it still featured an hors-d'œuvre or fish course before the main entrée and a pudding. These two meals were a mere preliminary to the real business of the day: the dinner. In the second half of the century the customary succession of courses was hors d'œuvre, soup, fish, entrée, roast, pudding, savoury and desert. Earlier on, the fashionable either dined *à la Française*, which involved the spreading out of two successive courses, each containing a selection of dishes, or were given the more labour-intensive and long-drawn out dinner *à la Russe*, at which each dish was presented and withdrawn by a flurry of footmen. Mrs Beeton's specimen menus for 'normal' family consumption show the scale of the daily effort and expertise required by even an ordinary family cook, and dinner parties were of course much more lavish. A choice had to be offered at each course, and the number of dishes increased with the length of the guest list. At a top-flight meal thirty or forty options were quite usual.

Quantity was equalled by quality. Elaborate sauces, gravies and creams had to be offered as garnishes, and without food processors or convenient little packets from the grocer even that simplest of puddings, the jelly, meant hard work. This is Mrs Rundell's recipe for orange jelly – delicious, undoubtedly, but hardly the thing for a modern working mum to whip up for a toddler's tea:

Simmer eight ounces of hartshorn shavings with two quarts of water until it reduces to one; strain it, and boil it with the rinds of four China oranges and two lemons pared thin; when cold, add

A supper buffet for ball room or evening party
(Mrs Beeton, *Household Management*)

the juices of both, half a pound of sugar, and the whites of six eggs beaten to a froth; let the jelly have three or four boils without stirring, and strain it through a jelly bag.[2]

Of course the mass of people had neither the time nor the money to eat in this style. At the very bottom of the social scale, wood sawdust was being made into bread[3]. It needed a great deal of yeast, and was 'improved' by the addition of cereal flour. Records of workhouses and hospitals such as this list of menus for the Grey Coat Hospital, Westminster, reveal the farcical contrast between the diets of rich and poor. The two events of the week were beef broth on Sunday and frumenty (a wheat porridge) on Wednesday:

Sunday	Breakfast	Bread and butter
	Dinner	Beef broth and peas
	Supper	Bread and cheese
Monday	Breakfast	Bread and butter
	Dinner	Bread and butter
	Supper	Bread and cheese
Tuesday	Breakfast	Halfpenny roll
	Dinner	Bread and butter
	Supper	Bread and cheese
Wednesday	Breakfast	Bread and Butter
	Dinner	Frumenty
	Supper	Bread and cheese
Thursday	Breakfast	Halfpenny roll
	Dinner	Broth
	Supper	Bread and cheese
Friday	Breakfast	Bread and butter
	Dinner	Peas porridge
	Supper	Bread and cheese
Saturday	Breakfast	Halfpenny roll
	Dinner	Milk porridge
	Supper	Bread and cheese

Such monotonous and nutritionally unbalanced diets were a nineteenth-century commonplace. Soups, pulses, cheese and bread were the staple foods. The kitchen appliances intended to relieve the work of the high-class cook had no relevance to the poor until living standards rose enough to allow them to eat nourishing and varied meals.

Laundry Work

The weekly wash was the heaviest of all the household tasks, a commonly acknowledged cause of breakdown in women's health. A

From millionaire's tea-party to cellar subsistence:
rich and poor at table, New York, 1864

**Washing-dolly and tub in use in the late nineteenth century
at Staithes, Yorkshire**

research project by the Maytag washing-machine company re-
constructed nineteenth-century washing conditions and estimated that
'The old washday was as exhausting as swimming five miles of
energetic breast-stroke, arm movements and general dampness
supplying an almost exact parallel'. Anyone who could afford the
money, paid someone else to do it. The washerwoman, ideally 'a
brawny female with muscular arms and a tireless back', took the
washing away on Mondays and returned it on Thursdays. Public
washing-grounds were very ancient institutions, centres of gossip and
community contact. They were generally set up near running water of
some sort, and provided tubs, boilers over open fires, wide tables and
clothes-lines.

Substantial country houses had their own laundries, and could
probably find full-time work for special laundry-maids. There would be
a washhouse, an ironing- and drying-room, and sometimes a drying-

closet heated by a furnace or gas. The washhouse had a range of wooden tubs and a stove to heat the copper wash-boilers. In the ironing-room stood a strong white deal table, about fourteen feet long, clothes-horses for airing, and a mangle for smoothing table and bed-linen. Starching equipment would be kept here, and another stove for heating the irons. Steam from that stove might be directed into drying-closets, as it was in Cardiff's extraordinary Castel Coch, a late nineteenth-century gothic extravaganza furnished with every available domestic convenience.

What exactly did washing entail? An account of old-time washing processes could make it clear why so few people used to achieve the standards of cleanliness that we take for granted today. Work began on Monday. Clothes were sorted, serious stains removed, and soaked in lukewarm water and soda. On Tuesday the real labour started:

> Early in the morning, fires should be lighted, and as soon as hot water can be procured, washing commenced; the sheets and body linen wanted to whiten in the morning should be taken first; each article being removed from the lye in which it has been soaking, rinsed, rubbed and wrung, and laid aside until the tub is empty, when water is drawn off. The tub should again be filled with luke-warm water, about 80°, in which the articles should again be plunged and each gone over again carefully with soap. Novices in the art sometimes rub the linen against the skin; more experienced washerwomen rub one linen surface against the other, which saves their hands, and enables them to continue their labour much longer. Besides economising time, two parts being thus cleansed at once. After the first washing, the linen should be put into a second water, as hot as the hand can bear it, and again be rubbed over, examining every part for spots not yet removed, which require to be again soaped over and rubbed until thoroughly clean; then rinsed and wrung, the larger and stronger articles by two of the women, the smaller and more delicate articles requiring gentler treatment:

> In order to remove every particle of soap and produce a good colour, they should now be placed and boiled for about an hour and a half in the copper, in which soda, in the proportions of a teaspoonful to every two gallons of water has been dissolved. Some very careful laundresses put the linen in a canvas bag to protect it from scum and the sides of the copper. When taken out, it should again be rinsed, first in clean hot water, and then in an abundance of cold water, slightly tinged with blue and again wrung dry. It should now be removed from the wash-house and hung up to dry or spread out to bleach, if there are conveniences

for it, and the earlier in the day this is done, the clearer and whiter will be the linen.[4]

Lengthy and boring as the last two paragraphs may have been to read, they were only a small extract from Mrs Beeton's six pages of instructions, and dealt only with the relatively simple 'white wash'. Laundry was made even harder work by the fashions of the time. Comfortably remote from the wash-tub, ladies dressed themselves in layer upon layer of delicate fabrics, trimmed with ribbons and lace which had to be removed and sewn on again every time the garment was washed. In winter, shift, chemise, petticoat and pantalettes were *de rigueur* foundations for overdresses of merino wool or bombazine trimmed with fur. All clothes were made from natural fibres – silk, wool, linen and cotton – which required great care in handling to avoid shrinkage, crumpling and colours running.

Clothes were not only washed by hand. It is very difficult to imagine a world without ready-made clothes, and yet it is only just over a hundred years since every stitch had to be made manually. The female members of a household spent a large part of their leisure time with a needle of one sort or another in their hands – plain sewing, tatting, crochet, knitting or embroidery. No drawing-room was complete without its sewing-box or table, and servants too were expected to sew in any quiet hour of the day. In lower-income groups it was not just sewing for the family that made life miserable. For many wives, the only way to make ends meet was to take in ill-paid 'piece-work', ruining their eyes and their health by sewing late into the night by inadequate light. Although the clothes were bought from professional tailors and seamstresses, it was women's sweated labour that made everything from high-society finery to the most basic of masculine garments:

> Two o'clock in the morning chimed the old bells of St Saviours. And yet, more than a dozen girls still sat in the room into which Ruth entered, stitching away as if for very life, not daring to yawn or show any outward manifestation of sleepiness. They only sighed a little as Ruth told Mrs Mason the hour of the night as a result of her errand, for they knew that, stay up late as they might, the work-hours of the next day must begin at eight, and their young limbs were very weary.[5]

In *Ruth* Mrs Gaskell described the misery of girls bent over the frills and furbelows of an overdue ball-gown. Tom Hood's famous ballad, *The Song of a Shirt*, publicized such exploitation even more vividly:

'The Broken Contract', by M. Ellen Edwards, 1886:
a tragedy that paralleled those of the earlier seamstresses

With fingers weary and worn,
With eye-lids heavy and red,
A woman sat in unwomanly rags,
Playing her needle and thread –

Stitch, stitch, stitch,
In poverty, hunger and dirt,
Sewing at once, with a double thread,
A shroud as well as a shirt.

O men with sisters dear,
O men with mothers and wives,
It is not linen you're wearing out,
But human creatures' lives!

House-cleaning

The furnishings and fittings of prosperous homes in the last century displayed just as magnificent a disregard for practicality as did the clothes of their inmates. There were acres of highly polished mahogany, quantities of brass and copper lamps and fire-irons, intricate glass chandeliers, epergnes and vases, heavy velvet curtains and upholstery. Coal-fires in every room, candles and oil-lamps meant a constantly reimposed layer of dust, grime and soot, and without vacuum cleaners dust tended to be redistributed rather than banished. As with laundry work, it seems worth spelling out in detail the actual process of house-cleaning in order to give the most vivid picture possible of what was involved in attaining the exacting standards of a Victorian housekeeper such as Mrs Haweis:

> A fair-sized room takes full three hours to clean properly, and the housemaid must not begin later than ten on such mornings. All the ornaments have to be removed to another room or packed onto a central table and covered with a clean dust sheet, like the chairs, which should be rubbed and brushed *before* turning out the room; then comes the sweeping, after which the housemaid will make time to run down for her 'lunch' of bread and cheese and glass of – let us hope not beer. The dust takes half an hour to settle, and during this process a few ornaments can be washed or metal goods polished. Then comes the tidying and the beeswaxing, and last the dusting.[6]

In order to get through the rooms of a large house, cleaning fortnightly is advised, and a timetable might run:

	First week	Second week
Monday	Servant's bedroom and another	Two small bedrooms
Tuesday	Drawing-room	Library
Wednesday	Washing, stairs and rods	Washing, stairs and rods
Thursday	Best bedroom and dressing-room	Waiting-, school- or odd room
Friday	One or two bedrooms	Bathroom, or other
Saturday	Upper passages	Central passages

This was just morning work for one housemaid. She was expected to dress to answer the door in the afternoon, and, if not too busy with callers, clean the plate and the lamps, and fit in a couple of hours needlework.

There seems to be no truth in the view that our great-grandparents willingly tolerated much more dust and dirt than we do today. As long as they could afford to be kept clean, they not only sent maids scurrying around their over-furnished houses but ordained an annual spring-cleaning as well. Traditionally it started on the 25 March, when fires were left off for the summer. If the master and mistress of the house were fortunate enough to have an efficient housekeeper, they exited completely into hotels or lodgings. The sweep would be invited in, and then the empty fireplace made less desolate by decorating it imaginatively. A looking-glass or trellis might form a foil for plants – creepers, nasturtium and clematis were all popular. Pots of maidenhair fern, lobelias or begonias could be embedded in moss underneath them. Also popular were cascades of paper or tinsel fronds which could be bought from the ironmonger or improvised from strips of worn-out muslin.

In the preliminary paragraph of her lengthy chapter on the subject, Mrs Beeton summarized the annual cleaning process:

> All white-washing, painting and general repairs, should be done in the spring, and during the cleaning carpets should be taken up, well-beaten and turned so as to bring the worn pieces out of sight. Care must be taken to match the design of the carpet. All ornaments should be carefully washed, cleaned or relacquered. Curtain poles taken down, washed with vinegar, and rubbed bright with furniture polish. Looking glasses cleaned. Chairs and sofas recovered or invested with loose chintz covers. Wallpaper rubbed down with quartern loaves. Ornaments placed in fire-stoves, and white summer curtains hung up in place of damask or chintz, which should be well-shaken, folded in large folds, with a couple of handfuls of dry bran laid between each fold, and a piece of camphor placed in the drawer or box in which they are kept . . . locks should now be taken off, cleaned and oiled, bell wires adjusted, and bell-handles tightened if necessary.[7]

Not only was cleaning thorough to a degree that certainly makes my housekeeping slipshod; all the polishes and soaps with which a respectable lustre was given to furniture, stoves, boots, windows and floors, had to be made at home. Exotic as ingredients such as pounded galls and hogwood chips, ivory black and spirits of wine seem on the pages of the recipe books, they must have been messy and tedious to mix. Wooden tables and draining-boards were scoured with a mixture of lime and sand.

Despite this cult of cleanliness, few kitchens were free of bugs of one sort or another. Haweis recorded a particularly disgusting infestation.

> In a house I once lived in, only newly built, which should have been free, the beetles would collect in corners of the kitchen ceiling, and hanging to one another by their claws, would form huge bunches or swarms like bees towards evening, and as night closed in, swarthy individuals would drop singly on to floor, or head, or food, or whatever happened to be under them. This nice

**Berendsohn's poison could be spread as a paste or puffed about
through bellows, New York, 1864**

state of things was not resented by the maids. They only said,
'you can't help beetles'.[8]

Cleanliness was the more difficult to achieve in the absence of
running hot or cold water in the house. In 1851 bathrooms were a rare
novelty, although interest in them was growing. In previous ages, if one
bathed at all, the public baths or a portable tub was all that was
available. The decision to make the long tub the standard way of taking
a bath was an uncertain one, arrived at surprisingly late in the
nineteenth century. Earlier on, keen hygienists debated the respective
merits of steam-baths, gas-heated baths, sea-bathing, and icy showers
taken – in Austria at least – under the gushing spout of an open-air pipe
hacked from split tree-trunks and fed by a natural spring. In the home,
a shower- or small hip-bath was more usual than a long tub. Not
everyone advocated bathing – many doctors thought it could be a

debilitating practice, tending to effeminacy. A more powerful dis-
incentive to widespread tubbing, however, was the heavy labour
involved in preparing and clearing up after the fortunate bather.

To begin with, a very large quantity of water had to be pumped up
and carried to the washing copper or kitchen boiler in bucket-loads.
Eventually rather less hot water than we would find adequate, but
much more than the housemaid enjoyed carrying upstairs, would
arrive at the bath-tub. This, in the best sort of 'Upstairs, Downstairs'
household, would be arranged on a bath-sheet beside a fleecy rug in
front of a blazing fire in the bedroom. Screens cut off draughts, a huge
towel warmed on the fender. The idle rich stumbled out of bed, sipped
their morning tea among the suds, squeezed soft unguents over
themselves through giant sponges, were patted dry by a neatly
uniformed maid and wrapped in a thick Turkish-towelling robe. Then
all the paraphernalia of cleanliness was whisked out of sight.

Whisked? The scullery-maid had to lug the cold scummy suds down
several flights of stairs to the nearest sink. The bath, originally a hefty
affair of wood lined with lead, had to be dragged away, cleaned and
dried. Towels and the bath-sheet were laundered after every use. It was
hardly surprising that bathing in less wealthy households was a
sketchy, infrequent affair. At the other end of the social scale, a small
tinned metal tub was brought out in front of the kitchen fire once a
week, and the family took turns to bath in it. But in the rapidly growing
cities, there might not be enough water for even a weekly bath.
J. Riddall Wood, a contemporary critic, gave evidence on slum
conditions in Liverpool in a parliamentary report of 1840:

> There is a good supply of water for the poor, if they had a means
> of preserving it. The water is turned on a certain number of times
> a day, four hours perhaps, the poor go to the tap for it; it is
> constantly running, and each poor person fetches as much as they
> have pans to receive; but they are not well supplied with these
> articles, and in consequence they are frequently out of water. It is
> not sufficient for washing or anything of that kind.

Edwardian Bermondsey was even worse off than nineteenth-century
Liverpool. Alfred Salter's childhood home there was described by his
biographer Archibald Fenner Brockway:

> The house was one up, one down, with a small scullery and no
> backyard except a shut-in paved area three foot deep. Drying and
> washing was done in the front court, where at the other end there
> was one stand-pipe for twenty-five houses with the water 'on' for
> two hours daily, though never on Sundays. There was no place to

Queues at the street plug, Bethnal Green, London
(*Illustrated Times*, 1863)

wash in, no other water to wash in. There was no modern
sanitation. There was one WC for the twenty-five homes and a
cesspool. Queues line up outside that WC, men, women, and
children, every morning before they went to work . . . There was
no possibility of decency, modesty or wealth for these people . . .
the conditions of thousands of other homes were the same.[9]

Earth-closets and cesspits were the rural solutions to the problem of
sanitation – in the crowded cities there was just not enough room for
them. Better-off homes might be equipped with a water-closet; their
early imperfect design meant that they frequently became blocked and
were never completely flushed. Night-soil men collected the cities'
excrement and sold it to the nearest farmers; as cities became larger,
such trade grew less practicable, sewers more inadequate and rivers
badly contaminated. Sir Edwin Chadwick compared army discipline in
such matters with the urban chaos in his 1842 *Report on the Sanitary
Conditions of the Labouring Poor of Great Britain:*

The towns which never change their encampment have no such
care, and whilst the houses, streets, courts, lanes and streams are

polluted and rendered pestilential, the civil officers have in general contented themselves with the most barbarous expedients, or sit amidst all the pollution with the resignation of Turkish fatalists under the supposed destiny of the prevalent ignorance, sloth and filth.

The latter-day pashas were shaken from their complacency by the mid-century epidemics of cholera and typhoid, epidemics that hit the rich as well as the poor. Sewers were one of the principal sources of infection, so houses with some pretence of sanitation were actually more at risk than homes without drains at all. When the Prince of Wales himself narrowly escaped death, real progress was set into motion, and the extraordinarily well-designed sewage network, one which still underlies our cities today, began to be constructed.

In conclusion, it is evident that although today's poor have undoubtedly benefited from the technological advances and mass-production techniques which have made labour-saving appliances relatively cheap and easily obtainable, it is possible that today's rich have experienced a decline in standards since the disappearance of the nineteenth-century servant class. However sophisticated a cooker or washing-machines, owning more than one of them does not make laundry better finished or sauces more subtly flavoured. Machines do not operate in the same way as people – for example, it is not worth programming one to iron, stitch down and perfume the pages of *The Times* every morning in the way a good butler once used to do. One of the by-products of the mechanization of the home is that domestic tasks have been simplified and ways of everyday living standardized to an extent undreamt-of in the bad old days when the Little Match Girl looked longingly through the windows of the wealthy.

Nineteenth-century gadget-consciousness: a bottle-jack put to novel use as a baby-bouncer (*Punch*, 1863)

2

Of Pig-iron and Parlourmaids

The bias of the nation is a passion for utility. They love the lever, the screw, the pulley, the Flanders draught horse, the waterfall, windmills, tidemills . . . Their toys are steam and galvanism.

Ralph Waldo Emerson, *English Traits*, 1833

In 1851, as the dramatic increase in patents registered between 1750 and 1850 shows, invention was a well-filled profession.

Number of British patents sealed each decade			
1750–9	92	1800–9	924
1760–9	205	1810–19	1124
1770–9	294	1820–9	1453
1780–9	477	1830–9	2453
1790–9	647	1840–9	4581

Britain was a world leader in industrial technology, and that technology was a vital prerequisite for the mechanization of the household. Without the right metals and the right sources of energy, the Industrial Revolution's achievements could not have been translated into domestic terms.

As later chapters will show, many of the prototypes of our most familiar domestic appliances were made of wood – the Yorkshire Maiden washer of 1750, Thimmonier's 1830 sewing-machine and Sharp's 1851 gas stove. Cast iron was much better suited to accurate and cheap mass production, but its availability was limited by the declining supplies of timber for charcoal. In 1709 Abraham Darby discovered that coked coal could be used to smelt iron, and in 1784 Henry Cort patented and developed the puddling and rolling process which produced a more purified and durable form of bar-iron. Charcoal fuel had meant manufacture scattered wherever wood was available. The use of coal, often found in the same area as iron, meant that mining, processing and final manufactures could all be carried out by the same or allied firms in one district. This produced good iron of uniform texture and reliability, and enormous operational economies. Cheap iron stimulated invention. 'Iron-mad Wilkinson' of Staffordshire made everything from ships to razors from iron and steel, coined his own iron money and insisted on being buried in an iron coffin under an iron monument. Cast iron could replace expensive hand-wrought iron, hand-carved wood and some of the brass used in domestic appliances.

Its disadvantage lay in its brittle quality. Massive-looking pieces of metal cracked if mishandled, and its efficiency for precision engineering was limited. Good quality, mass-produced steel was also needed. In the 1860s, Henry Bessemer developed the tilt furnace, making it possible to heat iron to the temperature necessary for its conversion into steel in large quantities. A chain of other improvements led to the establishment of a steel industry able to provide the metals and alloys indispensable to the advancement of iron technology.

The dynamic of the Industrial Revolution had been steam. Although domestic steam-engines were built – one even powered a sewing-machine – they were evidently not practical. The constant stoking necessary, the noise, dirt and heat and the danger to children, combined to make them unfit for use in the home. The first domestic machines were powered by hands or feet, using rotary motion. Given the sophisticated gearings of the early nineteenth century, the breadth and application of this simple principle was enormous, as an editorial in a trade gazette pointed out:

Year by year domestic inventions of every kind are increasing; and no matter whether we desire to clean knives or make stockings, peel potatoes, black shoes, make butter, wash clothes, stitch dresses, shell peas or even make our bread, all we have to do is turn a handle. We need not even mind the baby now, we can put it into a domestic appliance and it will mind itself, and if we have bad teeth, and consequently impaired indigestion, we need not trouble to masticate our food, but can put it through a machine and, of course, turn a handle. This is a regular handle-turning age, and we may soon expect to wash and dress ourselves, clean the windows, scrub the floors, lay the table, make our beds, and do every household operation through the same medium. We shall then only require a handle to appease a stormy wife, quiet a screaming baby, and pay the tax collector, and our domestic happiness will have reached perfection.[1]

Despite such optimism, handle-turning could be heavy work, and many housecraft experts expressed their doubts as to the merits of some of the early machines. Experiments with heavy mangles have shown that they could involve more labour than wringing the clothes out by hand. Handles could only be turned as fast as human energy and the quality of engineering allowed. Ironically, just as the technology of the bicycle and the motor car was perfecting such improvements as ball-bearings, domestic appliances turned to other sources of power. Arguably the cheap, energy-saving advantages of hand-turned appliances have never been adequately explored.

The mains services of water, gas and electricity which we take for granted today were only introduced into the average home in the early twentieth century. They made domestic lighting and heating far less trouble, as well as providing cheap and efficient sources of energy for machines in the home. Piped water was known as early as the eighteenth century, but it was an unusual luxury within the walls of a house. The growth of towns made its absence a serious health hazard, until the 1849 Public Health Act was passed as a result of Edwin Chadwick's enlightened campaign. Obviously, until unlimited tap-water was available in most homes, there could be no market for washing-machines or bathroom fittings.

Piped hot water had evidently become an accepted feature of better-class homes by the time Anthony Trollope published *Barchester Towers* in 1853, but perhaps not much before then. The expectations of the redoubtable Mrs Proudie clearly exceeded those of her predecessor:

Surely the palace should have been fitted through with pipes for gas, and for hot water too? There is no hot water laid on anywhere above the ground floor; surely there should be the means of getting hot water in the bedrooms without having it brought in jugs from the kitchen?

The bishop has a decided opinion that there should be pipes for hot water. Hot water was very essential for the comfort of the palace; it was indeed a requisite in any decent gentleman's house.

Such hot water would have been circulated from the kitchen range, a plumbing operation undertaken by only the most decent gentlemen of the time – but Mrs Proudie was a Russian vine among social climbers. As demand for it increased, however, and the kitchen range was replaced by the gas or electric stove, geysers and immersion heaters were developed to bring a former luxury within almost everybody's budget.

Hydraulic engineering was widely used in industry, and piped water was also regarded as a possible source of domestic energy. Water-

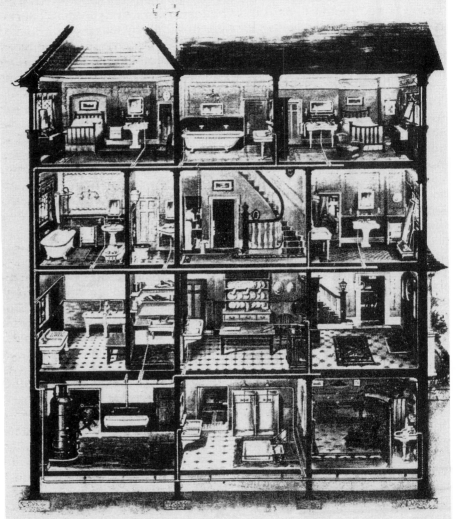

A cross-section of an early fully plumbed house in Ewart's Califont
water heater advertisement

motors, which fitted onto taps or underneath the appliance itself, were made to power vacuum cleaners, hair-dryers and sewing-machines. Like sophisticated handle-turning, it became fashionable once electricity was widely available, and remains extraordinarily unexploited. Perhaps one day inventors will turn again to what seems a most practical, cheap and pollution-free source of domestic power.

The most curious aspect of the development of coal gas as a source of domestic power was the length of time before it was used for anything except lighting. It had been toyed with for this purpose by various eighteenth-century experimenters living in coaling districts. In 1684 a Mr Clayton, rector of Crofton in Yorkshire, set light to pin-holes in a bladder of gas for the amusement of his friends. Some hundred years later, William Murdoch, Boulton and Watt's chief Cornish Engine builder, lit the rooms of his house at Redruth, Cornwall, by gas. He and Samuel Clegg pioneered the application of gas in industrial lighting. One of the first places to be lit was the famous Ackermann print factory in London. The jets were placed outside the windows, partly as a logical extension of daylight, partly to prevent the heat and fumes of the unrefined gas from affecting the workers.

The Gas, Light and Coke company began laying mains in Westminster in 1814, and by 1816 twenty-six miles of cast-iron pipe had been put down. The service pipes, known as barrels, as they were made on the same principle as ships' guns, were sometimes improvised from actual guns, the worn-out ordinance of the Napoleonic Wars. By 1825, the Lord Mayor of London's Mansion House had 2,062 burners for the benefit of the staff, but in his own parlour the mayor used only candles, as the gas lights were considered too hot and smelly. However, it was quickly recognized that for industry and places of entertainment, gas was far safer than candles. Theatres, cockpits, prize-rings were soon equipped with the unnaturally bright flares of gas burners.

Once techniques of purifying gas had been improved, and better burners and pressure-governors devised, the use of gas in the home became a matter of course. Gasworks were built in all considerable towns by 1849, and many country mansions had their own private gasholder in the grounds. In 1884, when William Sugg, the most talented nineteenth-century designer of gas appliances, wrote his book, *The Domestic Uses of Coal Gas*, he looked back at the achievements of the previous thirty years with pride, not unmixed, perhaps, with a defensive note. 'What a wonderful industry is gas manufacture, and how little its chief product deserves such erroneous epithets as "noxious compound" and the like which have been so freely bestowed upon it.'

By an 1869 Act of Parliament, the quality and constancy of the gas-supply required from the companies was specified, and in the 1880s Dr

**Early experiments with gas lighting were not greeted
with enthusiasm by Londoners**

Karl Auer, later Baron von Welsbach, invented the incandescent gas
mantle. It gave a more intense light, and used much less gas by
cloaking the naked gas flare with a cotton fabric impregnated with
thorium and cerium.

Although the gas that was piped into people's homes early in the
century could have been used to power all sorts of domestic appliances,
little interest was shown in exploiting its potential for water-heating,
room-warming, cooking, ironing or refrigeration. Only a handful of
cooking appliances were shown at the Great Exhibition, and none of
them were taken seriously. Michael Faraday had experimented with
the absorption principle of gas refrigeration as early as 1824 and
Ferdinand Carré had produced an ice-making machine worked by gas
in 1862, yet it was not until 1922 that gas refrigerators were developed.
Fears of explosion, faults in pipes and fittings and lack of exact

knowledge of its calorific value delayed serious development of its most important domestic function, heating, until later in the twentieth century.

Oil was a viable alternative source of power for heating and lighting, particularly useful in country areas where mains pipelines did not exist. At first animal and vegetable oils were used in lamps. Experiments with shale oils and asphalt in the 1840s and 1850s led to the development of paraffin, a light, relatively pleasant oil, which was to light the lamps of half the world by the end of the century. It would also be used for space-heating and cooking, but remained an auxiliary to coal and gas in Britain. In the United States, the boring of numberless oil wells in the 1860s led to the development of a vast oil industry. The crude oil was broken down into 'illuminating gas', paraffin wax, lubricants, fuel oils and excellent lamp oil. By 1874, Pennsylvania was producing ten million 360lb barrels a year. Only one by-product was regarded as useless and dangerous – gasoline, better known in this country as petrol. Oil was to the United States what coal was to Britain, and millions of homes grew to rely upon it as the basic fuel for heating and lighting.

All these sources of energy were replaced or displaced by the development of electricity. As Siegfried Giedion put it cogently in his excellent 1945 study of the development of technology, *Mechanisation Takes Command*, 'It meant to the mechanisation of the household what the wheel meant to moving loads.' As a source of light and heat it is cleaner, simpler and more convenient than any other fuel, and the application of the small electric motor to vacuum cleaners, washing-machines, food-mixers, sewing-machines, floor polishers and dish-washers has been seen as lightening household labour enormously. Nevertheless, as I will argue in chapter 10, it was the small electric motor more than any other invention which led to the development of domestic machinery along sadly isolationist channels, and took interest away from the community-based alternatives proposed by such thinkers as Charlotte Perkins Gilman and Mrs Havelock Ellis.

Electric lighting had been experimented with early in the nineteenth century – the Admiralty installed a carbon-arc light in the South Foreland Lighthouse in 1858. Carbon arc, although satisfactory for public lighting, was too brilliant and hot for the home, and it was not until 1878 that the American Thomas Edison and the Englishman Joseph Swan independently invented incandescent carbon-filament lamps for domestic use. Batteries, dynamos and electric motors, although still cumbersome and often inefficient, were also being developed to a degree that made the question of electricity supply to private homes as well as factories and public buildings a matter of great interest.

The first house in the world to be completely lit by electric light was the Glasgow home of the eminent scientist Lord Kelvin. In 1881, incandescent light blazed from his 106 one-time gas burners, now converted to electrical use. He even improvised what must have been the first-ever electric bedside light from a battery-powered Swan bulb fastened to the curtains by a safety-pin. His installation was powered by a dynamo driven by a gas-engine. In the same year, Sir William Armstrong, famous for his hydraulic experiments as well as his work with electricity, used a water turbine 1500 yards from his house at Cragside to light forty-five lamps. Most of them were veiled by ground-glass globes, reported *The Engineer* on 17 January 1881, although 'in the passages and the stairs the lamps are for the most part without glass shades and present a very beautiful and star-like appearance, not so bright as to pain the eye in passing, and very efficient for lighting the way.'

Thomas Edison and Joseph Swan joined forces to electrify the world, and the Edison–Swan company still exists today. The power stations at Deptford in London (1889) and Brooklyn, New York (1890) were the prototypes for generating stations all over Western Europe and the United States. In 1891 an American electricity manual could already envisage mains current being provided to power clocks, burglar and fire alarms, doorbells, a sewing-machine, a record-player, an electric fan and an electric stove.[2] By 1902, 8 per cent of American homes had mains electricity, and by 1948, 78 per cent. France, Germany, and other European countries were quick to follow suit, but progress in the United Kingdom was slowed down by the 1882 Electric Lighting Act. Still smarting from the notorious profits made by the railway, water and gas companies earlier in the century, the British government attempted to protect the public from exploitation by allowing tenure of plant for only twenty-one years, fixing prices and limiting each undertaking to a single municipal area. Despite an aggregate capital of £15 million, the companies formed between 1882 and 1883 to carry out public electricity supply were demoralized by the web of restrictions, and not one of the sixty-two provisional orders granted to companies in 1883 was taken up. The 1888 Electric Lighting Act improved investors' prospects by lengthening tenure to forty-two years, but local authorities still held far-reaching powers which made profitable development by private companies uncertain.

Besides the haphazard development of networks, the low voltage of public supplies held back the spread of electrically powered appliances in the British home. Private generating plants could solve these problems for mansions, hotels and large institutions; they produced electricity by a dynamo powered by steam-gas, oil or water engines. Enough power could be supplied to work sewing-machines, knife-

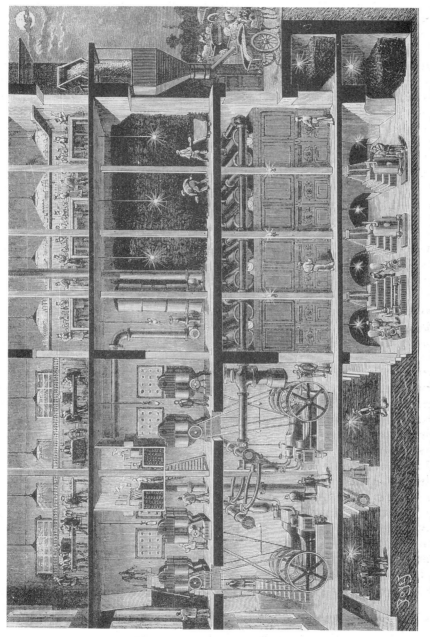

Edison central generating plant, Brooklyn, New York, 1890: the model for the world's electrification

grinders and coffee machines, as an article to Spong's 1887 household manual illustrated, but it was still a matter of attaching a belt-drive to machines originally intended to be hand-operated – there were as yet no specifically electrical appliances.

The first major British company to make electric fittings for the home was the General Electric Apparatus Company (GEAC) later the General Electric Company. It began operations in a London warehouse in the 1880s, virtually making appliances to measure. A customer was asked to describe what he wanted, and then a manufacturer was found to make it. The big electrical engineering companies, more concerned with industry, were not interested in such specialized work, and so GEAC used small workshops. Although such individual attention was flattering, it was bound to be costly. Meanwhile, in the United States fewer local restrictions had allowed a much more rapid spread of electrical appliances, and a very large market for them quickly developed. Westinghouse, Thompson and Houston, Hoover and Frigidaire became household names in the United States, and since their mass-produced goods were very competitive in price, they were soon as familiar in British homes. Subsidiaries were set up – British Thompson Houston in 1894 and British Westinghouse in 1899.

Prospects for British companies began to improve in the twentieth century. The electric tramways of the 1900s required much more power than street lights, and this could be extended for residential use. A new Electricity Act in 1919 appointed commissioners to divide the country into administrative districts, each with its own Joint Electricity Authority to co-ordinate and encourage the provision of effective supply, and the Government allocated £20 million for plant. In the First World War, 95 per cent of munition factories were electrically powered, and such widespread industrial use gave the domestic consumer confidence. Moreover, the women who signed up as wartime factory workers went back to their homes after the War with a proper understanding of the benefits of an energy source that had once been widely mistrusted. In 1924 the Electrical Association for Women was founded, and under its first director, the engineer Caroline Haslett, it became an effective political pressure group for furthering the spread of electricity to all homes. It issued a magazine, *The Electrical Age for Women*, and organized travelling exhibitions and electrical cookery classes in schools. But when Margaret Partridge and Caroline Haslett set up their own company to make electrical appliances and supply electricity, they were hampered by legislation, originally aimed to protect factory workers, which forbade women to work the off-peak hours (10 p.m. to 5 a.m.) necessary to maintain round-the-clock supplies.

As networks spread more generally, better heavy-load cables were developed, and lower tariffs were offered to households using power points as well as lights. The Central Electricity Generating Board and the National Grid were set up in 1926 with a ten-year plan for the provision of cheap, reliable and standardized electric power. This led to a great expansion in the numbers of electrical appliance firms in 1927, the heavy engineering electrical giant, English Electric, entered the domestic market with cookers, bowl fires and irons. But it was already difficult for British firms to compete with the long-established American companies which dominated the refrigerator, washing-machine and dishwasher sales, and the British Vacuum Cleaner Company, the first makers of suction cleaners, found it had to meet the challenge of the excellent machines produced by W. 'Boss' Hoover of Ohio.

With the economic depression of the early 1930s, Britain left the gold standard and abandoned the free trade policies which had made her such an attractive market for foreign firms. Sterling depreciated 30 per cent in terms of gold and the dollar, and the 1932 Import Duties Act put a 20 per cent duty onto imported domestic appliances. It became more economic for American companies to build factories in Britain, and new British firms were able to set up. Morphy Richards started production of radiant electric fires and irons in 1936, and their assembly-line techniques, learned from Henry Ford, cut the costs of such appliances by up to 40 per cent. At the same time, low interest rates brought a boom in house-building, a direct cause of increased demand for appliances, especially cookers. By 1931 there were some 1.3 million electric cookers in Britain, 400,000 vacuum cleaners, 220,000 refrigerators, and 60,000 washing-machines. By contrast, American homes boasted machines in their millions rather than thousands. The economies of scale that American manufacturers were able to make, given such a volume of production, put British firms at a permanent disadvantage.

It was not only government miscalculation and the consequent legal obstructions that slowed down the introduction of labour-saving machinery in British homes. Because of deep-rooted differences in social structure, public demand for such machines was far greater far sooner in the United States than in Britain. Inventiveness was certainly not lacking in Britain – between the 1850s and the 1870s the patent records show a flood of ideas concerned with domestic matters, and trade journals such as *The Ironmonger*, the *Journal of Domestic Appliances* and the *Sewing Machine Gazette* were set up to disseminate and stimulate inventions. But again and again the pattern was repeated: an invention was originally thought of and toyed with in Britain, rapidly perfected and efficiently marketed in the United States, then exported back to Britain.

In his *American and British Technology in the Nineteenth Century*, H. J. Habbakuk suggests that the United States' rapid adoption of labour-saving machinery in all fields of industry was a result of the shortage of unskilled labour, and the high wages therefore demanded. He quotes an early nineteenth-century commentator, E. G. Wakefield: 'Where land is very cheap and all men are free, where everybody who so pleases can easily obtain a piece of land for himself, not only is labour very dear . . . but the difficulty is to obtain combined labour at any price.' It was unskilled labourers who were most attracted by the farming alternative to factory work. Moreover, a high proportion of the early nineteenth-century immigrants to the United States were skilled craftsmen, the only people with enough capital and energy to cope with the major upheaval of emigration. If it was in effect easier to find men to make power-looms than to work hand-looms, mechanization was bound to be encouraged. 'Everything new is quickly introduced here, and all the latest inventions', wrote Friedrich List in the 1820s. 'There is no clinging to the old ways. The moment an American hears the word "invention" he pricks up his ears.'[8] This situation contrasted very strongly with the position in England, as George White made clear in his 1846 *Treatise of Weaving*: 'Such a state of society where, as with us, labour generally exceeds the demand for it, has a tendency to beget an indifference to its improvement.'

Britain was also held back from experiment with the new mass-production, highly mechanized techniques developed in the United States by her original forwardness in industrial development. Whereas the Americans could start from scratch with new equipment, British manufacturers were hampered by their unwillingness to scrap existing plant. Moreover, organized labour in Britain was afraid that such improvements would cost them their jobs. In the United States, the introduction of labour-saving methods in industry meant higher rates of production by an otherwise inadequate labour force. Since this led to higher wages, there was a positive incentive for workers to try new methods. American canal navvies spontaneously developed the first bulldozer (a horse-drawn one) to speed up their work.

The implications of those attitudes were twofold. Not only could domestic appliances be made more quickly and cheaply in the United States, but they were also welcomed more eagerly in the home. Women played an important part in American industrial and agricultural life, and they also had to run their own homes with a fraction of the British domestic labour force. There were nearly three times more servants per head of population in Britain than in the United States. There was also a profoundly different attitude to the whole idea of a 'domestic class'. Catherine Beecher expressed it well: 'In England the class who go into service are a class, and service is a profession. In America, service is a springstone to something higher.'[4] Mrs Beecher, cousin of Harriet Beecher Stowe, the famous authoress of *Uncle Tom's Cabin*, was as well known to her American contemporaries as Isabella Beeton was to English housewives. She found the existence of servants in a democratic state, 'where all are made to be free to rise and fall as the waves of the sea', almost as paradoxical as the keeping of slaves. 'We cannot in this country maintain to any extent large retinues of servants . . . every mistress of a household knows that her cares increase with every additional servant. A moderate style of housekeeping, small, compact and simple, must necessarily be the general order of life in America.' Gadgets that made housework easier were seized upon for use in the home with the same enthusiasm that marked the introduction of machinery in factories. In Britain, however, it was not until the wholesale desertion of the servant class during and after the First World War that middle-class housewives were forced to look seriously for easier ways of running their houses.

The disappearance of servants – the 'domestic revolution', as Theresa McBride describes it – was clearly an important stimulus to the introduction of domestic appliances. But the relation of servant-keeping to domestic appliance adoption is more complicated than a simple matter of cause and effect. As McBride points out, 'While domestic labour was plentiful and cheap, servants were used to take up the slack in the evolution of domestic technology.'[5] To put it another way, despite the fact that they were a dying breed, they had a powerful influence on the shaping of the mechanization of the home. They encouraged people to think of machines as replacing servants, rather than enabling a quite new form of domestic management to evolve.

Male servants, commonplace in the seventeenth and eighteenth centuries, began to find other occupations at the beginning of the nineteenth century. This was partly because industrialization offered more attractive jobs, but was also a direct result of the punitive tax put on their heads in 1777 in an effort to increase conscripts for the American War, and not repealed until 1937. Not only did this lead to a decline in the number of menservants, but it contributed to a polarization of labour in general. As Susanna Whatman's eighteenth-century *Housekeeping Book* shows, farm-workers and outdoor servants had often pitched in with household tasks; the vigilance with which excisemen enforced the high tax payable on menservants meant that domestic tasks became specifically women's work in a way that had not been typical of earlier household patterns. In Ireland, where no such tax existed, menservants continued to be employed and male and female domestic occupations were quite interchangeable. Caroline Davidson cites the Irish gentlewoman Dorothea Conyers's comment in 1920: 'Every Irish servant will do everyone else's work cheerfully, the men come in to help the maids to polish the floors and shoes, and the maids are quite willing to feed the horses if all the men are out'.

Until the 1900s there was actually an increase in the proportion of British households employing female servants, a reflection of the urbanization of the population and the rapid growth of the middle classes. Servants were the more necessary in grimy cities, and invaluable in the inconveniently tall and narrow terrace houses crammed together by speculative builders. They were also an indication of status. In his survey of York in 1902,[6] Seebohm Rowntree took the keeping or not keeping of servants as marking the division between those of the working class and those of a higher social scale. Numbers mattered too: according to J. A. Banks, Victorian society hostesses arranged their guests at the dinner-table according to the number of servants they kept.

Evidently the huge hierarchies of servants in the grandest families could defeat their object, as a clear-sighted American observer, R. H. Dana observed in his *Hospitable England in the 1870s*:

> Lord Charles and I set up the lawn tennis. It involved pretty hard work, and a good deal of stooping in marking off the lines with whitewash by means of a brush and long strings. Countess S . . . said she was sorry to have us work, but they had no servants who could do it . . . There were standing about in abundance, both outdoors and in, men quite capable of doing this work, but no-one was found whose duty it would be.

While such jobs were the height of a servant's ambition, shortage of domestic staff was not a problem. William Lancely's autobiography *From Hallboy to House-Steward* (1925) gives a good insight into the attractions of that world:

> Few servants are really overworked, and it is only in exceptional places that they are underfed. In businesses you must carry on during the stated hours, no matter how you feel. In service it is not so; one can get a rest at any time of day, and they have good beds to sleep in and airy rooms to live in, and in the large houses a change yearly from town to country. The country life is very easy in many places, and the surroundings pretty. As a rule in business you are fixed to one desk or counter year in and year out, craving for two weeks holiday to come round.

That was life at the top. Most servants were much less well-cushioned from the realities of household management. It used to be assumed that middle-income families employed at least three servants cook, parlourmaid, and housemaid. However, the 1871 census records only 93,000 cooks at a time when the upper classes officially numbered

Staff of a house in Black River Falls, Wisconsin, with the tools of their trades
(Charles von Schaik, 1905)

about 50,000, the upper-middle classes around 150,000 and the middle classes 600,000. In fact, with an income under £300 a year, only one servant could be afforded. Paying income tax, levied on all incomes over £160 a year, was a rough guide to membership of the middle classes. So it looks as if very considerable numbers of supposedly middle-class people must have had only one or two servants. Theresa McBride quotes a Labour Department study of London's households in 1894 which stated that 27 per cent of servant-employing households had only one servant and 35 per cent more had only two. Patricia Branca, in *Silent Sisterhood*, estimates that the typical middle-class family had only one general servant and a nursemaid while the children were small. In such households, lampooned by the Grossmith brothers' *Diary of a Nobody*, the wife spent much more time scrubbing, dusting, cooking and washing than she did queening it in the parlour with callers. Her maid-of-all-work was likely to be between fifteen and twenty years old, untrained and fresh from the country.

At this level, small, individual labour-saving machines were welcomed, as an 1881 series in the *Girl's Own Paper*, 'Margaret Trent and How She Kept House' makes clear. It mentions such appliances as washing-machines, mincers and gas fires with approval – 'With only one servant, the very great saving of labour quite compensated for the slight additional expense'. It also makes it clear that already servants like Margaret Trent's 'highly superior person' Anne had to be managed tactfully. Margaret dons gloves and a pretty pinny and sets to among the delicate drawing-room ornaments herself in order to encourage Anne's commitment to her job. In vain – the writing was already on the wall. Within thirty years a girl like Anne would no longer consider domestic service.

Why did servants leave the home? There were vociferous complaints about employers' meanness over food and living-quarters. Service could mean a sixteen-hour day spent in a gloomy basement kitchen. While factory girls were respectfully called 'Miss', servants were summoned by their surnames, or by some completely alien name which their employer happened to find easy to remember. It was very common for every successive footman in a house to be called by the same simple name – generally James or John. Undoubtedly the disappearance of male servants must have made the private lives of female servants bleak, and the average employer felt 'followers' from outside the household should be discouraged or forbidden. Such interference in their private lives was increasingly resented by the independent-minded girls of the 1890s. While wages, including board and lodging, were substantially higher in service than in other jobs, none of these petty annoyances weighed too heavily. But by the early twentieth century domestic wages, although not actually lower than many unskilled occupations, were not as much higher as they had been.

Even more influential was the opening up of alternative white-collar occupations to girls who would once have automatically gone into service. The new state schools both kept the very young out of the domestic labour force and provided them with basic skills that expanded their career prospects. The aptitude shown by girls for the newly invented typewriter led to the gradual disappearance of the male profession of clerk. Shop assistants, primary-school teachers and nurses were all attractive options, and domestic service was more and more often regarded as a last-resort job. The war economy struck the final blow:

> The Great War undoubtedly upset service, and this is not to be wondered at by those who know the servant question. The war called for hands to help, and many servants responded to the call. The work they were asked to do was a novelty to them, the pay was big, and they had short hours, hundreds being spoilt for future service through it. It made those who returned to service unsettled. They had money to spend and time to spend it when

**The new trend: Margaret Trent in protective gloves and apron greets
a surprised friend** (*Girl's Own Paper*, 1881)

not at work . . . and to come back to one or two evenings a week
was to them a hardship.[7]

In short, they felt human instead of subservient. Between 1900 and
1951, the numbers of men and women in domestic service shrank from
over 1.5 million to 178,000. Although the exodus of domestic servants
was lamented by the conservative upper and middle classes, there were
a significant number of women who apparently welcomed the
challenge of running their own homes. As family size was reduced they
found themselves with less child-linked housework and far better
physical health. It became acceptable to live in a small well-designed
suburban house with only a daily servant instead of a living-in maid,
and the breezy manuals for the servant-free of the 1920s contrasted
refreshingly with the heavy formality of Mrs Beeton and her ilk. It was
also natural to look hopefully at the new domestic technology for
positive assistance in saving labour.

But in what context? Interestingly, these were the years when the
home looked most closely to industry for guidance on how to manage
its affairs. Time and motion studies were all the rage in factory
management and in 1913 Christine Frederick published her 'Housekeeping with Efficiency' articles in the *Ladies Home Journal*: 'Didn't I,
with hundreds of other women, stoop unnecessarily over kitchen
tables, sinks and ironing-boards? For years I never realised that I
actually made 50 wrong motions in dish-washing alone, not counting
others in the sorting, wiping and laying away.'

The servantless household, she continued, offered the only oppor-
tunity for a family to follow 'exact standards'; it encouraged family co-
operation and offered a chance for training children. So the first
reaction to coping with the disappearing domestic servant was to
reorganize housework, to bring 'scientific efficiency' into the home.

Lilian Gilbreth, whose husband had been a professional time-and-
motion man as well as a highly involved father, had brought up twelve
children on just such principles. She was asked by a gas company in
1930 to study the kitchen as an industrial production problem. She
managed to reduce cooking operations from fifty to twenty-four, but
found organization very difficult because of the heterogeneous nature
of the domestic appliances then available. Nor was it altogether realistic
to apply time-saving principles which could save millions of vital
seconds in one factory to the task of saving a few vital seconds in a
million homes. It is ironic that an attempt was made to learn from
industry, but not in spheres that might really have helped – industrial
cleaning techniques, for example, or professional laundry work and
carpet cleaning. Ultimately all that the craze for 'scientific management'
did for the housewife was to waste her time on the elusive task of self-

organization. In *For Her Own Good*, Barbara Ehrenreich and Deirdre English have argued that it was a way of filling a 'domestic void' which opened out in front of housewives as household management became an easier task. I think their timing is wrong. There was still far too much hard work to be done around the house in the late nineteenth and early twentieth century for too much time to be a problem except among the most prosperous. But it is a much better argument applied now, to late twentieth-century housewives who assiduously measure out their long lonely hours with patchwork and pickle-making.

A more important aspect of scientific management was its significance as a measure of how housewives regarded themselves. Rather than being driven down into a servile role by the exodus of the old hired domestics, the housewife was attempting to achieve professional status by describing the daily round as domestic science, home economics, or even 'œkology', as Ellen Swallow Richards christened it in 1873.

Richards, the first women chemist to study at the Massachusetts Institute of Technology, only turned to domestic matters because her career path was effectively blocked by the male domination of science. But she was no feminist – the ultimate aim of the Domestic Science conventions held annually from 1899 to 1907 at Lake Placid in the Adirondack Mountains was to keep womankind contentedly in the home, to counter what she saw as 'the disintegration of the family group' with a scientific approach that would make housework more interesting. Women should ask themselves, Richards wrote, 'Can I do better than I am doing?' 'Is there any device which I might use?' 'Is my house right as to its sanitary arrangements?' 'Is my food the best possible?' 'Have I chosen the right colours and the best materials for clothing?' 'Am I making the best use of my time?'[8]

If women were not to be servants but professional managers of their homes, then whom were they to organize? Only themselves. Children were now in full-time education, and men had not been fair game as household assistants since the separation of their workplace from the home. Domestic technology, because it started as a way of helping out servants, ended up as a way of substituting for them. Millions of twentieth-century Margaret Trents are still wrestling with maintaining domestic order using technology founded on this essentially irrelevant concept: mechanical servants. The fact that inventors are still toying ineffectually with domestic robots shows how inextricably domestic management is thought of in terms of substituting machines for servants. In this sense, domestic technology is still in the pre-revolutionary stage that textile manufacture was before the days of the cloth-mills. I think it will become clear in the following chapters, which trace domestic technological progress in detail, how often this thinking distorted the development of labour-saving devices.

Prestigious Broadway salesrooms of Grover and Baker in New York, c.1862

3

The Mechanical Tailor

A little further on, you stop before a small brass machine, about the size of a quart bottle, you fancy that it is a meat roaster; not at all. Ha! it is a tailor! Yes, a veritable stitcher. Present a piece of cloth to it; suddenly it becomes agitated, it twists about, screams audibly – a pair of scissors are projected forth: a needle set to work; and lo and behold, the process of sewing goes on with feverish activity, and before you have taken three steps a pair of inexpressibles are thrown at your feet, and the impatient machine, all fretting and fuming, seems to expect a second piece of cloth at your hands. Take care, however, as you pass along, that this most industrious of all possible machines does not lay hold of your cloak or greatcoat; if it touches even the hem of the garment it is enough – it is appropriated, the scissors are whipped out, and with its customary intelligence the machine sets to work, and in a twinkling another pair is produced of that article of attire for which the English have as yet been able to discover no name in their most comprehensive vocabulary.

Giornale di Roma, 1852

This extract from a facetious Italian article was one of the very few press mentions of sewing-machines at the Great Exhibition. There were in fact six machines on show, none of them approaching the artificial intelligence fantasized by the Italian press. Presumably their performance was positively bad; otherwise it is difficult to explain the lack of interest in what was very soon to be the most spectacularly successful of all domestic appliances.

There was no shortage of would-be inventors of sewing-machines, but at this point no one person had grasped the numerous essentials necessary to a workable machine: a stitch that remained locked, a needle pointed at the eye end, a shuttle carrying a second thread, a continuous supply of thread from a spool, a horizontal table, an overhanging arm, a continuous cloth-feed synchronized with the needle motion, thread or tension controls, a presser-foot and the ability to sew in a straight line.

The first machines imitated hand-sewing, using crimped wheels to force material down a long needle, but this motion could not be made a continuous process. A London cabinet-maker, Thomas Saint, made a machine for 'completing Shoes, Boots, Splatterdashes and Clogs' in 1790, but no more than the patent survives. Its forked needle pulled thread through the material to form a chain-stitch, a common early answer to locking the stitch without a second thread. In France, Barthelemy Thimmonier made a large wooden machine, also sewing by chain-stitch, and actually set up production in the 1830s, making army uniforms at record speed on eighty machines. Unfortunately, a mob of tailors who felt their craft was threatened destroyed his machines. Although Thimmonier persevered, producing a machine that could make 200 stitches a minute, which he exhibited at the Great Exhibition, it was certainly not as efficient as the machines developed by American inventors in the 1840s.

No single one of these inventors was responsible for the sewing-machine. The great entrepreneur who drew together all the necessary elements from the numerous machines patented was Isaac Merritt Singer, but credit should be given to the more original minds whose work necessarily preceded his. Elias Howe patented a machine in 1846 which solved the problem of passing the needle right through the material by using a second thread and shuttle. His machine was still too like hand-sewing for rapid work; it could make only eighteen stitches before the material had to be lifted off and repositioned on the feeding-pins. But it was fast enough for Howe to challenge five of the speediest seamstresses in Boston to a race, and he succeeded in finishing five seams to their one. Despite this triumph, the stunt failed – there were no orders at all for the machine. A clue to at least one of its deficiencies was given in Bradshaw's 1848 patent, which mentioned Howe's machine as 'a very bungling device', causing frequent and unavoidable breaking of the needle.

Benjamin Wilson went into partnership with Nathaniel Wheeler to produce a very finely engineered machine. Their second model was patented in 1851 and weighed only 6.5lbs, a striking contrast to the 55lb machine patented on the same day by Isaac Singer. The Wheeler and Wilson machine used a thin circular bobbin, rather than the long shuttle more common at the time, and this principle, although it lay in abeyance for a hundred years or so, is now featured in all modern machines. More immediately important was the four-motion feed introduced in the same machine. This is the system, familiar to every sewing-machine user, by which small teeth rise to grip the cloth, slide it

**Wheeler and Wilson's machine (1851) had a slim circular bobbin
similar to that of modern machines**

along under the needle, sink to release it, then rise again for another
bite. The Wheeler and Wilson machine was a neat low shape, with a
simple one-piece needle arm swinging up and down in a short arc, and
a slightly curved needle. It 'attracted general notice for its beauty of
finish and its easy, rapid and silent manner of working' when shown at
the 1862 Exhibition in London.

The Grover and Baker was one of the best selling of the first
machines. It was patented in 1850, and used a double chain-stitch fed
by two cotton-reels, one under and one over the cloth-plate. This was
criticized by some as wasteful of thread and bulky of stitch, but its ease
of operation and the decorative qualities of the double chain-stitch
made it a popular machine, particularly for industrial use. In fact,
modern high-speed machines have to work on this principle in order to
be able to use two reels of thread big enough to cope with the 7,000
stitches they make in a minute. It was also the best-looking machine
ever made, with neatly turned legs skirted with a cast-iron frill, and
provided with a carrying case.

Clearly there was an exceptionally stimulating atmosphere for
inventors in the early 1850s. Ten patents were filed in 1849, and many
more machines were made. Isaac Singer saw one of these, a Blodgett
and Lerow, and decided he could improve on it. He used a horizontal
table to hold the cloth, instead of the vertical feed bar used by both
Howe and Blodgett. A wheel under the table with short pins in its rim
projected through a slot on the table, so the cloth could be fed
continuously to the needle. A presser-foot held it firm, and a heart-
shaped cam connected to the handle made a straight needle descend

vertically from the rigid needle arm into the cloth. No other machine looked at all like Singer's at the time he invented it, but it is the machine that would seem most familiar to modern eyes.

At this point, sewing-machine history was confused and hampered by the 'sewing-machine war', a battle precipitated by Elias Howe. He claimed that his patent covered the use of a grooved eye-pointed needle carried by a vibrating arm, and the system of making a lock-stitch with a shuttle. He offered to sell Singer the American rights to his patent for $25,000. Singer made one of the few mistakes of his career by throwing

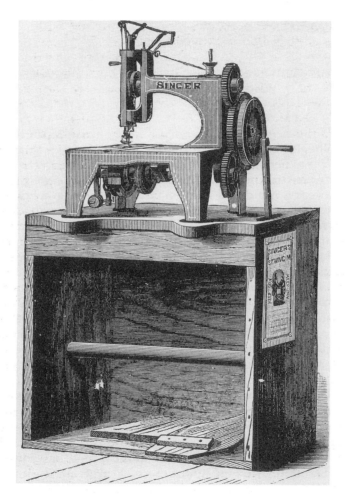

Singer's first machine (1851) came in a packing-case that converted into a treadle and stand

Howe out of his workshop. Howe then began a long series of lawsuits against Singer and the other manufacturers, and, cunningly, their customers. Some companies settled with Howe immediately in order not to demoralize the public, but Singer fought it out. He lost, however, and had to pay Howe $15,000 and a royalty of $25 on every machine sold. The price of the Singer at that time was around $100. Ironically, when Howe came to manufacture machines himself, he found that he could not make one without infringing on the patents of the very inventors he had been hounding. Singer had meanwhile revenged himself by buying up as many of the early patents as he could, in order to sue other manufacturers and recoup his losses to Howe. The situation could benefit nobody in the long run, and through the good offices of Orlando B. Potter, President of Grover and Baker, twenty-five manufacturers set up the Combination in 1856. This was the archetypal patent pool, and provided a pattern followed in the aircraft, automobile, cinema and radio industries, where similar clusters of invention had occurred. The four principals were Singer, Grover and Baker, Wheeler and Wilson, and Howe. They agreed to cross-license their patents, and all other manufacturers had to pay them a fee of $15 dollars on each machine sold. Of this Howe and Singer each received a third, because they controlled the most important patents. The patent pool mono-polized the industry until 1677, when the last of the patents expired. Then at last many hundreds of other manufacturers were able to start production, and the prices of sewing-machines dropped rapidly.

Singer was a colourful character in his own right, with two wives, numerous mistresses and twenty-four children. Much inclined to showmanship, he deserves special mention, since his selling techniques were adopted by domestic appliance makers generally. At a time when it was doubted whether women ought to manage machines at all, he employed attractive-looking young women to sit in a Broadway shop-window and sew away efficiently. His company was the first to set up agencies, first all over the United States, soon all over the world. Each employed at least one salesman, a female demonstrator and a competent mechanic. Competitive spirit ran high – too high in one case, when the Singer agent at Tacoma, Washington, shot dead a Wheeler and Wilson representative and was lynched. A more acceptable selling technique was the $50 trade-in offered to buyers for 'any inferior or wholly worthless machine'. Community leaders such as clergymen and newspaper editors were offered machines at half-price. The most effective boost to sales, however, was Singer's adoption of the credit system of selling. A few furniture-makers in New York and some clockmakers in New England had sold goods locally in this way, but Singer was the first to extend it nationally. It was the only way in which an average family, with a per caput income of about $500 a year could afford the $100 Singer machines. It was also a very attractive buying system for the housewife, who easily envisaged herself saving a few dollars a week to gain such an enormous domestic benefit.

Much cheaper machines were produced. James Gibbs, son of a Virginian mill-owner, saw a woodcut illustration of a Grover and Baker machine and tried to work out for himself how it sewed. Since he could not see the underthread, he assumed that it had a rotating hook underneath, and developed a very efficient little chain-stitch machine on that principle. He formed the Willcox and Gibbs company in 1857, making machines for about $30 each, and became one of the most successful makers of industrial and domestic machines. Elias Howe, a millionaire twice over from his patent licence, never actually made any successful machines himself. He did give an interview on the state of the industry to the *Englishwoman's Domestic Magazine* shortly before his death in 1867. He said that some 750,000 machines had been made in the United States by that time, 52,219 in the last quarter of 1866 alone. He believed that at least half as many again were being made by unlicenced companies operating from Canada. In 1863 there were 300 British and 648 American sewing-machine patents filed, and another 1200 applied for. The average price of these machines was around $30.

In order to compete, even the favoured beneficiaries of the Combination had to develop novelties and attractions. Most early machines were treadle-powered, since on the whole inventors had considered them as best suited to commercial use by tailors and seamstresss. As the potential of the domestic market became apparent, beautifully decorated machines appeared, and hand-operated 'work-box' models appeared. The first Singer Family, or Turtleback, machine, was a frail affair and not a great success. It was only made for three years after its introduction in 1858. Its successor, the enormously popular Singer New Family machine, was sturdier, but still much lighter and prettier than the massive industrial Singers. It was made for nearly 20 years, and about 4 million were produced in all. Its 'fiddle-base', prettily embellished with gilt foliage, was set into a variety of cabinets, some beautifully simple mahogany, others extravagantly elaborate, and costing five times the price of an unadorned machine.

Such portables were not only popular because they were cheaper and smaller than the clumsy early treadles. In some quarters they were felt to be more seemly. Rumour had it that the foot movement of the treadle was 'injurious and dangerous' to women. The *Englishwoman's Domestic Magazine* felt it necessary to correct this. 'It is untrue, save in those happily rare cases of internal complaint, or of natural, or rather unnatural delicacy. In the ordinary way, ladies may and do work their treadle machines at all times with perfect impunity.'

American machines were exported to England, but there were also

British and European firms making sewing-machines. The Excelsior, made in the 1860s by Whight and Mann of Ipswich, was a very impressive machine, beautifully engineered, with generously solid brass accessories. The machinist sat straight on at the machine, rather than at one side of it, and the underthread ran from a reel instead of a bobbin. Whight and Mann also made a lock-stitch machine similar to Wheeler and Wilson's, which was praised by *The Ironmonger* as 'remarkable for its extremely elegant bronzed iron stand in tripod form and of classic design, which by its weight and structure secures great stability to the machine.'[1] Three caryatids gazed pensively out from underneath it, and it was loyally named the Alberta, after the Prince Consort.

Charles Judkin had shown a sewing-machine at the Great Exhibition in 1851. It was intended for industrial use, and claimed to make 500 stitches a minute – perhaps this was the busy little tailor admired by the Italians. It held the cloth vertically, passing it over a toothed roller. The needle ran horizontally, and the shuttle was always visible, working in a carrier in the front of the machine. The Judkin machine of the 1860s was very different, a dainty little object 'suitable for Boudoir or drawing-room'. It had 'achieved a reputation for its simplicity, durability and certainty' by 1869. It closely resembled James Weir's very popular 55s sewing-machine, when in its turn was an English piracy of a Canadian machine patented by Nettleton and Raymond in 1858. Weir's machines have survived fairly well – probably because they are so pretty to look at – but mechanically they are disappointing.

The German sewing-machine became well-established in the 1870s, with such companies as Pfaff, Junker and Ruh and Frister and Rossman. Quantities of German advertisements flooded the British trade gazettes from then on, and there seem to have been few genuinely British firms among the major manufacturers. American and Canadian companies set up companies to make their machines in Britain just as their relations in other domestic appliance fields would do in the 1920s. The mass-production techniques which they had been able to develop thanks to their enormous home markets meant that they had learnt to make more efficient and cheaper machines than anything the British could offer.

There were a few British successes. William Jones of Guide Bridge, Lancashire, took out his first sewing-machine patent in 1869, and the firm was still trading a hundred years later. His first domestic machine was a lock-stitch, with a striking snake-like needle arm, standing on a decorated figure-eight shaped base. Made between 1879 and 1909, the peak years of the British Empire, its unpainted parts were heavily metal-plated, and it was supplied in a steel carrying-case to withstand tropical heat and damp.

The vigour of production of the early years led to some abuses, *The Ironmonger* warned its readers of the pitfalls in selecting suitable machines. 'We find sewing-machines still the subject of no little amount of prejudice, mainly due to the performance of the machines "made to sell" '. This seems reasonable enough. Apparently, 'of the host of machines which crowd the market', a large number were 'utterly inefficient'.

Although one must pity the gullible seamstress landed with an ornate but useless lump of metal, the enthusiasm for sewing-machines produced some delightful novelties. Patents were filed in the United States for some extraordinary variations on the basic lock-stitch or chain-stitch machines. In one, two cherubs stand supporting the cotton-reel and a harnessed dragon-fly carries the thread to the needle. Another was shaped like a pair of scissors. A British company sold a fascinating and surprisingly efficient little lock-stitch machine which fitted into a tin box measuring only 8 by 2.72 by 1.5 inches. It was originally patented by Rosenthal of Berlin in 1881, and was manufactured with some improvements by the Moldacot Pocket Sewing Machine Company of London from 1886. It screwed into a table edge, had a half-inch wide shuttle, and produced a passable stitch when its top was pressed down. Charming machines in the form of animals and people were made. Clowns, horses, dolphins frolicked over the once tedious task of stitching by hand. Grandest of the animal kingdom was Kimball and Morton's 1886 Lion. Meant for serious use as well as drawing-room ornament, this came in two versions. The treadle beast stood soberly at attention, his forepaws swinging back when in action, and the drive-shaft and gears hidden under the table. The hand-operated Lion had a more rampant casting. The lion reared up lugubriously over some low iron cliffs, which hinged back to reveal paws clenched around the presser-foot and needle. The head swung open to house the cotton-reel, and the operating handle was placed unobtrusively low on the side of the mahogany supporting plinth. But my personal favourite of all the excited frivolities that celebrated the great new era of freedom that the sewing-machine was felt to mark for women was Steinfeld and Blasberg's 1893 Princess. You could argue with the name. Dressed demurely in blue, she sits with a needle clenched in her hand, her head rising and falling rhythmically as a handle is turned to make her sew. Woman as machine: a powerful symbol of the profound muddle at the heart of the domestic appliance industry.

As well as arriving in strange shapes, machines could be supplied with tempting accessories. The Pedal Zephyrion was a fanning attachment, which swept soft breezes over the seamstress as she worked. To amuse children, a pianola device could be fitted into the lid of one treadle machine, and dance-music supplied by energetic

**Kimball and Morton's Lion (1886) was a conventional lock-stitch
machine in unusual disguise**

footwork. The reverse of this device was the piano which could be
made to sew by 'an ingenious mechanism' that fitted under the
keyboard. A trade journal announced this French invention with
jocular enthusiasm in 1893:

> This machine will have its disadvantages in thickly settled
> communities. Hereafter it will not be a question of how many
> sewing machines run in a cloak factory or sweat shop, but how
> many pianos. Musical talent will be at a premium when it is
> generally known that the Russian hymn will run up a baby's
> bonnet, the walzing Faust will sew a flannel vest, the intermezzo
> of Cavaliera Rusticana will turn out a complete suite of Ypsilantis,
> and the Battle of Prague not less than three topcoats for young
> men.[2]

A few useful improvements were made to the generally very efficient
machines made by the bigger companies. Positive take-up was
introduced in 1872, in the form of the familiar lever through which the
thread runs from the tension screw to the needle. It jerks up the thread
after it has looped round the shuttle and so completes the stitch. In
1879, Singer patented the oscillating hook, a variation of Wheeler and

Wilson's rotary hook, which is now featured in nearly all modern machines. Little more could be done mechanically until an alternative source of power was available, so in the last two decades of the nineteenth century attention was devoted to externals. Cabinets worthy of eighteenth-century libraries housed treadle machines disguised as Davenport desks. A fine specimen of these is in the excellent Bartlett collection at Reading University. After a glorious zenith of fine castings and delicate ornament, *fin de siècle* degeneration set in. Machines became fat and florid, with drawers drooping down to their casters. Individuality disappeared; all the machines sported the same heavy arm and cam-operated vertical needle bar. Designs were aimed to disguise rather than exhibit – drop-head machines, which sank down into a table-top, were introduced in 1896. People no longer showed off their machines in the drawing-room; they became utilitarian tools, indispensable, but no longer objects of wonder.

' "Man never is, but always to be blest". If with one part of his brain he invents a labour-saving appliance, the other lobes immediately create as much new labour as the apparatus saves.'[3] The immediate response to the sewing-machine was a tremendous elaboration in fashionable dress, paralleled only by the ambitious architecture of wedding-cakes following the invention of royal icing. Many seamstresses found themselves working harder at their machines than they had done with their needles. Constant treadling was exhausting, and so other sources of power began to be explored.

Steam might seem an unlikely means of power in the home, although it was used in factories to drive Judkin's first machine and others. However, a French engineer called Daussin constructed a steam-engine for domestic use in 1884. Its two-pint boiler could be put on a kitchen range and from there the engine would power a sewing-machine. Its speed was controlled by a pedal underfoot and a braking disc. *Scientific American* showed the Tyson motor, powered by steam, gas, oil, or petrol, driving a sewing-machine in 1880.

Equally unlikely was the patent applied for in 1875 which showed a dog in a treadmill replacing human foot-power under the machine. The Royal Society for the Prevention of Cruelty to Animals intervened, and more conventional ways of exercising pets have triumphed. Edison, of telegraph and phonograph fame, constructed a sewing-machine powered by sound. A membrane was mounted level with the seamstress's head. All she had to do was to talk into it and the sound-waves were transformed into power to work the machine.[4] Theoretically Edison was right. The vibrations of the diaphragm mechanism were transmitted via a metal spring to a wheel on a shaft with a heavy flywheel. But he did not take into account the modulations of the human voice, which caused irregular movements. He suggested that poetry be recited or books read aloud to keep up the flow of sound, but no doubt this was more tiring than treadling in peace.

The water-motor was a more realistic alternative, and did in fact power many sewing-machines in the 1880s. It worked efficiently, driven from the household supply, and using a small jet of water to drive round cupped floats attached to a wheel. A machine in the Bartlett Collection still has one attached to its treadle, and trade gazettes recommended them highly. 'Wheeler's Eclipse Percussion Spade Mill Water Motor Excels All' ran the punchy slogan of one Preston manufacturer. A little later disenchantment had set in:

> I often smile when I hear of new motors for sewing-machines. I remember well the Empire water motor introduced in 1879. It sold quite well for a time, and cost only a penny a day to run, but is now quite obsolete. I have seen so many motors, spring, water, and electric, tried out on sewing-machines, and none of them has been a financial success. Will a sewing-machine motor ever command a sale? Not until it costs about half a guinea.[5]

Within a decade the Old Hand would have to eat his words. Electricity was the long-term solution to powering sewing-machines, although the first electric motors were so bulky, smelly and unreliable, that he could be forgiven for doubting their potential. The Griscom Electro-motor, shown at Philadelphia in 1882 was battery-driven, with six one-gallon cells enclosed in a large box. It was supposed to last for several months of normal household use, and the speed of the motor could be controlled by the depth to which its zinc and carbon plates were immersed in fluid. 'The apparatus is very complete, and were it not for the dislike of women to have anything to do with mysteries of a chemical or electrical nature, it would doubtless soon win its way to popular use.'[6]

In fact such supposedly silly feminine foibles were quite justified by the inadequate earthing, insulation and guards of the early machines. Another neater motor was illustrated in an 1891 book, *Electricity in Everyday Life*. In 1911 a Singer machine appeared with a fairly bulky mains-driven motor attached below its drop-head casing, but it had a treadle too, just in case. In 1921, the 99K, the first Singer with only an electric motor to power it, was produced, and sewing-machines seemed to have joined the ranks of the other appliances whose domestic future was assured by the small electric motor.

For a time the domestic trade boomed. As well as making sewing much easier work, electricity opened the way for all sorts of elaborate stitchery. 'Replete with the latest and most approved mechanical devices, the Singer 201K is the supreme achievement of many years experimental work by the ablest sewing machine designers and engineers', declared a 1940 advertisement. There was no longer any need to seduce the customers with gay decoration and novelties. Sewing-machines became unashamedly ugly and severely functional.

Since the 1950s, the situation has changed. The sewing-machine effected a commercial revolution in the rag trade as well as overturning the drawing-room workbox. Cheap machine-made clothes, curtains and linen can now be bought for less than it costs to make them at home, and making clothes is a pleasurable hobby rather than an unavoidable chore. In the effort to maintain domestic demand, styling has improved and accessories have proliferated. Sleek, furnished with electronic memories and digital windows, modern machines are capable of performing small miracles of elaborate embroidery. The control panel of the New Home Memory Craft 6000 has as many buttons as a TV equipped to receive satellite. Touch a few of them and flocks of penguins or tribes of crocodiles march forth to order; you can sew a poem in Palace Script, or print out as many daisy-trimmed name-tapes as you need. To people who enjoy sewing for its own sake, such machines are luxurious aids, but their original function as domestic labour-savers has almost entirely disappeared. The example of the sewing-machine illustrates the most successful possible labour-saving appliance – one which has completely removed the task from the home.

The most famous of all washerwomen:
Beatrix Potter's Mrs Tiggywinkle

4

Laundry Work

Lily-white and clean, oh!
With little frills between, oh!
Smooth and hot – red rusty spot
Never here be seen, oh!

Beatrix Potter, *Mrs Tiggywinkle*, 1905

There are two possible solutions to the back-breaking labour of wash-day: to send clothes and linen out to a commercial laundry or to develop small efficient machines to wash it at home. Any one who could afford to do so sent out their washing in the nineteenth century; today most people take it for granted that they will need a machine in their own home. How did the system change? Why didn't the mechanization of wash-day simply mean more efficient cheaper laundries rather than reintroducing work into the home? Part of the reason lay in the bad reputation acquired by the early laundries for destroying clothes, part in the same bad logic that left the housewife bent alone over her little gas stove: the idea that machines could fill the vacuum left when domestic servants faded away. Finally, as the price of small domestic machines dropped, they were the obvious alternative to the women who had always washed at home because they could not afford to send clothes out to the laundry.

The laundry processes best assisted by machines are rubbing clothes clean, wringing them, tumbling dry and ironing. Domestic washing-machines, mangles and wringers, tumble-driers and irons all owed much of their development to the commercial laundry machines that they have succeeded in replacing for home use.

Washing-machines

Simple tools which had long been used to make washing easier inspired the first inventors. Earliest of these was the 'dolly', perhaps so-called because of its appearance – a two-armed handle on the top of a stout stick, with a cluster of legs below. It was also known as a posser, from the Middle English *poss*, to pound or beat. It was wielded in a wooden tub full of hot suds and dirty clothes, and remained popular in rural areas until well into the twentieth century.

The Canadian Washer, illustrated in the *Journal of Domestic Appliances* in 1881 was a slightly more sophisticated tool. A copper cone replaced the cluster of legs, and operated on the force-pump principle. The washer lifted it clear of the water at each stroke, forcing air down into the water and creating a suction effect that was supposed to be very effective in loosening dirt.

The washboard is perhaps the best known of the pre-machine washing aids. A frame of hardwood filled with corrugated iron or zinc, it became mass-produced in the second half of the century. *The Ironmonger* dated its introduction from the 1860s, but there is evidence of a 'new, improved' type in 1859. Crude, home-made versions had probably been in use for some time. One ingenious adaptation of the 1890s came even closer to the original inspiration of human knuckles. Six wooden balls, each about an inch in diameter, were attached to a strap that fitted round the hand to provide an easily manipulated tool. This echoed one type of early washing-machine, as did the two corrugated rollers on a handle produced a little earlier.

The first known reference of any sort to mechanizing washing methods seems to be a letter of 1677 which mentions Hoskins's idea for a machine 'whereby the finest linen is washt, wrung and not hurt'. The first patent taken out in Britain was in 1691, perhaps concerning the same machine, but no details survive in either case. Significant steps in invention did not begin either in Britain or the United States until the late eighteenth century, and were on the whole aimed at textile industries or city laundries. At least one, however, seems from its name to have been designed for domestic use. Invented in 1792, it was called the 'Washerwoman's Assistant or Housewife's Economiser'.

The first American patent for a washing-machine was filed in 1805, but the industry did not develop much until the 1850s and 1860s – crucial years for so many domestic appliances. In 1869 domestic machines were still scarce, although 2000 patents had been taken out. Interestingly, it was in this year that Catherine Beecher wrote: 'Whosoever sets neighbourhood laundries on foot will do much to solve the American housekeeper's hardest problem.'[1] She recommended that every dozen families should share a communal laundry; an idea which, if generally taken up, would have meant a huge saving of individual expense, time and effort.

In Britain, the take-off of the new invention was equally slow. Seven machines were displayed at the Great Exhibition, mainly commercial ones. It was not until the late 1870s that the idea of domestic machines became widely accepted and they could win the ultimate accolade of inclusion in the 1883 edition of Mrs Beeton: 'What the sewing-machine is to the seamstress, the washing-machine is to the laundress; the one will soon be as indispensable to family comfort as the other.' One might note *en passant* that the sewing-machine ceased to become a domestic necessity once most clothes were made outside the home – there was no good reason why the washing-machine should have stayed within it.

The slowness with which washing-machines developed is partly explained by the enormous variety of approaches attempted by inventors. In retrospect it is easy to select those machines that were relevant to progress, but at the time it was not, and frequently dissatisfaction was expressed as thousands of unsuitably designed machines failed to live up to the extravagant claims made for them.

Vertical-axis machines with a central agitator, rotating-cylinder machines on a horizontal axis and machines imitating the movements of the human arm reflected attempts to mechanize the dolly, the boiling copper and the washboard. One of the first vertical-agitator machines was described in the *Gentleman's Magazine* in 1752, with a sketch of its workings. A wooden tub had a dolly permanently fixed through a lid. It was called the Yorkshire Maiden, and said to have been 'long in use in Yorkshire and now claimed by three new inventors in London'. The design hardly constituted a machine until it was powered by rotary notion, an improvement of the 1850s. Mr Harper Twelvetrees, a prominent British washer- and mangle-maker, produced some of the most impressive versions of this hand-cranked type. Their only drawback was that continuous rotary motion tended to tangle the clothes round the dolly. An American model patented in 1869 had the dolly attached and geared to the base rather than the lid. This was developed into the very effective Pan-American and Canadian Red Star machines, which used a reciprocating motion. This meant that clothes were churned around in both directions and were less inclined to knot together.

An American patent of 1846 showed a machine that imitated the washerwoman's arm movements. A curved arm slid over a bed of rollers, squeezing the clothes against them as if against a washboard. Such machines, and perhaps the washboard too, were descended from large-scale machines in use since the late eighteenth century in French and English textile manufactories. Bradford exhibited an English version at the 1862 Exhibition. The rollers hung in a flat frame, and clothes had to be fed in and held in place manually. It was useful for articles requiring hard rubbing, such as new shirts and collars, but was not recommended for the general wash of large items, or for flannel or

duty has been decreaſing for theſe ſeveral years, ſo that the laſt year's amount thereof did not exceed 11000*l.* Therefore the only method that remains to prevent *running* of *ſtarch,* and the fraudulent practices in powder, is to remove the cauſe, by lowering the duty to ſuch a *medium* as may encourage the trader.

Let us ſuppoſe the duty on *ſtarch* reduced to a fourth part, the price then will be too low for the temptation of running it, and the following computation will ſhew what effect this reduction muſt have on the conſumption.

It is adjudged, at the loweſt, that there are 8000 barbers and peruke-makers within *London* and the *weekly bills,* that after this regulation muſt conſume at leaſt 6 lb of powder per week each ; which, at the preſent duty of 2*d.* per lb. will amount to the annual ſum of £. 20,800

Then ſtating thoſe of trade, excluſive of *London* and the *weekly bills,* to be 30,000, and that they (together with what is conſumed by all the nobility, gentry, &c.) make uſe of the like quantity of 6 lb. of powder per week each, the annual amount will be 78,000

The ſum of which being the total of the annual duty ariſing from powder only, is . 98,800
The fourth part thereof is 24,700
The laſt year's amount of the whole duty is 11,000

Then the advance from the conſumption of powder, by this regulation, will exceed the preſent duty by the annual ſum of 13,700

Then admitting, that every family in *England* and *Wales* make uſe of only two ounces of groſs ſtarch each, the duty thereon will produce the annual ſum of 123,210
The ſum from powder, as above, is 98,800
222,010

The fourth part whereof is the annual duty of 55,502

As from this eſtimate there appears ſuch a general advantage to the *land-intereſt,* and advancement of the *revenue,* by lowering the aforeſaid duty, it is preſumed that this expedient will not fail of meeting with all the ſucceſs that it juſtly merits ; which ſhould be the deſire of every well wiſher to his country, as it is of *Yours,* &c.

Jan. 16, 1752. J B.

A Machine for waſhing of Linnen, called a Yorkſhire *Maiden.*

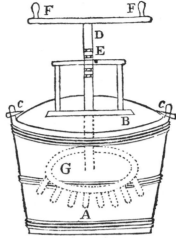

A, A tub 19 inches high and 27 diameter at the top, in which the linnen is put with hot water and ſoap.

B, A cover to the tub, which fits it very cloſe, and is faſtened to the tub by two wedges c c.

D, An upright piece of wood, which goes through a hole in the middle of the cover, and is kept to a proper height by a peg at E.

F F, Two handles by which it is turned backward and forward.

G, A round piece of wood faſtened to the end of the upright piece D, in which round piece are fixed ſeveral pieces like cogs of a wheel.

*** This machine, which has been long in uſe in Yorkſhire, came by degrees into Derbyſhire *and* Leiceſterſhire ; *and now is claimed by* three new inventers *in* London. See Daily Advertiſer, Jan. 20, *where 'tis aſſerted that it will* FIRST three dozen ſhirts within the hour.— *There is a ſmall difference in the form, but the operation on the linnen is the ſame in all* ; *that is, to make it paſs and repaſs quick thro' the ſoapy water.*

Mr URBAN,

YOU have metaphyſical correſpondents ; perhaps ſome one of them may give an anſwer to the following query :

In what does the identity of ſenſible things conſiſt ? or, when may two or more minds be ſaid to have the ſame perception ? L. M.
Reflexions

First known washing-machine: the Yorkshire Maiden
(*Gentleman's Magazine*, 1752)

wool. Of more general use was Chatterton and Bennett's Float Washer, made in Manchester in the 1860s. 'It imitates exactly the knuckles of a vigorous washerwoman, only of course acting in a moment on a surface of clothes a hundred times as large' explained the *Journal of Domestic Appliances*. Although this energetically abrasive system would not be suited to electric power, it remained popular in hand-cranked machines for many years. The American Montgomery Ward mail-order catalogue offered an Old Faithful Self-working Washer in 1926 which differed only slightly from the 1846 type.

Rocking or oscillating machines were related to cylinder machines, but did not rotate. They were the most highly recommended of hand-operated machines because of the gentle way they operated. 'A common complaint against washing machines is that they destroy clothes. There is nothing in the Vowel which can destroy clothes in any way', the *Journal* reassured its readers in 1885. The Vowel machine thus praised was one of a series, the A, E, I, O and U machines, made by Mr Bradford of Saltram. The earliest was described by Kinnear Clark in his account of the 1862 Exhibition. It was patented in 1861, and consisted of an almost square box which rocked and vibrated on its axis. The inside was lined with ribs of wood to increase the friction on the wash. It had some drawbacks – the clothes did not circulate very well, and it was very heavy to work. Later versions were improved by being geared to the turning handle. Mrs Beeton's 1883 edition praised the Vowel E: 'This machine will wash twelve shirts, or a large blanket or counter-pane, and the ease with which the machine is worked is surprising.'

The 1880s and 1890s saw the heyday of the noblest washing-machines of this type – ornate cast-iron giants approaching half a ton in weight and standing six feet high. Competition for the rapidly growing market was intense, and periodicals of the time were full of extravagant double-page advertisements by warring manufacturers. The Cherrytree 1893 Spray Washer boasted 'a very attractive oscillating motion which causes the water to rush through the articles being washed at every turn of the handle'. An American inventor, Mr Morison, patented the ultimate in comfort in 1908. The operator could remain seated throughout the proceedings, and 'A tub of clothes can be washed in six minutes by a mere child.'[2]

The type of machine with the greatest future ahead of it was the cylinder machine. This too was descended from textile workers' machinery rather than domestic aids, although it was to some extent related to the old washing-coppers. It was the only machine to envisage in-built water heating. A patent of 1782 shows a wooden cylinder machine, powered by a large flywheel and handle. The perforated inner casting held the clothes and revolved through the hot suds in the outer cylinder on the same principle as a modern front-loading machine. J. T. King made two American versions of the cylinder machine. His 1851 model was fairly small and could have been used in the home. More immediately influential was his large commercial machine, in use in New York by 1855. Its outer cylinder was about two metres in diameter and was heated from below by a fire of wood or coal. Inside was another perforated cylinder, revolved by huge belts attached to an industrial steam engine. The clothes boiled for about twenty minutes, and it was the boiling rather than the gyrating of the cylinder that was calculated to clean the clothes.

Thomas Robson's 'portable washing-machine' was described in the *Practical Mechanic's Journal* in 1858. A corrugated drum inside its cylinder was rotated by hand, but the machine seems too small to have been very efficient, unassisted by the boiling that was a feature of King's washer. The 1862 Summerscales Dashwheel was regarded as the best of the domestic cylinder machines. Much faster because of the rocking motion of the dashweel, it had a reciprocating rack-and-pinion mechanism at the side so that it turned in two alternate directions, and so avoided tangling the clothes. It also had brushes for coarse washing inside the cylinder. These could be reversed when fine material was being washed.

Two cylinder machines foreshadowed the integral heating element of modern machines. Pearson's Marvellous Steam Washer, first exhibited in 1862, was heated by charcoal or gas. A handle turned its small cylinder, and its 1885 advertisement claimed that it was easily operated by a child. Even more interesting was the Factotum, invented in 1893 by Dr Money. Not only did it have a gas heating element to boil the wash as the cylinder turned, but it converted into a crude version of a tumble-drier. Once the clothes had been washed out and wrung, they were returned to the machine, shut in with a wire shield instead of the door, and rotated over warm air from the gas 'for an hour or two'. The Factotum could also be provided with a water motor to save the manual labour of turning the cylinder.

Opinions varied as to the effectiveness of these hand-operated machines. They were certainly very hard on clothes, but so too were the laundries, and the knuckles, washboards and dollies of the washerwoman. The machines seem to have been widely used in both Britain and the United States by 1900, but their price and small capacity meant that they were best suited to smallish middle-class households. Grander establishments had enough washing to run their own laundries or to use commercial ones, and poorer families could not afford to buy a machine. They were ideal for such a household as Margaret Trent's, who provided her one servant Anne with 'a convenient little washing-machine and wringer'. By rising half an hour earlier than usual on a Tuesday morning 'Anne was able to do the small

**Pearson's Marvellous Washer gave the traditional wash-boiler
washing-machine motion over a bed of charcoal**

household wash herself without extra help, and without the other work
of the house getting in arrears. She sprinkled and folded on Tuesday
evening, mangled on Wednesday and ironed on Friday.'[3]

Randall Phillips did some arithmetic to prove the worth of washers in
his *The Servantless Home* (1922). A week's wash for a household of four
adults would cost £10 10s at the laundry. To hire a washerwoman for
two days washing and ironing at 4s. a day would cost, including firing
for copper and irons, about 16s. With a washing-machine it would be
necessary to have the washerwoman in for only one day's washing and

one day's ironing. Moreover, less boiling and soap would be needed, so nearly 6s. a week could be saved. Since by then a simple hand-operated machine cost only about £8, it clearly paid for itself within a matter of months. Moreover, many households would feel that they could manage without a washerwoman at all with such a machine.

Two things are worth noting in Randall Phillips's argument. The expense of the laundry explains why it seemed obvious to turn to domestic machines. Only mass use of laundries could make them operate on a sufficiently large scale to be cheaper than hiring a washerwoman. Secondly, it is clear that women were stretching themselves to take on more work with the aid of the washing-machine in order to solve the immediate problems of staff. Writ large in every aspect of house-management this would mean disabling themselves from taking on employment outside the home.

Other contemporary authorities were less enthusiastic than Phillips about the merits of the early machines. In 1922 Gowans Whyte wrote that 'The labour needed to work the hand-operated machine is so little short of hand-washing that they have never come into general use.'[4] Christine Frederick wrote of the United States in 1913 that 'Washing is done in most houses without washing machines and with only a common boiler.'[5] The fact remains that great numbers of machines were sold. A *Journal of Domestic Appliances* survey in 1892 recorded 996 dealers in England, and Siegried Giedion assumed the American market to be much more buoyant than that. 'English interest in mechanised laundry rather weakened in the nineteenth century, while the American quest for a device to lighten the laundering burden of the housewife became even stronger.'[6] Giedion did not use the British trade gazette sources, so his picture may be a distorted one. On the other hand, many of the British dealers were probably selling commercial and imported machines. This contrast in enthusiasm was again a reflection of the fact that in Europe the decline in domestic service did not disrupt households seriously until the First World War, whereas in the United States the Women's Movement and assertions of sexual and racial equality had undermined domestic labour well before the end of the century.

It was the electric motor that made domestic washing-machines successful. The first crude attachment was attempted by the American A. J. Fisher in 1908. Its exposed belt-drive gave careless users frequent shocks and water motors were still a more popular option at the time. Wide local variations of current and voltage made it difficult to include a motor in the structure of the machine, so at first motors were sold as separate units. Once electrical networks were set up and current became easily and cheaply available, the American washing-machine industry boomed – no revolutionary mechanical development was needed to electrify the old hand-operated machines. In 1926, 900,000 machines were sold at an average retail price of 150 dollars, and in 1935, 1.4 million were sold at an average retail price of only 60 dollars. One large mail-order firm cut its prices to a record $29.95 in 1936. What was originally a luxury to help out the servants of the rich was rapidly becoming a domestic commonplace.

In Britain, demand for electric machines came later, mainly because of the slower extension of the electrical networks. The British National Grid, the system by which electricity is distributed to different parts of the country, was not set up until 1926. By then it was difficult for British machines to compete with the cheap mass-produced imports from Hoover, Maytag, Thor and such American giants.

One of the first washing-machines with an integral electric motor was the Thor. The earliest model had a white enamelled tub, raised on legs, with a revolving cylinder of hard whitewood inside. It contained 'lifters to carry the clothes up out of the water and then let them fall again of their own weight into the foaming suds'. It also had a powered wringer. Like the early vacuum cleaners, it ran from an electric light socket, and was supposed to use only a pennyworth of electricity a session. Other electric machines were cast iron, copper in a steel frame, or all wood. Twin-tubs were soon developed, at first featuring an electrically powered agitator which was dipped into the appropriate tub, not unlike the arm of a food-mixer. In fact, one curious phenomenon of the 1920s, the Mulparvo ('much in little') claimed to combine washing clothes, washing dishes, beating eggs and mincing meat for sausages in one adaptable whole.

The Hotpoint BTH electric washer was chosen for King George V's 1935 Jubilee House – its advertising copy described lyrically how 'the specially designed gyrator, swinging backwards and forwards in the unique square-shaped tub, gently forces the creamy soap-laden lather through and through the texture of the fabric, cleansing the dirtiest garments, and yet without fear of damage to the daintiest of lingerie.' Finished in blue stove-enamel, with adjustable legs to suit the height of the owner, it was very reasonably priced at £25, or £35 with a roller–ironer fitted underneath. Even more space-age in concept was the Thor Electric Servant. Its white cabinet fitted the new streamlined kitchens, and its motor was adaptable to a degree that challenged even the Mulparvo. Attachments included an ironer, a food-mixer, a stirrer, a masher and a radio.

Increasingly these efficient electrically powered machines began to challenge the better-off household's dependence on laundries as well as easing the task of those who washed at home from necessity. This piece of copy from an advertisement for the Universal washing-machine in the 1920s is an interesting illustration of the shift in opinion that was necessary before home laundry work became as much a matter of course as home cooking.

> She sneaked away to wash! She did not want to be seen, nor did she want it known that *she* washed the family clothes. It seemed humiliating work which stamped her with social stigma.
>
> TODAY the sensible woman takes pride in doing her own washing. She calls in the neighbours to see how little work *she* does and how much the UNIVERSAL electric washer *does for her*.
>
> DON'T pity the woman who does her own washing. The pity is for you!

Advertisements for electric washers blossomed thickly in the women's magazines of the mid-1920s, and many calculations were offered as evidence of their economy. The average life of a machine was estimated at twenty years by *Ideal Home* in 1926. At a maximum cost of £60, this meant only £3 per annum, plus about £2 for electric current and soap. Costs were falling dramatically as demand increased. The 20 per cent import duties of the early 1930s and the abandoning of the gold standard stimulated British industry, but although several American firms set up factories in England, only 60,000 electric machines were being produced annually by the end of the 1930s, compared with a figure closer to 2 million for the United States.

At this time washing-machines did little more than take the heaviest labour – rubbing and wringing the clothes – out of washing. They had to be filled and emptied, stopped and started. Many inventors became preoccupied with the dream of a fully automatic washing-machine, with integral heating elements, a timing device and pumping and drying mechanisms. The two types of machines suitable for such development were the vertical-agitator and the horizontal-cylinder machine. As early as 1878 a prototype of a power-driven single-tub washer and drier with two speeds had been made. By 1911 automatic control devices were patented. A clock or electric motor set off an electromagnet or operated a hydraulic device to open and close the valves connecting power to the washing cylinder. In 1922 a British patent for an automatic speed-change device was issued, and in 1925 a similar French patent appeared. There were no practical results until about 1939, and the extremely high prices of the first attempts at such intricate mechanisms made such machines the dream furniture of the 'kitchen of tomorrow'. A contest to design this appeared in *McCalls* in 1944, and results revealed that 'Most of the women who voted cherished the idea of owning an automatic washing-machine. This vote of approval is five times as high as for either spinner or wringer types.' As washing-machines became cheaper, they became the most sought-after of all electrical appliances: 29 per cent of British families owned machines by 1958, 64 per cent in 1959 and 77 per cent in 1981.

Today washing-machines are automated far beyond most house-holds' requirements. Few families can take advantage of the dozen or more programmes that their machines offer because they rarely have a full load of, say, silks and delicates, or woollen garments. The most commonly used programme is coloureds, at a warm temperature, using one of the biological detergents which have arguably taken more work out of wash-day than the machines themselves. It is increasingly common to soak a few oddments in detergent and handwash them, reserving the machine for only one or two full washes a week. The old sums that used to make machines an economy no longer work nearly so well. Instead of lasting twenty years, machines are only credited with five years' life. The service contracts necessary to see to see to the mechanical intricacies of the new machines add more to the cost, and since repairs are apparently beyond the brief of most washing-machine mechanics, replacement parts are another major item of expense. If the time taken to load and empty the machine, and to hang out and fold the clothes, is taken into account, it is much more economical to take a load once a week to a service launderette than to have an expensive machine – or two if a tumble-drier is also necessary – standing about unused for most of the week. The alternative is to share a machine between several families. Condominiums, apartment blocks and housing associations are increasingly turning to the scheme for communal laundries voiced by Catherine Beecher back in 1869.

Mangles and Wringers

The distinction between the wringer and the mangle has been forgotten with their disappearance from everyday use. Wringing was simply squeezing moisture out of the clothes to help dry them, but mangling was a form of ironing; it smoothed and glazed table linen, sheets and so on. Often the same machine was used to wring and mangle, but whereas all mangles could wring, not all wringers could mangle.

The simplest aid to wringing, its use recorded as early as 1780, was to stretch linen between two hooks, turning one of them to squeeze out the water. Ten years an improvement in the shape of a netting sack was mentioned. This technique only imitated manual methods, and, with mangles as with vacuum cleaners and sewing-machines, it was not until someone approached the problem in a fresh way that mechanically aided methods succeeded.

A more significant stage in the development of the mangle was the use of wooden cylinders, round which clothes were wound and then

beaten with flat pieces of wood called batlets. These can be seen in
many folk museums, often beautifully carved. The first mangle was a
mechanized version of this operation. Known as a box-mangle, it was a
massive affair, perhaps 6 feet by 4. It consisted of a low wooden table
on which clothes twined on wooden cylinders were placed. Over them
was placed an oblong wooden chest filled with large stones and
mounted on runners at the side of the frame. It was propelled over the
rollers by straps attached at each end of the box and passed over an
upper roller carried round by a winch. 'The labour of working it is
excessive', commented Webster and Parkes (1841), 'not only on account
of the strength required to move it, but from the continual reversing of
the motion; for scarcely has it been got into motion by great exertion,
than it becomes necessary to turn it back again.' An improved machine
on a permanent stand, and worked by a handle, won George Jee a
silver medal from the Society for the Advancement of Arts, Manufactures and Commerce in 1779, and such mangles could be found in
the laundry rooms of large country houses such as Vinters in Kent or
Erdigg in Clwyd. The rack and pinion mechanisms and fly-wheels
which made such machines operable by a single washerwoman were
not generally introduced until Baker's machines of the 1830s and such
mangles were, of course, far too bulky and expensive for the average
home. Professional laundries used them, and, foreshadowing
launderettes, allowed individuals to come in and smooth on them for a
small charge. By the 1930s, the electric roller–ironer had replaced them
in most laundries, but one was still in use in a Sussex laundry in 1953.

The first mangle to sound like the domestic upright model was
described in a 1774 patent granted to Hugh Oxenham. It had three
rollers, and springs to apply pressure on to the clothes. More common
than springs in other early models were heavy weights hung on long
levers, as in Thomas Oxenham's 1797 machine, or Robert Webster's
1812 model.

The three-roller mangle had no major advantage over two-roller
types, and required a more complicated mechanism, so most
machines had settled for two by the mid-nineteenth century. One
cylindrical and one octagonal roller was a curious feature of the
machine in Stephen Chubb's 1805 patent, but this was probably too
harsh on the cloth to be generally adopted. Most of the early machines
calculated that the linen would be wound round one of the rollers, and
some had mangle-cloths, known as brattices, in which a collection of
smaller items could be secured. A flannel cloth might be wrapped
round one roller to protect shirt buttons. Frames were of wood, until
improved techniques of coal-smelting led to the availability of cheaper,
easily cast, iron. Two of the five machines shown at the Great Exhibition
were in iron frames.

Mangles used three methods of applying pressure. Weights and levers were cumbersome and did not adapt to different thicknesses of cloth, but continued to feature, sometimes as an auxiliary to springs, until as late as 1895. Spiral springs at each end of the mangle were popular because of their neat appearance, but experts such as Kinnear Clark regarded them as less efficient. 'A woman gives one screw perhaps two or three turns, and the other six or seven, the consequence being that the ends of the shafts and the rollers do not get the equal pressure which is essential.'[7] Some idea of how hard the giant mangles were to operate was given by the Maytag Company's research into the old-fashioned wash-day. They concluded that mangles added to the labour of wringing out clothes rather than lessening it, although turning was made somewhat easier by the refinement of chain drive, first single, then double. The need for careful and lengthy treatment of the wood used for mangles made them unsuited to mass-production methods. Quarter-cleft rock maple was used for the rollers, first cut to hexagonal shape, then rough-turned and bored to make seasoning more thorough. Every roller was seasoned for twelve to eighteen months before use. Seasoned pine was used for the boards and table-tops, and cypress for the washer-boxes. If oak was used, it had to be seasoned for two years before it was sufficiently dry to resist moisture.

When vulcanized rubber was developed, and rotary cranks became more sophisticated, the wringer began to take over. Compact, easy to operate and gentler on clothes, it could either be attached to the top of a washing-machine, screwed to a table-top or sink, or mounted in a light frame. Its very convenience was, however, a source of suspicion to many housewives – it was hard to believe that anything so puny would do the work of the massive mangle. Of course it could not compete with its smoothing function, but more efficient irons and roller–ironers were soon to take that over.

In 1882, Mr Bowden of Soho, London, produced a last effort to compete by developing a drop-down mangle. The first version of this device combined the large kitchen table of the time with an equally substantial mangle. It was a very attractive piece of joinery, with elegantly rounded, though necessarily solid legs and a removable flywheel of about two feet in diameter, which slotted in while mangling was in process. The rest of the machinery, the two large rollers and drainaway slopes for wringing, tucked away under the table-top. 'The idea is a good one. The wonder is that it has never been thought of before', wrote the *Journal of Domestic Appliances*. Whittaker Brothers redeveloped the idea in the 1930s, and their oak table-wringer and mangle, 'a piece of furniture to grace any room', proved that there was room for a mangle even in small flats. Later they added an extension to convert the table to a dining-table. Disconcerting for guests, perhaps,

THE DOMESTIC APPLIANCES EXHIBITION.

SOME TIME ago we expressed an opinion that at the above exhibition some surprising novelties would be exhibited, not only for aiding domestic labour, but fo economising the many articles consumed in the house. In these go-ahead days, a year is quite sufficient time for the invention of numerous wonderful improvements, and the discovery of many alto- gether new systems of mechanism, and therefore it is not surpris- ing that at the Agricultural Hall are exhibited a number o domestic appliances which now, figuratively speaking, make thei first bow before the public, and only ask a fair trial to become appreciated. Year by year domestic inventions of every kind are increasing ; and no matter whether we desire to clean knives make stockings, peel potatoes, black shoes, make butter, wash clothes, stitch dress, shell peas, or even make our bread, all we have to do is to turn a handle. We need not even mind the baby now ; we can put it in a domestic appliance and it will mind itself ; and if we have bad teeth, and consequently impaired digestion, we need not trouble to masticate our food, but can put it in a machine, and, of course, turn a handle. This is a regular handle turning age, and we may expect soon to wash and dress ourselves, make our beds, clean the windows, scrub the floors, lay the table, and do every household operation through the same medium. We should then only require a handle to appease a stormy wife, quiet a screaming baby, and pay the tax collector, and our domestic happi- ness would have reached perfection.

The Agricultural Hall has been thronged with visitors at night, and the last few evenings it has presented a very crowded appear- ance. There are altogether upwards of two hundred exhibits, which is an increase on last year. We shall first notice :—

WASHING, WRINGING & MANGLING MACHINERY.

MR. W. BOWDEN, Soho Bazaar, Oxford-street, W.

At this stand we notice something new in wringing machines, which will be welcomed by those householders whose space is

When used as Table.

limited, it is a mangle, a wringer, and a kitchen table combined and the three illustrations we give will at once make clear to the

reader what we mean. These machines are as large, as strong and as serviceable as any ordinary wringer or mangle, and when not

When used as Wringer.

in use the fly-wheel can be quickly taken off, and the whole folds down under the table top out of sight, the operation not taking more

When used as Mangle.

than a minute. The idea is a good one, the wonder is that it has never been thought of before.

MESSRS. HOLMES, PEARSON AND MIDGLEY, Keighley.

Several specimens of the well-known " Royal Washer," the " Cyprus " wringer, the " Excelsior " wringer and other laundry machines were shown by this well-known Keighley firm. An in- spection will show that they are carefully made and their simplicity and effectiveness is beyond all question. This firm have recently opened a London depôt, at 5, New-street, Bishopsgate, E.C., where a large stock of their manufactures are warehoused. This Depôt

groping to fit their knees around the protuberances, but apparently it proved 'an unqualified success'.

Both mangles and wringers became unnecessary once spin-drying washing-machines succeeded twin-tubs. Roller–ironers and drip-dry fabrics made smoothing an easy task, and finally tumble-driers completed the sophisticated equipment of the modern laundry.

Irons

From the aesthetic point of view, the history of irons is one of sad decline – a host of specialized, beautifully designed tools disappeared to make way for one rather dull electric appliance. However, the goffering-irons, crimping-boards, cap-smoothers, slickenstones, lace-dollies, presses and flat-irons involved a great deal of hard work and skill.

In 1851, flat-irons were the basic tools of the trade. They varied in size and shape. Triangles were the most common, ranging from vast 10 inch by 4½ inch models, weighing nearly a stone, to dainty 4 inch by 2½ inch ones for fiddly corners and tiny gathers. An oval shape for delicate fabrics was also popular. The smallest versions of these were the cap-irons, used to perfect the frills that a self-respecting Victorian lady might change twice daily. In 1870 an American housewife called Mary Florence Potts patented a double-ended flat iron with a detachable handle. This meant that the handle could be made of a comfortable material such as wood, since it need never be close enough to the fire to burn. These 'Mrs Potts' irons', as they were universally known, were usually sold in sets of three irons, one handle and a stand. Two bases could thus be heated up while the third was in use. A long-handled iron rod was also supplied, to move the hot bases from the fire, and the conveniently rounded handle could be fitted on quickly by a knob attached to a small latch. The bases varied in weight and shape, thus providing a most useful all-purpose ironing set.

Cleaner in use, since the base of the iron did not have to go near the fire, was the box-iron. This was a deep iron, somewhat cumbersome to hold, hollowed out inside with a door sliding up at the back. Through this was inserted a slug of iron, heated red-hot on the stove. Greater initial heat meant that the iron could be used for a longer period, and it remained much hotter. Similar in principle was the Italian, or 'tally', iron, without which Queen Elizabeth I and her contemporaries could not have had their exquisitely crimped ruffs. It consisted of up to six smooth tubes of various sizes mounted on a vertical or S-shaped pedestal. A poker made to fit the inside of the tubes was heated in the fire, and inserted into the tubes to heat them up. Then the collar or ruffle could be pressed onto the tube.

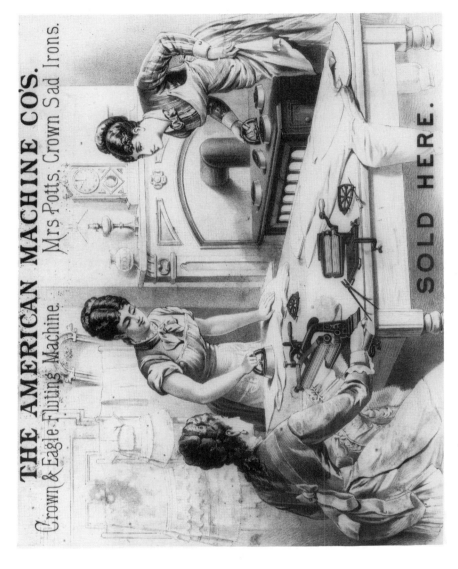

Set of Mrs Potts's irons and two sizes of crimping- or fluting-machines: note tongs for iron slugs

The mechanical successor to this tool was the crimping- or goffering-machine. Screwed or clamped onto a table, this looked like a tiny mangle. It had brass corrugated rollers about six inches long. Frills were inserted at one side, a slug of metal pushed into the rollers as into a box-iron, and a handle turned to propel the material through. Different sizes and shapes of rollers could be fitted on, to provide for all varieties of pleats and frills. The first patent for this machine seems to have been taken out in the United States by Susan R. Knox in 1866.

Commercial laundries and large households could make use of special laundry stoves such as those produced by Smith and Wellstood in the 1860s. These were completely enclosed, thus minimizing the dirt picked up by the iron, and were specially designed to hold as many flat-irons, slugs for box-irons and Italian pokers as possible. Pyramids, hectagons and octagons were mounted upon each other to provide the maximum number of flat surfaces. Such improvements in heating methods, and the cheapness and simplicity of the tool, led flat-irons to continue in use even after the Second World War. However, it was clear that a self-heating iron would be a far more attractive appliance, and experiments with different fuels were frequent.

The first type of self-heating iron was the charcoal iron. It resembled a box-iron, but contained slow-burning charcoals which provided a continuous heat for an hour or so. It had a squat chimney behind the handle to help combustion, and was usually supplied with a curved shield to protect the hand from the heat. Very large, it was often beautifully decorated, chased and fretted with leaves, flowers or animals. One superb example in the London Science Museum was made in about 1850. It was supplied with a pair of brass bellows, blind-stamped with a willow pattern. Irons such as these are still made today for such countries as Czechoslovakia and India, where electricity is often non-existent in rural areas.

The *Practical Mechanics Journal* described an oil-heated iron in 1861, but this does not seem to have come into general use until later in the century when the availability of paraffin made it less risky to use. An interesting 'plaiting' (pleating) machine, heated by lard, lard-oil or sperm-oil was advertised by Kendalls in 1882. It could make fifty to eighty pleats a minute, of any size up to 1¼ inches in depth and 12 inches in length. These fuels were not really suitable for domestic use, although paraffin-irons did become popular, particularly where gas and electricity were slow in becoming available. They were alarming-looking appliances, with large spherical reservoirs for the paraffin, or even petrol, perched behind the handles. They had to be well ventilated, and this gave scope for imaginative designers to deckle the sides of the iron with wavy slots, grooves and other patterns.

Gas was much better suited to the task of ironing. Most town houses

**Adaptable electric travelling-iron which converted to
boil water for morning tea**

in the late nineteenth and early twentieth centuries used gas for lighting, so it was easy to employ it for ironing too. At first irons were not directly heated by gas; it was merely an alternative fuel to heat flat-irons. The Little Gem smoothing-iron (1879) involved this simple use of gas, balanced on a gas burner to heat up. Larger irons could be supplied with their own gas ring. A set of two Champion irons (1891) came with their own ring and a length of tubing to attach to a gaslight outlet. In hot weather such appliances were far less oppressive than working close to a kitchen range with flat-irons in the time-honoured fashion. More specialized iron-heaters were made by Parkinsons. They had space for four or more irons to be slid in over burners, and, since they were semi-enclosed, were economical to run. These were for domestic use. Parkinsons also made a gas laundry stove which held up to fourteen irons on its many-facetted sides.

More grandiose, and perhaps not for the ordinary home, was Furlong's elegant Shirt Collar and Cuff Ironing and Polishing Machine (1881). The weight of the iron was taken by an overhanging arm, and a complicated system of sockets gave it freedom of movement. Most innovative of all, it used a continuous supply of gas to heat the iron. But this was by no means the first directly heated iron. In the 1850s, the American firm of Lithgows advertised a 'gas-heated smoothing iron for tailors, hatters, and family use', with an illustration showing a lady using an iron connected to the gasolier by a gutta-percha tube. 'Time alone must bring it into universal use' ran the caption. Old habits died hard. Parsimony seems to have held most households to the flat-iron, especially while it was the comfort of the servant rather than the mistress of the house that was at stake. Gas irons were certainly in use, both in England and the United States in the last years of the century, but they sound potentially dangerous. With no thermostatic control except the instinct of the ironer they were an undoubted fire risk, and gas fumes in a confined space would have been unhealthy. Like charcoal and spirit irons they had to be fitted with heat shields. Examples survive made of brass, bronze and iron, and later models were nickel-plated and enamelled. By the 1920s many of the earlier drawbacks were overcome, and familiarity with the use of gas for cooking made them potentially more easily accessible. Had it not been for the evident advantages of electricity, they might have continued in use. There is still one long-established London hat-maker who uses them today because he finds their performance so satisfactory.

The electric iron was one of the first applications of electric power in the home. In 1882 a patent was granted to H. W. Seely of New Jersey for a carbon-arc iron. This does not appear to have been a success. His second patent showed an iron placed on an electrically heated stand. A French version of the carbon-arc iron had a vertical square-sided spindle which was turned by a key to adjust the separation of the two carbon electrodes. In use it was 'a handful of blinding light, flying sparks and weird noises'. Few of its users survived.

In 1895 advertisements appeared in Crompton's catalogues for an electrically heated iron. It weighed 14lbs and cost £1.10s. It resembled a large flat-iron, but was made in two pieces, screwed together. The connection was through the handle, like the electric saucepans of the time. Inside it had an electrical resistance heating element basically similar to that of the modern iron.

The first commercially produced electric irons in the United States appeared in California in 1904, sold by Hotpoint. Westinghouse were quick to follow, and published a series of newspaper advertisements to educate the housewife in its advantages. Ironing could now be done in the open air, they pointed out – perhaps on the veranda. 'Never immerse the iron in water' was a commonly given warning. Nor should the iron be left on all the time one was ironing – 'If an electric iron is left on unnecessarily for five minutes, enough electricity is consumed to burn a lamp for 69 minutes . . . A habit should be formed of disconnecting the current once the iron is really hot.' To make this easier, many irons had a switch on the iron itself. Thermostats were not introduced until the 1920s.

Prettiest and most versatile of the first electric irons is a little travelling-iron now in the London Science Museum. Immaculately chromed, with a basketwork handle, it fitted into a metal case which doubled as a water-container. The iron could be set face upwards in its stand and used as a hotplate to brew up a holiday cup of early morning tea.

In the 1950s, steam-or-dry irons appeared, making it possible to iron fabrics with a light-weight iron that forced steam through the material as it was pushed over it. Thermostats became finely tuned, and base-plates stainproof and non-stick. Although today's machines are much more fragile than the old simple electric irons, they make ironing a pleasant and relaxing task. The most striking contrast between the early irons and modern ones is in their weight. No housewife used to believe that a light iron could do much good, and on average a large iron weighed 10lbs and a small one 7lbs. Today an iron rarely weighs as much as 1lb.

Laundry work today takes a fraction of the time and effort that it used to demand. But it is not only the machines and the magical detergents that have transformed the tasks. Revolution is not too strong a word for the changes in dress in the last hundred years. One could not possibly toss the clothes of an 1860s Victorian lady into even the most versatile of modern washing-machines. As well as simplification of styles, synthetic 'easy-care' fabrics have made frequent washing of clothes a simple matter. And much more frequent it is too – the other side of the coin of modern fashion simplicity and ease of laundering is that people wash their clothes far more frequently and have more of them in their wardrobes than ever before. Managing the washing is still a major chore – especially in families with children. That it is a domestic task rather than a service industry is a historical accident. If laundries had become more efficient and cheaper instead of declining in the face of the mass production of small domestic machines, the household could have been relieved of a considerable burden.

'Puffing Billy', Booth's horsedrawn vacuum cleaner at work
in London, *c.*1910

5

House-cleaning

A busy woman is accustomed to say that her idea of the house of the future is one that can be cleaned with a hose.

Maria Gay Humphries, *House and Home*, 1896

The most drearily recurrent of household chores used to be dust removal. An endless variety of brushes was listed in the early manuals. Telescopic curtain-brushes, double banister-brushes, carpet-whisks, hearth-, stove-, boot-, velvet-, hat- and library-brushes augmented the basic indispensable trio of hair broom, bass-brush and scrubbing-brush. For all that, much of the dust was redistributed rather than removed. Machines to contain the dust instead of stirring it up have made the modern home infinitely easier to keep clean.

Carpet-sweepers

Street-sweeping machines were the inspiration for domestic carpet-sweepers. Joseph Whitworth's 1842 patent showed an endless belt of brushes, chain-driven, and was widely introduced into the United States in 1843. Although much too large for domestic use, it inspired the spate of designs for carpet-cleaning machines which appeared there in the late 1850s. Five patents were granted in 1858 and nine in 1859. They all centred on the idea of a cylindrical revolving brush turning in a chassis, mounted on rollers or wheels, and pushed over carpets at the end of a long handle. The principle of the carpet-sweepers produced today is exactly the same.

The British Society of Arts did mention such a machine in 1859, likening it to street-sweeping machines, but it was American manufacturers who were the first to develop domestic carpet-sweepers. Foremost among them was Melville Reuben Bissell, of Grand Rapids, Michigan. In the back of his small crockery store, apparently to cure his own allergy to the dust from the straw used to pack china, he constructed the Grand Rapids, soon to be a household name all over the United States and Europe. It was patented in 1876, when the Bissell Carpet Company was formed. The most prominent early British manufacturer was Entwhistle and Kenyon, already known for their roller–ironers and mangles. The Ewbank, first produced in the early 1880s, would 'sweep better than a broom, and at the same time will collect all the dust instead of driving it about the room to settle on furniture, curtains, pictures, etc., whilst pins, hair, threads, bits of paper or crumbs are unerringly picked up, and the colours of the carpet revived'. It was made in two styles – hardwood with japanned ironwork, or walnut with metal parts nickel-plated. Other makers were quick to enter this evidently promising new field, and soon a host of superficial trimmings were added to the basic machine. *The Ironmonger* surveyed the scene in 1889. 'Housewives in search of carpet-sweepers which do their work effectively and make no dust about it should have no difficulty in suiting themselves at the present time, unless indeed the number of patterns all claiming to be the best should prove an *embarras de richesses* and puzzle them which to choose.'

Bissell dominated the market. The Gold Medal and the Grand Rapids were his most popular models, and their quality was emphasized. 'We use only the finest lumber out of the state of Michigan, and incorporate therewith only the best procurable iron, rubber and material generally.' In the 1880s, Bissell could boast that his sweepers were 'in daily use in the households of HM the Queen and HRH the Princess of Wales'. Ball-bearings were an improvement of the 1900s. They gave the suspension of the brush more elasticity and made sweepers in all essentials what they still are today. By 1910 there were over forty superficially different varieties of Bissell sweepers. Children could contribute to the chores with the Bissell Baby, only 5 inches wide and costing 9½d. The Bissell miniature, 'suitable for ladies' use and works conveniently among furniture', cost 10s 6d in 1907, as did the basic Bissell Standard. The Grand Rapids, now with 'cyclo-bearings and greater brushing power' cost 13s 6d. Grandest of all was the Parlour Queen, 'a very powerful pattern for the thickest piles', at 17s 3d.

In 1930s aluminium castings began to replace wood – they made the machines much lighter and easier to manœuvre. Tattersall's All-British Boudoir weighted only 3½lbs. Its brushes were of real hair instead of bristle, and it was 'calculated to bring out every particle of dust without damaging the most delicate of fabrics'. Another machine of the 1930s, the Kwick-Kleen, attempted to steal some of the prestige of the new vacuum cleaners by imitating their appearance. In reality, of course, the carpet-sweeper could not begin to compete. Although still a handy tool for the occasional spill, its function has now been entirely usurped by the much more efficient and powerful electric vacuum cleaner.

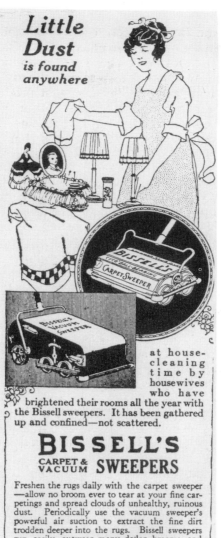

Little Dust
is found anywhere

at house-cleaning time by housewives who have brightened their rooms all the year with the Bissell sweepers. It has been gathered up and confined—not scattered.

BISSELL'S
CARPET & VACUUM SWEEPERS

Freshen the rugs daily with the carpet sweeper —allow no broom ever to tear at your fine carpetings and spread clouds of unhealthy, ruinous dust. Periodically use the vacuum sweeper's powerful air suction to extract the fine dirt trodden deeper into the rugs. Bissell sweepers run easily, outwear many dollar brooms, and lengthen the service of your floor coverings. A second sweeper for upstairs is a decided convenience. "Cyco" Ball Bearing Carpet Sweepers at $3.25 to $6.25; Bissell's Vacuum Sweepers $6.00 to $12.50—depending on style and locality. At dealers everywhere.

"The Care of Rugs and Carpets" is a help-ful booklet mailed free on request.

BISSELL CARPET SWEEPER CO.
Oldest and Largest Sweeper Makers
Grand Rapids, Mich.   Made in Canada, too

Bissell's cyclo-bearing and friction-powered vacuum sweepers improved the original Grand Rapids machine

Vacuum Cleaners

Vacuum cleaners were much slower in finding a workable form than carpet-sweepers, although cleaning by suction was first explored as early as 1859, a peak year for early carpet-sweeping patents. The two basic types, those with and those without brushes, were both formulated in the same year. In an American patent of 1859 a cleaner using only pneumatic action was described. It had four wide metal blades on a spindle. This was turned by gearing connected to the small wheels on which the sweeper was pushed across the carpet. Its effect was to blow some dust at least into the pan behind. It is difficult to imagine enough force being created to raise dust thoroughly, but the important principle of the fan was established. A few months later, the second type appeared. This featured a revolving brush which swept up dust, assisted by a draught produced by bellows. The air was then forced through reservoirs of water, which retained the dust, and out through side valves. Again, the motive power was the wheels on which the sweeper moved, which were connected by a rod to the bellows. These two machines had little success. The vacuum cleaner, electrified or hand-driven, did not become a portable household tool until well after 1900. Three massive forms of semi-industrial plant preceded it: the carpet-washer, a cleaner that forced air through carpets, and fixed-installation vacuum cleaners.

The first were steam-powered machines used by professional cleaners to wash and beat carpets which had been taken up and sent to them to be cleaned. Such machines were developed in the 1860s, and at first made no use of air either to suck or to blow dirt from carpets. They were more akin to industrial washing-machines, with large india-rubber beaters to pound the carpet as it was fed through the machine. An improved model of 1881 had the refinement of hot steam-filled pipes to kill moths and other insect predators, and, most interestingly, a rotary fan, which blasted air through the beater-chamber and up a chimney, taking dust and dirt with it.

By 1900 this had been developed by American inventors into a machine that blew compressed air through carpets. It was widely used in railway carriages and other public places, and eventually inspired the inventor of the first successful suction vacuum sweeper, H. Cecil Booth. Booth was a well-known British civil engineer, who specialized in designing bridges and fairground big wheels. He described his reaction to seeing the American cleaner when it was demonstrated at the Empire Music Hall, London in 1901:

> The machine consisted of a box about a foot square, having a bag on top, and to which compressed air at 90lbs pressure was

supplied. The air was blown down into the carpet from two opposing directions, while the box was pushed over the carpet, and the inventor trusted to the reflection from the surface under the carpet to drive dust and air up into the box. I remarked that I could not see how one could get the dust out effectively in this way, as much must be blown out sideways; further, a cushion or seat where there was no back to reflect the air could not be cleaned. I asked the inventor why he did not *suck* out the dust, for he seemed to be going round three sides of a house to get across the front. The inventor became heated, remarking that sucking out the dust was impossible, and that it had been tried over and over again without success; he then walked away. I thought the matter over for a few days, and tried the experiment of sucking with my mouth against the back of a plush seat in a restaurant in Victoria Street, with the result that I was almost choked.[1]

Booth was convinced that the irate American was wrong. Luckily he had friends who were prepared to finance his early experiments. Messrs Bryan Donkins and Company, of Bermondsey, gave him the freedom to work out a viable suction machine. It was clear from his specification that he was aiming at something more ambitious than merely brushing up dust:

The machine must be capable of . . . sucking the dust completely out from within and beneath the carpet or fabrics being cleaned . . . The current of cleansing air produced by the suction must pass into the machine from under and through the fabric being cleaned, and must be of considerable volume and move at a high velocity so as to have sufficient energy to pull the dust out of the fabric . . . The only practicable and economic method of producing the required degree of air and volume and vacuum necessary to give the air sufficient energy was to employ a power-driven suction pump.

Unlike many domestic appliances, vacuum cleaners have a detailed early history. Once his machine began to operate successfully, Booth was bombarded with lawsuits from a small army of disappointed inventors. In the records of these cases, many other attempts at making vacuum cleaners are preserved. Over thirty related patents had been filed in the United States and Britain in the last three decades of the century, but an analysis of these by Booth and his lawyers proved that none of them had all the elements of a successful machine, partly as a result of failures in design, but primarily because of the absence of an effective source of power. The only force greater than the friction-driven bellows mentioned was the unrealistic one of compressed air cylinders.

Booth's first machine, nicknamed 'Puffing Billy', was driven by a 5 h.p. piston-engine, powered by electricity or petrol. No brushes were involved; it extracted dust entirely by powerful suction through slot-shaped nozzles at the end of very long flexible tubes. Some machines were installed permanently in a building, with wall sockets for the tubes in every room like modern electric points. Much more spectacular were the mobile units, mounted on trolleys and drawn first by horses and later automobiles. Spring-cleaning could be completed in an afternoon, and 'vacuum tea-parties' were often held to witness the new wonder. The bright red vehicles of the British Vacuum Cleaner Company (BVC) would draw up outside the house, and white-uniformed men unrolled long tubes and passed them through the windows upstairs and downstairs. As the spectators sipped their tea and marvelled, the dust was extracted from everything cleanable with a minimum of fuss and disturbance. By men, let it be noted.

**Edwardian tea-party given to witness the transformation
wrought by vacuum cleaning**

Not everybody approved of the new invention. In its early days, the company was fined hundreds of pounds for illicit operation in public thoroughfares, until at last an appeal produced a decision that the machines were allowed to work in the streets provided that no obstruction was caused to traffic. There were also numerous suits concerning the alleged frightening of cab horses, but eventually the vans became an accepted part of the spring and autumn scene.

A vivid description of the early impact of vacuum cleaning was given in Arnold Bennett's novel *Riceyman Steps* in 1923. Even allowing for author's licence and a bookworm's disregard for housework, it suggests that there must have been a dramatic new vision of the extremes of cleanliness possible once Mr Booth's machines arrived. Henry Earlforward's peaceful life as proprietor of a soothingly dust-laden second-hand bookshop is completely upturned by his marriage to Violet, a girl with ideas of her own about household standards. He returns to his shop one day to find it apparently on fire – at least so the crowd outside and the red 'engines' at the door suggested:

As he hurried, without a word, from the train to the house, he was careful to avoid any appearance of astonishment or alarm. At any rate, the engines, both throbbing, were too small to be fire-engines, and the house was not on fire. What distressed him was the insane expenditure of electricity that was going on. And why was the shop open? The day being Saturday, it should have been closed hours ago.

He strode over a hose-pipe into his establishment. One side of the place looked just as if it had been newly papered and painted, and all the books on that side shone like books that had been dusted and vaselined with extreme care daily for months; almost the whole of the ceiling was nearly white, and the remainder of it was magically whitening under a wide-mouthed brass nozzle that a workman who stood on a pair of steps was applying to it. And Henry heard a swishing sound as of the indrawing of wind. He went forward mechanically into his private room, which, quite unbelievably, was as clean as a new pin. No grime, no dust anywhere! And not a book displaced. The books which ordinarily lay on the floor still lay on the floor, and even the floor planks looked as if they had been planed or sandpapered. He dropped into a chair.

'Darling, how pale you are!' murmured Violet, bending to him. 'This is my wedding present to you. I wanted it to be a surprise, but you've gone and spoilt it all with coming home so soon.'

The present misfired. Henry had liked the comforting patina of grime that used to surround him, and, tight-fisted to a degree, he found the price of the clean-up (£13, 'the wages of a morning char-woman for over three months') as abhorrent as 'the bare inhospitable look of the place'. The patient Violet's gradual disenchantment with married life is another story. What is interesting about Bennett's description is what it conveys about the dramatic effect of early vacuum cleaning. Evidently that morning char had never made anything like the impact of those powerful suction tubes. The amazement that greeted the first cleaning exhibitions suggests that a permanent veil of filth had clouded society until Booth's invention lightened its darkness.

One of the most famous jobs undertaken by the BVC was the cleaning of Westminster Abbey prior to the coronation of Edward VII and Queen Alexandra. The great blue carpet in the aisle was transformed. So impressed was the Royal Household that the Lord Chamberlain wrote to Mr Booth on the instruction of the King and Queen requesting a demonstration at the palace in their presence. The cleaner was fitted with a glass inspection-chamber so that the dust could be seen rushing away. Apparently their Majesties were astonished that the palace could be so dirty, and promptly ordered a machine. Demonstrations to many other heads of state followed: the French President in the Elysée Palace, the German Kaiser Wilhelm II and Tsar Nicholas II at Darmstadt, and Sultan Abdul Hamid in Constantinople.

Vacuum cleaning's contribution to health was believed to be confirmed after the Prince of Wales had an analysis made of the dust taken from his own residence, Marlborough House. Journalistic sarcasm had a field-day at the expense of royalty when the bacteriologists revealed that there were over 355,500,000 living organisms, many potentially lethal. An outbreak of spotted fever among naval troops stationed at the Crystal Palace during the First World War brought an Admiralty official down to the BVC. He made an optimistic request for 'one of those things you stick into the electric light fittings'. Booth grasped the scale of the problem and sent down a fleet of fifteen high-power machines. Within four weeks the dust, which had been inches deep on the spider-web girder-structure of the Palace, had been removed. Twenty-six tons of dust were buried, and the health of the men improved rapidly.

Permanent installations were made in the House of Commons and many London stores and theatres. They were more popular domestically in the United States, where the large number of apartment blocks made them a practical proposition. A vacuum system similar to Booth's had been developed independently, and at about the same time, by an American, David T. Kenney, but he did not patent it until 1903. His fixed installation in the Frick Building, New York, seems to have been the first of its type in the world. Fixed installations had many advantages before a light power unit was developed. But installation costs were high. With a typical dislike of capital outlay. Europe tended to prefer the occasional visit of a mobile plant.

German scientists were slow to admit the benefits of vacuum cleaning. In a series of tests with wet gelatine plates, they compared the dust raised by ordinary sweeping and that raised by a vacuum cleaner. Dr Berghaus and other hygienists concluded that it failed to save either time or labour.[2] Undeterred, Siemen were producing their Vortex cleaner for permanent installation by 1911, and an article in *Domestic Engineering* regarded it as 'undoubtedly the most satisfactory for nearly all purposes, especially for private houses, offices, workshops and all buildings of several storeys'. A catalogue of the time showed a cross-section of a house served by such a machine. The fixed plant throbbed discreetly in the basement. In the hall a butler gave his master's coat a quick once-over with one extractor tube. Next door a parlourmaid and a footman cleaned the sitting-room, each tube-in-hand. Upstairs the lady of the house preened in front of a looking-glass while her maid refreshed the feathers of her hat – by vacuum, of course.

Siemen's Vortex suction cleaner (1911): a permanent installation with sockets in the walls of each room

The development of the vacuum cleaner as a portable household tool was not then the only possible course. In fact, it required immediate compromise – a much less powerful vacuum. Machines like the foot-operated 1906 Griffith, or the hand-pumped 1910 Baby Daisy required two operators – one to pump or pedal and one to pass the suction nozzle over carpet, curtains and furniture. Such machines had no brushes, were labour-intensive, and cannot have been at all efficient. Many experts regarded them as tantamount to frauds, trading on the favourable publicity earned by the big machines. Arthur Summerton's *Treatise on Vacuum Cleaning* (1912) stated in its preface: 'We shall confine this treatise to stationary machines, as we believe satisfactory results in cleaning cannot be expected from portable machines.'

Although they were less good than fixed plants, such machines often improved on carpet sweepers, however. Models that could be worked by one person were developed. The BVC Good Housekeeping cleaner (1913) resembled an enormous bicycle pump – in reverse, naturally. The Star had a bellows fitted neatly into a can on its shaft, and after a little practice one operator could both guide the nozzle, pump the bellows and support the machine. Such manually powered suction sweepers survived the introduction of electric machines because they were much cheaper as well as reasonably efficient, and they were still being sold in large numbers in the 1930s.

Bellows machines with electric motors were the last stage before the light portable machines we know today. The Ideal, illustrated in the *Ladies Home Journal* in 1904 could either be operated by an obliging daughter, shown in a dapper sailor-suit, or by an electric motor. Booth in England offered the Trolleyvac (1906), a heavy box on wheels with an electric motor and pump which could be run off an electric light socket. Both machines were expensive – $60 and £35 – and rather cumbersome for convenient home use. In 1913 *First Aid to the Servantless* dismissed electric sweepers, which then weighed around 75lbs, as 'far too much for any woman to lift about, still more to carry up and down stairs'. They were relevant only to 'such establishments as keep men-servants, and with which it is entirely out of our province to deal here'.

The electric vacuum cleaner in its modern form was the vision of James Murray Spangler, an asthmatic school janitor of New Berlin, Ohio. Casting about for a way of making his job more suited to his health, he developed a sweeping machine. Although crude to look at, it has all the elements necessary for a successful portable vacuum cleaner. Made of tin, wood, and a broom-handle, it had an electric motor coupled to a fan disc and a cylindrical brush. Behind the motor and the fan, Spangler arranged one of his wife's pillowcases to catch the dust. The clear and simple drawing in the 1908 specifications showed that a flexible tube with a nozzle could be fitted into the machine for cleaning curtains and upholstery. Spangler was related to a leather goods manufacturer, W. H. 'Boss' Hoover. Hoover had predicted the disastrous effect of the new automobile industry on the old carriage trade, and was looking for an alternative enterprise. He began to manufacture Spangler's invention as the Electric Suction Sweeper. Soon it was known simply as the Hoover. Despite the initial high price of $75, the machine sold well enough for Hoover to be exporting to Europe by 1913, and by 1918 Hoover made nothing but electric sweepers and other domestic appliances.

W. H. Hoover's first Electric Suction Sweeper, patented in 1908 by James Murray Spangler

The very first model had the greatest charm. Smartly etched with a livery of gold on black, most of its body was filled by the very large fan and a motor mounted above it. The brush was almost completely separate from the main body, sticking eagerly forward in search of dust. It must have been heavy to push around the floor, let alone to carry up and down stairs, and by 1915 Spangler had improved it. His second patent shows a much smaller fan, revolving faster, and connected more directly with the brush and the air inlet. In 1918, the machine already looked curiously modern, with a light-coloured casing, rubber bumpers and trade-marked dustbag.

Like sewing-machines, Hoovers were well-suited to door-to-door selling. Hundreds of thousands were sold on the credit system to customers who saw them only as a dramatic improvement on carpet-sweepers and had never witnessed the wonderful efficiency of large vacuum-cleaning plants. Dealer organization quickly spread across the United States, offering generous upkeep and repair services to gain customers. Four years after specialists had expressed doubts about the value of portable sweepers, the Hoover and its imitators had become an American institution. They appeared in mail-order catalogues in 1917 at the very reasonable price of $19.45. By 1929, the *Encyclopædia Britannica*, then edited in the United States, stated that 'The light portable type is by far the most popular, and represents 95% of all vacuum cleaners in use.'

In Britain such cleaners took longer to be popularly accepted. Fears of electrocution had to be allayed. 'There is one definite quality in all reputable makes of vacuum cleaner – the possibility of a shock being received while one is using them is so remote as to be non-existent for all practical purposes', declared *Ideal Home* reassuringly in March 1930. Doubts existed as to the ability of domestics to cope with their mechanics – they were countered by such advertisements as this for the Ideal: 'It eats up Dirt . . . If servants work with it at all they must do thorough work. It means contented servants, and leaves them as well as their mistresses with more time and strength for other tasks.' Thirdly and more important, electric power was slower to become generally available in Britain, so many households could not use electric tools even if they wanted to.

British companies were quick to develop rival lightweight electric sweepers. Booth's Goblin, the Magnet and the Universal were the best-known makes. Swedish firms competed with the Electrolux and the Tellus. The Electrolux was purely a suction sweeper, with no brushes at all, but it had the advantage of a very light motor. The Tellus was attractively adaptable, capable of drying hair or clothes, working as a room-heater or cooling-fan, and of spraying paint.

A short-lived enthusiasm, which might be worth re-examining in view of energy shortages, was the water-powered vacuum cleaner. The Water Witch could be attached to a tap, and worked by suction. Dust washed away down the waste-pipe, and the whole outfit weighed about 23lbs. It cost $75, which was not cheap, but was sold as the bargain of a lifetime. 'Never wears out, will last as long as your building . . . and gives better results without machinery'. It had a long flexible tube like the Electrolux, and was very easy to use. The absence of dust-bags was a hygienic advantage, and the generous supply of accessories included a hair-dryer and a vibro-masseur.

The two basic electric vacuum cleaners – pure suction with a small tank, and the rotating brush and fan – remain essentially the same today. In 1926 Hoover added their beater-rod to alternate with the brush on the cylinder and so increase cleaning power. Bigger and better dust-bags, smaller quieter motors, and wider greedier nozzles evolved. Fans shrank, tilted to the vertical, and finally disappeared from sight. A single streamlined casing shrouded the works of the 1935 Hoover, and its portrait was splashed in a full-page, front-page spread over the 21 February edition of the *Daily Mail*:

IN THE NICK OF TIME FOR YOUR SPRING-CLEANING! . . .
£10.15s

Spring-cleaning was certainly transformed by the vacuum cleaner. 'To the modern woman, the annual ritual known as spring-cleaning need present few problems. If the march of time has brought the drawback of poor domestic service, it is of some comfort that the difficulties which beset the lady of the house of the Victorian era no longer torment her grand-daughter', declared *House and Garden* in March 1924. It recommended a Hoover vacuum cleaner, a Ronuk floor-polisher and buckets with built-in mop-drainers. 'Spring Cleaning is really a pleasure in this mechanical age, as housework has ceased to be a drudgery, and efficiency in this line has increased one hundred per cent', wrote *Vogue* thankfully in April 1928. More adventurous thinkers suggested that the once-yearly upheaval was now unnecessary, since homes could be kept so much cleaner all the year round.

None of these attitudes necessarily led to the manager of the house spending less time at the task of household organization. The work may have changed in nature – no more tea-leaves on the carpets or blood-gall on the floor-boards – but there was just as much of it. Instead of lessening the hours spent in cleaning the house, the mechanical aids were used by many to raise standards of cleanliness. The assertion that middle-class homes could be kept clean all the year round without the help of servants was hailed as one of the triumphs of the twentieth century, instead of being recognized as a tyranny just as great for the once proudly managerial housewife as that formerly exerted on her hard-working tweeny. Today Margaret Trent is no longer upright in gloves dusting the parlour – she is on her knees and alone.

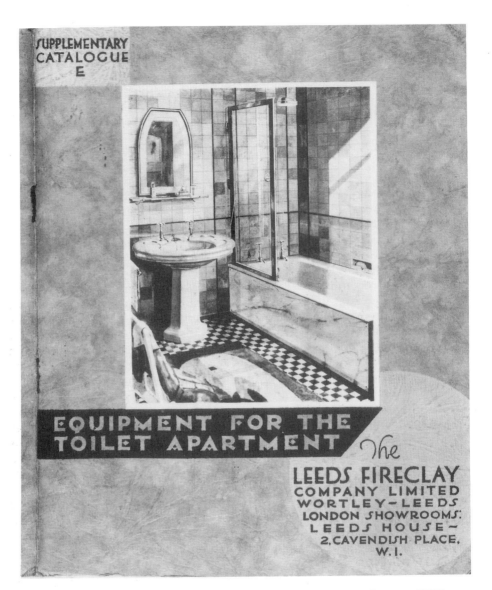

Art Deco bathroom from the Leeds Fireclay Company catalogue, *c.*1925

6

The Bathroom

. . . a little place of Easement of marble, with sluices to wash all
down.

From the inventory of Windsor Castle, *c.*1700

Few people realize how recent and half-hearted is our present custom
of immersing ourselves alone in a long tub of hot water. Communal
bath-houses, historically and cross-culturally, have a far longer history.
From Peking to Sparta, from Russia to Rome, bathing was an important
and very sociable ritual. Even late in the nineteenth century the merits
of several different methods of bathing were still being debated. Hot
bathing was approached with considerable circumspection. A bath of a
temperature between 98°F and 112°F was 'a powerful stimulant which
should never be used by persons in a state of perfect health, but is
employed only in cases of disease, and this should be always under the
direction of a medical practitioner'. Sea-bathing as a cure for consumption made the fortune of Dr Russell, who published his *Uses of Sea Water
in Diseases of the Glands* in 1753. Thousands of pale victims flocked to his
fashionable Brighthelmstone practice, and a spate of building justified
the memorial which still stands to Russell on the site of Brighton's
Royal Albion Hotel – 'If you seek his monument, look around you.'

The vigorous cold-water plunge, promoted among reformed public
schools of the Rugby type, originated in the fashion for hydropathic
treatments around the 1830s, and was reinforced by a renewed
enthusiasm for sea-bathing later in the century. In the 1870s, *Cassell's
Household Guide* described cold baths as 'one of the most refreshing
comforts and luxuries of life . . . calculated to make the whole body
rejoice with buoyancy and exhilaration of spirits'. It recommended a
temperature of 60°F, and warned that it was important to ensure that
one was in the right state of mind. 'If the mind is languid, gloomy,
fatigued or desponding, a cold bath may be attended by risk.' Five to
ten minutes was the limit for the 'delicate unaccustomed', and fifteen to
twenty for the robustly healthy.

Steam-baths were another option. As well as being popular in Scandinavia and Russia, they had respectable Eastern origins, and many public Turkish baths were set up in large cities in the second half of the century. Domestic versions were also popular. In 1854, the *Encyclopaedia Britannica*'s article on bathing declared that 'The vapour bath is infinitely superior to the warm bath for all the purposes for which a warm bath can be given. An effective vapour bath may be easily had in any house at little cost or trouble.' The simplest method was to heat a brick in the oven, place it in a basin and pour water over it while the bather sat close by, holding a towel over himself and the steam. Another, illustrated in the *Mechanics Magazine* in 1826, was to use a large bag, tightened around the neck of the bather, with an inlet for steam connected to a small water-heating apparatus. In 1882, an attachment to convert a long tub into a vapour bath was patented in the United States: a geyser-like device fed hot water along a pipe pierced with tiny holes.

Perhaps the best-known sort of steam-bath was the large wooden cabinet encasing all but the bather's head. A gas-heated version was described by William Sugg in 1884. It had luminous flames, and a self-regulating tap. A small boiler was thoughtfully provided to warm the feet, as early in the day the normal household boiler might not have heated up adequately to provide a foot-warmer. Under the seat were gas-burners with a small vessel of water set over them to provide the steam. Other steam-baths used paraffin or electricity to heat them. On the whole, however, the fashion for steam-baths did not survive the spread of plumbed hot water. Their main advantage had been the very small amount of water required. Today, as saunas, their benefits are better understood, and they are once more becoming popular. Interestingly, they also indicate a return to the more sociable bathing of former times.

Showers were among the earliest and most convenient methods of taking a bath, again requiring a very little absolute volume of water. One was sold among the possessions of Robert Burns's wife at her death in 1837, and an English hip-bath with shower attached was illustrated in an 1847 Birmingham catalogue. Thackeray's Pendennis had one as a matter of course in his otherwise shabby lodgings in a London Inn of Court. The 1851 Great Exhibition showed a wide range of showers, but only a few rather primitive bath-tubs. This may have been because the mechanics of the shower were of greater interest than a simple tub, but at a time when the transport and supply of water was a major problem, it is also likely that this economical method of washing was preferred.

Early showers were usually hand-pumped, on the principle still occasionally used in boats and caravans today. Fearncombe's 1866 catalogue showed several varieties, some attractively painted with flowers around their precarious-looking reservoirs. Such showers could be fitted over any shape of bath-tub – hip-bath, sponge-bath, or long-tub – and curtains draped the whole contraption. To release the water in the reservoir, a handle was pulled, and the water poured through its sieve-like base. Presumably one soaped oneself thoroughly first, then suffered a short deluge. Or perhaps the more experienced could control the flow by staccato jerks on the handle. Some had outlet taps on the cistern, but there seems to have been no provision for emptying the bath underneath except by jugs. It is possible that the used water was then pumped up again, and so drained off through the otherwise mysterious tap on the cistern. Certainly a shower described in *Scientific American* in 1878 used such a principle. The water circulated constantly, operated by a simple treading movement, rather as if one was jogging naked in the rain. Not tremendously hygienic, perhaps, but 'of particular advantage if a hot shower is required, as only a slight degree of heating is necessary'. An Englishman, Mr Noble, produced an ingenious 'bath in a suitcase' on the same lines. The pump was contained in a light metal box, the lid of which, divided and covered with cork, served as pedals to recirculate the water. Presumably the shower was hand-held, and history does not relate what happened to the water.

Like the vapour bath, the great advantage of the shower was the small amount of water it used. While water was in short supply it was an ideal method of keeping clean. It was especially recommended for poorer types of housing. W. P. Gerhard wrote of American city housing in 1895:

A great step forward in the improvement of tenement houses would be made if they were provided with bathing facilities. As at present constructed even the best have absolutely none. The reason is . . . that tubs without hot water would rarely be used . . . I am firmly convinced that the shower bath offers many advantages for the tenement houses . . . It is not necessary to provide a bath.[2]

As running hot water became a matter of course, baths asserted the primary importance they still hold today. In the next fifty years the shower ceased its separate existence in the English home. Towering, mahogany-encased, it crowned the bath-tub in its great Edwardian magnificence, then grew simpler, thinly glass-walled, and finally withered away altogether into a chromium-plated snake clinging to the tiles behind the taps. Only the energetic and time-conscious Americans preserved it as an invigorating and speedy washing aid. Recently showers have become more popular in England than ever before. Efficient built-in water-heaters, greater expertise in providing adequate pressure, and a new mania for scented cleanliness have made shower-rooms one of the most common home-improvements of the 1980s.

The key factor for comfortable bathing in a long tub was enough hot water. Carrying jugs of water upstairs was clearly too primitive, and alternatives began to be explored early in the century. In February 1827 the *Philosophical Magazine* illustrated a bath with its own heater. Its inventor, E. D. Thompson, claimed that it 'had stood the test of actual experiment'. Water passed from a storage cistern into a cylinder in a furnace, and thence into the bath. Unlike many later heaters, it provided a safety-valve for escaping steam. Cole's *Journal of Design* described another such bath in 1850, heated by coal, which a Mr Tyler exhibited at the Great Exhibition. Warriner's gas-heated bath was also mentioned. Its gas flames played on the underside of the bath itself, a technique that had obvious drawbacks. In a cheaper Warriner model, a heater could be attached to the gas-lighting bracket and then immersed in the bath-water. This method was a development of the ancient use of bricks – first heating them in the fire, then dropping them in the bath-water. Charcoal heaters, such as the aptly named Salamander, were a slightly more sophisticated variation of this principle.

The three methods of water-heating tried out in these early experiments – heating water in a boiler and piping it to the bath, immersion heating and heating at the point of use – are all still used today in the shape of central heating boilers, electric immersion heaters and geysers.

The geyser was invented in 1868 by Benjamin Maugham. Named after the Icelandic natural hot spring 'gusher' (*gjosa*: to gush), it was simple in principle. A water-tube spiralled or zigzagged its way through a cylinder containing gas burners. The first Maugham geyser was by far the best-looking of these usually unsightly appliances. Squatting on short curly legs, it rose in elegant piers of green-marbled metal to its brass-trimmed peak. Another popular type was the Boiling Steam Therma invented by an Oxford professor of chemistry, Vernon Harcourt. A continuous stream of water heated to 120°F could be obtained, at a rate of up to forty gallons an hour. Sugg recommended that it should be placed over kitchen sinks, in housemaid's closets, in bathrooms and nurseries. Such duplication had the advantage of not wasting heat by sending water around pipes, but the real reason was because these early geysers could not withstand internal water pressure. Gas was not the only fuel for geysers – Ewart produced an oil-fired model, and Jennings developed one fired by coke, wood or coal.

A link between the geyser and the household boiler which heated water for the whole house was the multi-point pressure geyser. The

The first Maugham geyser, marbled in green and gold,
patented 1868

first of these was the 1899 Ewart Califont, which could supply every hot tap in the house from its home in the basement. In a superbly detailed house cross-section, an advertisement showed its benefits for every room from the attic nursery to the billiard-room's cloakroom. However, the early geysers had their darker side. They were notoriously difficult to manage, and an enormous number of accidents resulted from explosions of gas or leakage of fumes into badly ventilated bathrooms. Eventually pilot-lights, interlocking devices between gas and water-jets, and thermostatic controls made taking baths under a geyser less hazardous, and today gas or electric point-of-use heaters are very popular indeed, especially for showers.

Just turn the Tap

Ewart's 1924 Califont geyser produced water hot enough to make tea

Preferable to the geyser for those who could afford it was a hot-water tank heated by first the kitchen range and later a special boiler allied to a central heating system. Small tanks had long been attached to the old coal ranges as a practical way of using the surplus heat they produced. By moving the tank up the chimney, water could be heated in a more systematic way by using the steam rising from the boiler in the range, forcing cold water to descend in another pipe, and so gradually heating a second tank. Eventually such tanks were moved to the top of the house, from where hot water could be gravity-fed all over the house. As long as pipes were kept unobstructed, the water-supply regular and the fire hot, this worked well. Disasters occurred when frost or mineral deposits blocked the pipes. 'We have fresh in our memory several of these lamentable occurrences', wrote *Cassell's Household Guide* in the early 1870s edition. 'The most prominent in our mind at the present is that which took place in the kitchen of Longlan Vicarage, Derbyshire, by which two women were killed and a third seriously injured. This explosion was preceded by several others in various parts, both in London and the country, of a like dangerous and fatal character.' Such stories probably explain why, despite adequate technology, such hot water systems were very slow to spread. By the 1930s the 'back boiler', set in the kitchen or sitting-room chimney, was a reliable means of providing hot water for the average home. More prosperous houses could indulge in the new central heating, and so obtain almost unlimited hot water.

Hot water and the extension of plumbing to the upper storeys opened the way for the development of the bathroom proper. One of the earliest, at Hanby House, is mentioned by Surtees in *Mr Sponge's Sporting Tour* (1853). It was furnished with 'every imaginable luxury', including 'hip baths and footbaths, a showerbath and hot and cold baths adjoining, and mirrors innumerable'. But twenty-five years later, as Samuel Hellyer pointed out, bathrooms were evidently still the exception rather than the rule:

> One might as well look for a fountain in a desert as for a bath in any of our English houses, or modern ones even, below a large rental. It is not too much to say that there are scores of villages in England without a single bath in the whole village, except perhaps in the rector's or squire's . . . to mention a bathroom to a landlord or householder is to paint before his mind's eye the Bankruptcy Court. And to talk of having hot water circulation throughout the house is to plunge the landlord into *hot water*.[3]

Hellyer was the most literate of authorities on sanitary technology. And if one can stand the generous litter of puns, his book makes very amusing reading, especially the stirring exhortation on the duties of the plumber in furthering human happiness and his bigoted diatribe against the new trade unions.

For some time, even where bathrooms were available, it was regarded as polite to allow guests to bathe in their own rooms if they wished. Mrs Peel advised in *How to Keep House* (1902) that 'There should always be a bath in the room and a bath blanket. If there are bathrooms, the visitors may prefer to use them, but the choice should be given.'

Another manual, written a few years later, advised that the bathroom should be reserved for lady guests, and gentlemen provided with portable tubs in their rooms. Besides being a flagrant case of sexual discrimination, this reflected the increasing comfort of the bathroom. It was rapidly becoming a most luxurious and desirable part of the home.

Many metals were experimented with for bath-tubs, and Hellyer gave a useful run-down of the options. Earliest and most common in everyday use was the wooden tub lined with sheet lead. This lasted well, but could never be thoroughly cleaned. Zinc was good when new, but deteriorated rapidly. Wood lined with sheet copper looked splendid, and could be polished, but again was too soft, although 'for good houses' Hellyer recommended a first-quality taper-bath of solid copper. Porcelain, easily cleaned and durable, became increasingly popular among the well-to-do, but was criticized by Hellyer as being too heavy, slow to heat and usually too small. 'Maybe five foot is long enough for Zaccheus, but how is a Saul to stretch himself out in such a bath?' Marble was one of the most ancient and luxurious materials for baths, and Hellyer approved such baths – in summer at least. He warned that 'In winter, when a hot bath is needed, or when a bath is required for invalids, they not only look cold but strike so.'

Cast iron, the metal that was eventually to be accepted as standard for baths, was available in several different finishes – galvanised, enamelled or painted. All these techniques had their drawbacks. The finishes wore off, became rusty, or cracked. Painted baths were often very attractive. Strode and Company advertised an elegant bath, complete with gas heater, in 1879. The tub itself was iron, with a fringe of cast iron round it, and a tall conical heater standing sentinel at one side. A stylized frieze was painted around the outside of the tub, and a marbled look applied with tinted bath enamel.

Such elegance was less successful when attempted by a do-it-yourself enthusiast like the Grossmiths' Mr Pooter. At first he was delighted by the effect of the red enamel paint, dismissing Carrie's reservations. But when he took an extra-hot bath a few days later to counter a chill, he experienced 'the greatest fright I have ever received in my life':

> Imagine my horror on discovering my hand, as I thought, full of blood. My first thought was that I had ruptured an artery, and was bleeding to death, and should be discovered, later on, looking like a second Marat, as I remember seeing him at Madame Tussaud's. My second was to ring the bell, but remembered there was no bell to ring. My third was that there was nothing but enamel paint, which had dissolved with the boiling water. I stepped out of the bath perfectly red all over, resembling the Red Indians I have seen depicted at an East End theatre. I determined

not to say a word to Carrie, but to tell Farmerston to come on Monday and paint the bath white.[4]

Porcelain enamelling, the ultimate solution to lining iron tubs, was far from perfect in its early form. Although easy to clean, and long-lasting if handled with care, it was very prone to chipping. Cheaper white-glass enamels cracked and crazed with rapid changes of temperature, as they did not expand and contract as quickly as the metal underneath. Moreover, before assembly-line techniques were applied to bath-tub manufacture, this was a very slow process, and the tubs were therefore expensive to make. Lightweight, double-shelled, enamelled iron tubs were first made specially to order for Pullman carriages in 1900. By 1916, the United States had begun to mass-produce these tubs, and their cost dropped dramatically. Improved enamelling techniques made surfaces more durable, and over the next twenty years prices continued to fall. The Chicago mail-order house of Crane could sell a full set of bathroom fittings – bath, basin and water-closet – for $70 in 1940, compared with the 1910 price of $200 for a bath alone.

As the middle classes increasingly accepted the desirability of bathrooms, and manufacturers brought such luxuries within the reach of average incomes, architects had to devise ways of adapting existing houses and designing new ones to accommodate them. The small dressing-rooms next door to master bedrooms were an obvious target. Otherwise, extensions could be built over back kitchens, or bites taken out of over-large bedrooms. If no space at all was available, there was always the brilliant space-saving idea offered by the *Scientific American* in 1881 to consider. It looked like an ornate and well-polished wardrobe, complete with mirror and drawer handles, but opened out to unfold a bath-tub equipped with hot and cold water on tap. Similar devices, without piped water and so relatively portable, remained popular in American mail-order catalogues until well into the twentieth century.

The ultimate in bathroom luxury was achieved in Edwardian England. Catalogues show an enormous range of decorated baths, bidets, foot-baths, basins, water-closets, tiles, friezes, cabinets, looking-glasses and towel-rails. Fixtures looked like and were regarded as furniture, and as such were expected to reflect individual taste. Just as electrical firms in the 1870s had offered conversions to suit each buyer's taste, so did bath-makers. 'Available in various woods', boasted one catalogue, 'and can be modified to suit architects' requirements'. The ideal bathroom was spacious and full of incidental furniture – an armchair was quite normal. The most splendid baths were the grand L-shaped shower-and-bath combinations, such as Shanks' Superior Bath

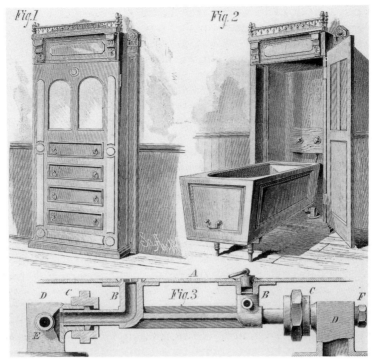

Victorian space-saving design: Damen's folding bath-tub
featured in *The Scientific American* in 1881

Cabinet, 'made in mahogany, walnut, or other wood'. Its balustraded crown, flanking columns and decoratively carved side-panels gave it a dignity unrivalled before or since. The London Science Museum has a splendid cabinet-bath, with a formidable array of controls for the shower. Water came from every possible direction: overhead shower or douche, waist-level spray, or plunge at tap-height. At a slightly increased cost a thrilling 'wave' was available, a sheet of water to cascade over the bather from toe to top.

Good-looking as it was, wood was far from suitable for bathroom use. Easily stained and affected by damp, the cabinets also became infected with a mouldy filth which could only be removed by dismantling the entire cabinet. So attention shifted to softening the naked lines of the cast-iron enamelled bath, better calculated to 'fulfil the sanitary requirements of the age'. Shanks' independent spray-, plunge- and shower-bath, 'with rolled edge and ornamental feet, finished outside to stand without any woodwork or enclosure whatever', was simpler than its wooden ancestors, but still commanding.

Early models still harked back to the cabinet years with a rather unpleasant mock-woodgrain finish, but within a few years the Independent appeared decorated in a confidently debased classical style all its own, the shower-head nodding triumphantly from the top like a nickel-plated sunflower.

Bathroom interiors were often as magnificent as the actual fittings. The most luxurious floors and walls were covered with sheets of marble; the most modest looked to linoleum or cork and varnished the walls thickly. The bathrooms in between were more attractive than either. Here the craft of the nineteenth-century potter reached its zenith in the casting and colouring of tiles. The most restrained were elegantly severe in black and white, but under the influence of Art Nouveau, much wilder fantasies were brought to life. Writhing plants and elongated wild-life tracked multi-coloured paths in bas-relief across floors, walls and ceilings. The range of subtle colour and the imaginativeness of the designs have made such tiles collectors' pieces today, but unhappily very few survive in their original settings. Windows too were made things of beauty in what was also a practical attempt to preserve modesty in pre-plastic-curtain times. Glass was leaded and stained, either in geometric shapes, or in a picture matching the themes of the tiles. More economically, they could be covered with opaque papers, patterned and coloured to give the same soft twilight effect.

Finally a heating system – perhaps the weakest feature of pre-electric bathrooms – was necessary. Coal fires were romantic but dirty, and needed constant attention. Oil-stoves smelt. Gas was probably the best option, as long as the room was properly ventilated. Heated towel-rails could take the chill off the air, but did little more if the room was large. The development of today's small bathroom was influenced by problems of warmth as well as considerations of space.

Although adopted rapidly by the middle classes, nineteenth-century bathrooms remained expensive, and it took some time for them to percolate down the social scale. In 1877 Hellyer, one of the great hygienic visionaries, illustrated a bath in the kitchen of an artisan's house which could be neatly disguised as a settle when not in use. It had no tapped water, but was so close to the kitchen range that it must have been easy to fill from the hot-water tank. But Hellyer was well ahead of his time. Many so-called philanthropists were unpleasantly acid on the subject of working-class washing. In 1905 Baillie Scott wrote dismissively:

> It must be frankly admitted that the average cottager would have little use for a bath, and in such families it is often only the children who enjoy a weekly tub. A recent inspection of some

model cottages in which the greater part of the scullery was taken up by a full-size bath left one wondering as to the probable use to which it would be put – a handy place for storing potatoes, perhaps.[5]

The Garden Cities of Hampstead, Welwyn and Letchworth set new standards of space and hygiene that were adopted by almost all architects. 'Even the smallest house must have its fitted bath', declared *Ideal Home* in March 1922. Tenements were still being built without bathrooms in the late 1930s, but by then they were just as exceptional as the model cottages with scullery bath-tubs had once been. Most new housing schemes included bathrooms as a matter of course.

Once the principle of a bathroom in every home was accepted, mass production of fittings brought prices down. From the 1920s the iron enamelled five-foot bath-tub with rolled-over edge dictated the size of the bathroom provided in new houses. Compact 'bathcells' had been envisaged very early in the United States. In 1853 a New Jersey hotel annexed one to every bedroom.[6] Catherine Beecher designed a flat in the 1860s which showed a tightly combined unit of bedroom, bathroom and kitchenette. American bathrooms were both earlier in arriving and far more functionally designed than European ones. Even the Fifth Avenue bathroom of a millionaire like George Vanderbilt was crudely laced with bare pipes.

The spirit of the Edwardian bathroom was not entirely lost in the new era of hygienic orthodoxy. Those who could afford to, still experimented with luxurious excesses. As financial superiority passed across the Atlantic, wealthy Americans began to set the trend in unusual bathroom design. *Home and Garden* printed a 'Letter from New York' in 1921 which showed how fashions had effectively reversed. Never mind the sanitary requirements of the age – it was back to the bathroom as total environment. 'The hospital effects that used to be considered good enough are quite a back number. The present ideal is something more like a boudoir. Some great ladies of the eighteenth century used to hold their receptions in the bath, and I can quite imagine myself doing so in some of the modern bathrooms I have seen'.

Marble was still most highly sought-after, but cosy chintz or white-wooden panelling was also recommended. A glass chandelier, an elaborate dressing-table and a water-closet disguised as a Louis XV chair, made the bathroom 'fit for the great ritual of self-adornment rather than a hasty wash'. The most expensive English magazines also showed extravagant bathrooms. A sunken bath of green Siberian marble in Chelsea Park Gardens recalled the Romans. Regency elegance was evoked by the surround of satinwood and ebony which boxed in a 1920s bath at Madresfield Court, Malvern.

By the 1930s, bathrooms were less nostalgia-bound. Mass-produced components became less blatantly utilitarian, and were designed in consistent styles. A *Vogue* article in March 1931 described modern bathroom luxury.

> When those beautifully enamelled gadgets for bathrooms were first offered us – soap dishes, special electric lights, cupboards, and sets of shelves – the effect was to produce a rather bristling type of room, everything gleaming and glittering and offering itself in a most eager and obvious way. Nowadays what we really like is to have everything recessed, concealed, smoothed away, and our bathroom walls are honeycombed with excavations for various gadgets instead of being spiky with things that jut out of them.

Colour came to the bathroom in the 1930s. It was a simple, total look, not the fairy-tale wilderness of the 1900s. Expensive baths grew more massive. To quote again from *Vogue*:

> The modish bathroom is no longer frigidly and hygienically white, but coloured like Aphrodite's sea-shell . . . At the Froy shop, in Bond Street, for instance, you have a choice of delightful colours – orchid, deep blue, Rose du Barry, Tang red, Ming green, and other shades . . . With ingenious lighting arrangements, you can change the whole colour of the bathroom at the flick of a switch . . . The simplicity of a huge block of glistening marble or enamel is entirely in harmony with the spirit of modern decoration. We like our metal fittings too of a massive-looking, simple type. The use of chromium for such fittings gives a gleaming finish that neither corrodes nor discolours.

Such bathrooms were rare luxuries. Right at the other end of the scale was the prefabricated bathroom which Buckminster Fuller produced in 1936. Every component, from the soap-holder to the bath, formed an integral part of the wall or floor. The wash-basin and water-closet faced each other with the raised bath between them, approached through a stable-door affair that demanded some agility to negotiate. The whole unit measured only 4 feet 6 inches by 5 feet. All the parts were stamped simultaneously out of a metal skin, easily mass-produced at minimal cost. Such extreme and impersonal solutions have not been adopted, except for submarines, aircraft and some Japanese hotels, but the experiments stimulated the production of cheap sanitary equipment, and helped to make the 'benison of hot water' available to all.

From Wash-stand to Hand-basin

Wash-stands are of very ancient origin. They appear in domestic interiors represented in medieval manuscripts and in Dürer's engravings. Curiously, medieval lavers were often more 'modern' than their eighteenth- and nineteenth-century successors, with small cisterns above them rather than a jug of water tucked underneath. Eighteenth-century wash-stands were beautiful pieces of furniture – naturally enough, since they were made to stand in the corner of a bedroom or dressing-room rather than being isolated in a purely functional room for washing. They were frequently triangular in shape, made of polished rosewood, walnut or mahogany, with holes cut for bowl, jug and soap-dish.

By the 1830s a new form of wash-stand had developed. Larger, with a rectangular marble top, this fixture had a bowl either standing upon it or set into the top, and a magnificent array of jugs, sponge-bowl, soap-dish, tooth-glass, water-bottle and container for false teeth set out on small shelves arranged around a mirror-faced back. Below stood a china pail with wicker handle and perforated tray for slops. All would be uniformly decorated. The catalogues of firms such as Wedgewood and Mason show the most delightful sets of 'toiletries' – blue transfer patterns of oriental scenes, lashings of purple begonias twined with irridescent emerald ivy, or Greek black-figure designs on terracotta. Mrs Panton even envisaged buying gas globes to match when she advised Edwin and Angelina to be sure to buy good ware and, somewhat cryptically, advised them to 'pay extra for the soap-dish.'[7] Sets of painted tin were a cheap alternative, while for servants a white enamelled bowl and jug was considered 'quite acceptable'.

Once running water was plumbed in throughout the house, the wash-stand could be replaced by a fitted basin. Instead of a removable bowl, the whole top was moulded from one piece of porcelain, earthenware or marble. The unsightly pipes for water and waste were, in England at least, usually concealed behind a wooden front. The Americans were less modest, revelling in the no-nonsense functionalism that was a characteristic of their bathrooms.

The cascading vegetable life which had swathed the artillery of the wash-stand was not immediately lost when the fitted basin was introduced. An Edward Johns design of 1880 shows azaleas trickling down to the waste-pipe, scallop shells coddling the soap, and a heavily marbled finish overall. Twyfords Chrysanthemums, Victoria and Roses, and Gobelin designs were splendid features of their 1900 catalogue. By then cast iron had replaced the wooden structures around many basins. Some supports were simple, others baroque. The

Athena Quadrangular Lavatory was upheld by filigree angels. A polished brass central pillar disguised the comings and goings of the water and held up a four-sided looking-glass complete with shelves and electrolier. With its brass taps, copper pipes, gun-metal wastes, vulcanite plugs and brass chains, the whole edifice must have cut a resplendent figure in those institutions far-sighted enough to equip themselves with it.

As the demand for cheaper basins increased, the one-piece porcelain enamelled fire-clay basin was developed, first mounted in brackets, and later on a matching pedestal. With mass production, hygienic and utilitarian simplicity was the essence of design. Taps became thinner and meaner, the old generously splayed brass spouts replaced by small-bore chrome or even china enamel. Patterns were unfashionable after the First World War; a lily-livered obsession with pastel confined colour ranges to a hundred shades of pale pink and green.

As bathrooms became common, basins became an intrinsic part of them, rather than a replacement for the wash-stand in the bedroom.

Edward Durell Stone's 1940 bathroom had a solid sheet of marble across its hand-basins

Wash-stands remained a useful alternative for many houses, relieving pressure on the bathroom, and a surprising number of 1930s three-bedroomed semi-detacheds were built with a hand-basin in the master bedroom. Recent affluence has extended this hand-basin to the bathroom or shower-room *'en-suite'*, contrived out of an old closet or by dividing an existing bathroom into two.

Water-closets

Least attractive of the old domestic chores was disposing of the euphemistically named 'night-soil'. An enterprising Manchester firm attempted both to ease the task and put the by-products to good use with a housemaid's barrow it advertised in 1859. This was designed to hold slops, ashes and night-soil. Once these had been collected, the maid was supposed to wheel the barrow over the garden paths to distribute the ashes, then around the flower-beds to manure the roses. A brush behind the front wheel distributed the spoil evenly as it fell. The environmentally conscious can only applaud such a device, but it is not altogether surprising that the mainstream of invention followed a quite different path.

Attempts to mechanize the closet began surprisingly early. In 1596, a godson of Queen Elizabeth, Sir John Harrington, described the workings of a water-closet in his *Metamorphosis of Ajax* ('jakes' was the current slang for a closet). He explained 'how unsavoury places may be made sweet, noisome places made wholesome, filthy places made cleanly' at a cost of thirty shillings or so. The illustrations that accompany his very clearly explained text are charming. The essential parts of the closet are shown, accompanied by an engraving of 'the rare engineer Archimedes'. Little fish are drawn in the cistern to show where the water was stored. The actual arrangement of the closet seems from the drawing to be a sensible one, with a cistern above for gravity feed, a smoothly finished seat over a bowl, and a connecting pipe controlled by a close-fitting screw 'to yield water with a pretty strength when you would let it in'. This was thoughtfully provided with a safety device 'that children and busy folk disorder it not'. Harrington also emphasized how important it was that everything should be watertight, and that the vessel should be left 'a foot deep in clean water' after use. A Harrington closet was installed in Richmond Palace.

This was a freakishly isolated case. Nothing more was heard of such closets for some 200 years, although Queen Anne was supplied at Windsor with 'a little place of Easement of marble, with sluices to wash all down'. In the eighteenth century, closets seem to have been more common in France than in England or the United States. A Parisian

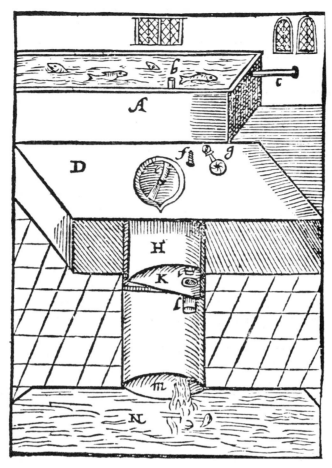

A. the Cesterne.
B. the little washer.
C. the wast pipe.
D. the seate boord.
E. the pipe that comes from the Cesterne.
F. the Screw.
G. the Scallop shell to cover it when it is shut downe.[53]
H. the stoole pot.
I. the stopple.
K. the current.
L. the sluce.[54]
M. N. the vault into which it falles: always remember that (   )[55] at noone and at night, emptie it and leave it halfe a foote deepe in fayre water. And this being well done, and orderly kept, your worst privie may be as sweet as your best chamber.

Design of the workings of Sir John Harrington's water-closet
(*Metamorphosis of Ajax*, 1596)

advertisement of 1759 describes a polished oak model with gilt fittings, but no patents at all were entered for water-closets between 1617, when the Patent Office opened, and 1775: an extraordinary hiatus. It may have been that closets were constructed as a matter of course by local builders, who did not consider patents necessary to immortalize any improvements they might make. Unfortunately, this means that few details of pre-1775 closets exist. The standard mechanism of the eighteenth century, if there was a sluice at all, was the pan-closet. This had an upper bowl of lead, marble or glazed pottery. Below was a large container, with waste-pipe, in which hung a hinged metal pan. When level, this formed a water-filled base to the upper bowl. By pulling a handle, it tilted down and tipped all, or nearly all, its contents into the bowl beneath. Its efficiency depended on the amount of water available to wash it out, but the lower bowl was difficult to clean and did not drain effectively.

In 1775, Alexander Cummings, a Bond Street watchmaker, invented the valve-closet. This, after Ernest Bramah's modification to the original inefficient valve, was to remain popular until the end of the nineteenth century. The closet actually had two valves, one to let the water in, and one attached to the 'slider' which controlled the outlet at the bottom of the basin. The interconnection of these valves made the pan a quick and vigorous flusher, although again not always guaranteed to dispose of everything, and rather too prodigal of water to suit the water companies. Hellyer improved on the Cummings closet with his 1870 Optimus. Its handle was more reliable, and the water-seal better constructed. Its workings could be concealed under smoothly joined and varnished woodwork or beneath the innocent white seat of a wickerwork armchair.

After the complete absence of patents between Harrington and Cummings, it is startling to find that there were nearly 300 entered between 1775 and 1886. None were very remarkable. The standard alternative to the valve-closet was the hopper, a conical pan that was supposed to be flushed by a rather feeble gush of water at the top. 'By the times it has twirled its way down the trap it has no energy to carry anything away with it', commented Hellyer. Such closets, cheap and easily constructed, were advertised as 'suitable for prisons, mills, etc.'

1870 saw the invention of two much-used closets. Neither was perfect. First Twyford realised how much of the valve-closet's cost was increased by complicated metal workings, and thought up his simple 'wash-out' closet. Hellyer remarked that this deserved its name, since the flush lost most of its force hitting the base of the bowl, and was not powerful enough to carry refuse down the trap. Twyford set the trap at the side of the bowl, in order to leave a little water at its base, but inevitably what remained was far from clean. The siphonic closet,

John's Itonia wash-down closet, with chrysanthemum decoration (1896)

invented in the same year by J. R. Mann, featured a fast flush, and had a siphonic jet to add force by injecting air through the waste-pipe. Its greatest advantage was its quietness in use, but its complexity could not compete with what was to become the standard design for closets, the 'wash-down' type.

There is some dispute as to who was the actual inventor of this familiarly shaped pan, with its S-bend, but D. R. Bostel's 1889 patent seems to be the first official recording of the idea. Water gushed straight down, across the pan, and through the S-shaped trap, thoroughly scouring the simple moulding, and leaving the necessary level of water to seal the waste-pipe. With improvements in cisterns, and in the force of water pushed through to the pan, the wash-down gradually replaced all other types. Today many of the older designs are actually illegal on grounds of hygiene or water conservancy.

More interesting than the somewhat uninspired mechanics of water-closets are the superb designs for sanitary ware that quite literally flowered between 1880 and 1914. Even the cheapest hoppers were available with pretty blue-and-white transfer patterns inside. The John's Itonia (1896) was lined with chrysanthemums, with a simply moulded pedestal, covered with more chrysanthemums. A decorated base to the cistern-pipe and the cistern itself provided more scope for the flowery motif, by now perhaps a little overwhelming. Ornate cast-iron supports held up the thick mahogany seat. Many designs were entirely inappropriate. Shanks' Lion pattern of 1896 seemed an unnecessary indignity for the king of beasts to endure, nor was the John's wide-mouthed Dolphin of 1880 a much happier concept.

'Low-down' suites with the cistern just above the pan were introduced in the 1890s, but could not offer the impressive pressure guaranteed by the ceiling-high cistern until more intricate flushing mechanisms were developed. Such mechanisms remain unsatisfactory, particularly in hard-water districts, but the neat, all-of-a-piece look is preferred to the reliable old thunderers from on high, and sanitary considerations have seen off the germ-harbouring intricacies of the highly decorated designs.

There is no denying the domestic convenience of a private bathroom. Public baths remain popular, but they now have a quite different function – fitness rather than cleanliness – and generally lack the atmosphere of a community meeting-place. Meeting head-on while doing a racing crawl is no fun. But the latest aquatic leisure domes give new opportunities for friendliness, whether by lying companionably in the warm bubbles of the jacuzzi or steaming sociably in the sauna. The ancient tradition of leisurely bathing with friends in warm water, the most relaxing and pleasant of all human pastimes, may be coming into its own again.

A well-loaded open range with two ovens and central fire

7

From Roasting-spit to Trained Lightning

No Nation can be free when half the population is enslaved in the kitchen.

Lenin, possibly apocryphal, quoted by Ann Oakley, Housewife, 1974

In 1851, cooking was a sweaty chore, requiring long-term planning. Just over a hundred years later, it is a pleasant task, initiated by the flick of a switch, and rated the most popular part of domestic labour by the housewives who participated in Ann Oakley's survey in the early 1970s.[1] Although this chapter will only consider changes in the hardware of cooking, the actual range itself, it has to be remembered that the cooking revolution has other aspects. First, the major function of the live-in servant was to get up early enough to light the kitchen range, and so provide hot water and breakfast for the family. Permanently burning ranges, and gas and electric power made this unnecessary, so easing, perhaps even speeding up, the exodus of the resident servant. Secondly, food that was once taken down to the neighbourhood bakery to be cooked is now always cooked at home, almost always by a woman. From this point-of-view, the new cooking methods lessened community co-operation, increased the domestic load on the housewife, and wasted energy. Today the wheel seems to have come full circle, and the latest trend towards takeaway food services is in a sense a hopeful sign of liberation, making serious cooking an occasional pleasure rather than a daily duty.

Coal-fired Ranges

The principle of the iron range was straightforward: concentrate the heat source, and cooking will be quicker, surer and more economical.

In 1806 an American inventor, Oliver Evans (1755–1819), produced a combined fireplace boiler and cast-iron oven. Soon many ironmasters were adding more or less efficient grates and iron ovens to their domestic wares. Benjamin Thomson, better known as Count Rumford (1753–1814), an American member of the British Royal Society, built well-insulated ranges so far ahead of his time that it will be more appropriate to discuss them when describing the ovens of the 1930s (see p. 120). The most prolific time of invention was between 1850 and 1880, when the struggle between open and closed, or 'close' ranges was fought out.

Open ranges were the first improvements on open hearths – a basket grate set between an oven and a hot-water tank. Anne Cobbett defended them against their successors, the ranges with closed-in fire-boxes.

> The few close ranges that I have seen do not give me satisfaction. It is certainly desirable that every *possible* saving should be made in the consumption of coals, but it is not possible to have cooking in perfection without a proper degree of heat; and as far as my observation has gone, meat cannot be well-roasted unless before a good fire. For a family of moderate style of living, nothing can equal the common kitchen range with a boiler for hot water at one side and an oven at the other. It is a great convenience to have a constant supply of hot water, and an advantage to possess the means of baking a pie, pudding or cake; and this may always be done when there is a large fire for boiling or roasting. There is a great difference in the construction of these ovens. We have had several, and only three have answered.[2]

The type of range she described could have a large or small fire, depending on how one adjusted the movable plate that slid across the fire-basket. The front bar of the grate often swung forward to provide a support for pots and pans. Spits and other mechanisms of the open hearth could be fitted across the front of these ranges. More convenient in a small house was the bottle-jack. This was a bottle-shaped, brass-enclosed clockwork turnspit, which could be hung from the mantelpiece or meat-screen. When wound up, its hook revolved to turn the joint in front of the fire. Mrs Beeton had her reservations about this early rotissomat. Although 'an article of great consequence', it was 'a troublesome one, being frequently out of repair.' When there was a good meat-screen, 'A stout nail and a skein of worsted will, provided the cook be not called away from the kitchen, be found to answer the purpose.'

Simple and good as cooking on an open range could be, there were several drawbacks to such uncontrolled heat. Unless a good fire was kept in, there would be no hot water or hot oven. Keeping the fire burning steadily all day required constant attention and skill – both qualities notoriously absent in most domestics. Ten tons a year of coal was not unusual consumption in a moderate-sized kitchen. The effect of naked heat and the open chimney on food could be unpleasant and dishes frequently arrived in the dining-room 'smoked'. Pots and pans were very hard to clean, even with the aid of ashes, fine sand and much elbow-grease. Sometimes ancillary charcoal ranges were substituted, particularly in summer, for light cooking and the making of preserves, but clearly some more efficient cooking appliance was badly needed.

Closed ranges, with a small fire behind iron doors, hot-water tank and hotplates, and flues to guide the heat around the oven, proved difficult to perfect. The most notable of the many examples shown at the Great Exhibition was the Leamington. This name became a description of the type, just as Hoover became synonymous with vacuum cleaner. Saltram House, a National Trust property near Plymouth, still has a Leamington, a giant model standing free in the centre of the kitchen, with its flue running under the floor to the old

Kitchen at Saltram House, Plymouth, with free-standing Leamington close range. The fireplace retains older methods of spit-roasting, including a bottle-jack

chimney. It has two ovens, clearly marked for roasting and baking, and its makers claimed that, were its dampers but properly adjusted, meat could be as satisfactorily roasted in the oven as in front of an open fire. The damper was an iron plate at the top of the oven which slid to and fro to alter the amount of hot air circulating around the range. When I fiddled with the knobs and levers which operated the Saltram range-dampers, it seemed impossible to judge how far open they were without removing massive sections of hotplate. The more complicated the range, the more dampers it had, and a cliché of contemporary domestic fiction was a red-faced cook struggling with the dampers to the smell of burning meat.

'We cannot but regret,' wrote Catherine Beecher in 1869, 'that our old steady brick ovens have been almost completely superseded by those ranges which are infinite in their capacities and forbid all general rules.'[3] An Ipswich local newspaper of 1851 was more luridly critical:

> Immense furnaces are kept in gigantic kitchen ranges of which the object seems to be to produce the smallest possible result at the greatest possible cost. The health of the cook is injured by the inter-tropical heat maintained. The whole dwelling-house is pervaded with clouds of subtle soot, coal, and ashdust, and consequently the paint, furniture, clothing, linen and the very surface and indentations of the human frame are discoloured and begrimed.

A badly constructed stove could be positively deadly, as a letter to *The Expositor* pointed out in 1853 after an incident when three people died from the fumes given off by a stove: 'Sir, there can be no more deplorable picture than a nation which professes scientific eminence, when it tolerates loss of lives, as in a recent London case, by the use or abuse of coke. We see hundreds of these poison machines exposed for sale – a sheet of round tin filled with coke and without a smoke tub, ticketed at 18s to £8.6s.'

By the 1880s, closed ranges were improving. In Mrs Panton's 1888 *Kitchen to Garret*, she enthused over 'picturesque kitcheners, with blue-tiled backs, delightful ovens, and broad expanses of hotplate over the fire'. The 1882 Patent Economiser was a popular and fairly efficient close range of this type. It had separate ovens for roasting and baking, with dampers to adjust them in what were still considered quite different cooking operations. Baking required a close, medium heat, and roasting a hot fire with air circulating freely. This distinction, only recently reasserted in modern cookery by the appearance of rotissomats and barbecues, was at the heart of the open/close controversy. Ultimately convenience was preferred to perfect roasting, and ranges such as the Patent Economiser were accepted as superior to the open gates. They used smaller, cheaper coal, and were much less oppressive for the cook. A panoply of accessories accompanied them: plate-rack, plate-warmer, meat-hooks, racks and double dripping-pans. Prices ranged from £18 for a normal model, or as much as £28 for a four-oven model.

A popular American alternative was the free-standing close range. This was a development of the room-heating stove invented by Benjamin Franklin in the 1780s, and wasted none of its heat on the brickwork of the fireplace. Since such stoves were portable, they suited the nomadic life of the Western pioneers, and were a stand-by in the army camps of the American Civil War. They were also ideally suited to the temporary homes set up by the British as they extended the network of the Empire world-wide. Smith and Wellstood were one of the largest and most successful British manufacturers of stoves of this type. James Smith emigrated to the United States in 1832 at the age of sixteen and established a successful hardware business in Mississippi. As the climate did not suit his wife they returned to Scotland in 1841, where he established a factory to produce American-style stoves for the British market in partnership with a childhood friend, Stephen Wellstood.

By the 1880s, Smith and Wellstood made forty-three different models of stoves and kitcheners, the smallest of which cost only 7s 6d. The Enchantress, sold complete with two iron pots, a large ham-boiler, a tea-kettle, a potato-steamer, two frying-pans, a gridiron and eight iron baking-pans, cost a very moderate £3 3s. A hot-water attachment could be supplied, and, if one favoured roasting in front of the fire, the fire-doors could be swung open and a Dutch oven (a capacious meat-screen) put in front of it. Reflecting linings concentrated heat inside the oven, and a jacket of insulating material on the back and sides of the stove helped to economize on fuel.

The next thirty years saw the steady development of Smith and Wellstood, and in 1912 a catalogue was produced which is a fine combined tribute to the wilder fantasies of iron-casters' imaginations and the vast extent of the British Empire. The ranges and stoves could burn virtually any fuel – coal, wood, turf, kraal fuel, or anthracite. Every one of the 200 or so varieties was solemnly christened before it left Bonnybridge, Scotland: the African, the Australian, the Coastal Grand Pacific, the Durbanian, the Fortress, the Indess, the Kipling (for territorial camps), the Lioness, the Mrs Sam, the Plantress, the Maoriess, the Sultana, to name but a few of them.

Over the years, the Smith and Wellstood catalogues provide a very useful summary of changes in the design of cooking ranges. The Mistress was Gothic Revival, with massive hinges across its doors. The

Typically American, free-standing stoves, such as the 1876 Uncle Sam, wasted no heat on the chimney brickwork

**Earliest of the Smith and Wellstood free-standing kitcheners:
the Enchantress, £3 3s complete in 1885**

President approached the neo-Baroque, with curling foliate hinges, while the Sultana was a riot of Art Nouveau convolutions. The Edwardian Pearl was much calmer – sedate and functional, its decoration was reduced to a few geometric doodles and the SW monogram. Hinges were mere hooks and the boiler unadorned iron. A new development was the U-shaped tube which passed from fire to water-tank, conducting heat from one to the other most effectively. When supplied with the 'Elevated Steel Hot Closet made of Planished Steel Plate, with Nickel-plated brackets, Top, Side and Bottom Bands', it began to look not unlike the modern kitchen range. However, for all these shifts in design, every successful model in the firm's history remained available: the planned obsolescence that afflicts today's trade was unthought of. There was still an Enchantress in 1912.

Besides domestic and hotel ranges, Smith and Wellstood reflected Edwardian prosperity in their selection of yacht stoves – the Spanker,

Stewardess, Jack Tar and Skipper. The final refinement was the Hostess caravan stove, an ideal model for the gentlemen gypsies who lumbered around the countryside in vast and luxurious 'land yachts'. All its trimmings were nickel-plated, the back-skirting was fitted with 'hand-painted view tiles', and the main body of the stove was 'porcelain-enamelled in Green Majolica'. The Hostess foreshadowed the household ranges of the 1920s which could be had enamelled in every pastel colour of the rainbow. Enamelling was stimulated by the challenge presented by the smooth, easily cleaned surfaces of the new gas and electric cookers, with which coal ranges were finding it increasingly difficult to compete.

The solid-fuel range owed its long-term survival to two things – a new fuel and a totally revolutionary design for a constantly burning cooker. Anthracite, slow-burning enough to stay in all night, and so clean in use that little flue-cleaning was required, had been a by-product of Welsh collieries for years before it came into general use in Britain. It was again the servant problem which increased the appeal of so convenient a fuel, and overcame the prejudice in favour of open, or at least openable, fires.

One of the earliest anthracite ranges was the Treasure, shown by its maker Mr Constantine, at the Smoke Abatement Exhibition in 1882. A vivid picture of the scale of the pollution problem in the late nineteenth century was given in the Marquis of Lorne's speech when he opened the exhibition. He was so impressed by the Treasure that he declared 'Were the public but to avail themselves of such appliances, we might one day see roses blooming in Kensington Gardens.' The journalist reporting the speech added sadly that 'Any such great result as this is doubtful in the extreme.' By the 1890s, Mrs Beeton was also recommending the Treasure as less smoky and expensive than a coal range, and capable of keeping in all night. By the early twentieth century almost all manufacturers of ranges could supply them to burn anthracite as well as coal.

The second reason for the survival of solid-fuel ranges was the brilliant rethinking of cooker design achieved by a Swedish scientist, Gustav Dalén. Interestingly, Dalén's idea had been anticipated as early as the 1800s by the extraordinarily inventive Count Rumford. Faced with catering for masses of infantry, Rumford had designed a thickly-insulated close-fire range, \standing free of the chimney brickwork, with wells sunk into the hotplate to hold the pots. Each hob had a small fire underneath it, and there was an extra grate set in the side to warm the cook in case he complained of feeling cold. But, although many sitting-room fireplaces were 'Rumfordized' on the Count's draught-improving plan for open fires, none of his contemporaries thought of applying his army scheme to their kitchens. It was not until Dalén, blinded in a laboratory accident and so confined to his own home, set his mind to the waste of energy and general drudgery of cooking meals that the Aga, a superbly efficient insulated solid-fuel cooker, was produced.

The idea was basically very simple: a massive metal fire-unit kept at a very high temperature, around 900°C, by the thermostatically controlled combustion of the solid fuel inside it. This heat was both stored in the fire-unit and radiated or conducted to the hotplates and ovens – there were no convection currents to cause heat loss. The hotplate was part of the fire itself, and could boil a pint of water in less than a minute. The other, heated by conduction, was always at a low temperature for simmering. Similarly, one of the ovens was always maintained at a high temperature for roasting, and the other at a gentle heat for slow cooking. What made the Aga so economical in use, although it was burning day and night, was the thick layer of insulating material all around it – six inches deep all round and weighing about 250lb. It was

A 1930s four-oven Aga. Still popular, many original Agas are in daily use fifty years later

guaranteed not to use more than 1½ tons of coal a year, a fraction of the amount consumed by other ranges. Smoothly enamelled, with self-cleaning ovens, it was, wrote a profile in *The Engineer*, 'a difficult product to describe objectively'. Its only drawback was its price – half a ton of carefully machined metal was far more expensive than lightweight gas and electric cookers. However, fuel economy was calculated to compensate for the initial cost within five years, and certainly, once bought, an Aga lasted a lifetime.

That there is still a demand for Agas, and similar stoves like Raeburns and Esses, is an interesting phenomenon. There are probably more economical methods of cooking and heating hot water, nor does the isolated farmer's need for an efficient solid-fuel range apply to the many city-dwelling owners of Agas powered by gas, oil and recently electricity. They certainly cook superbly, but undoubtedly the real basis of their appeal is that they offer a warm heart to houses which, because of the tyranny of the central-heating time-clock would otherwise be distinctly chilly.

Cooking by Gas

For many years after gas was introduced into the home, it was used almost exclusively for lighting. It was not until after the First World War that the supply of heat became its most useful domestic function. This delay was partly because of the difficulties of supplying and measuring gas outlined in the last chapter, and partly because of not unreasonable public prejudice against its poisonous and explosive potential. The Royal Commission organizing the 1851 Great Exhibition stipulated that no apparatus could be exhibited which was 'in practical operation through the agency of gas'.

Despite this discouraging background, there were some enthusiastic early experimenters with gas-cooking. The earliest recorded is the Moravian Z. A. Winzler's gas-cooked dinners served in a gas-heated dining-room in 1802. The Aetna Ironworks, near Liverpool, produced the first British gas cooking apparatus in 1824. It was merely a gun-barrel, twisted into the shape of a tennis-racket, and pierced with small holes. It could be placed horizontally to fry or vertically to roast. Without any oven-like additions, the unadorned descendant of the Aetna Ironworks' twisted gun-barrel was of course the extraordinarily useful and adaptable gas ring which quickly became a commonplace of kitchens and sitting-rooms. Firms such as John Wright and Company of Birmingham offered gas rings to suit every pocket and inclination.

The most famous of the first gas cooks was Alexis Soyer, who did a great deal to win recognition for gas cookery by installing gas stoves in his kitchens at the Reform Club, Pall Mall, in 1841. The sort of stove he used – essentially a development of the gas ring – was described in the *Gas Gazette* (1847).

> The gas jets are enclosed in a circular sheet-iron case, with the cooking vessels all fitted to the same, so that while the cooking process is going on there is none of the waste that takes place with the coals and the ordinary chimney . . . The meat is surrounded by small jets of flame, an arrangement by which the necessity of turning it is completely obviated.

Stoves such as Soyer's and Leoni's, shown at the London Exhibition of 1862, had their disadvantages. Although the principle of loading the gas jet – as yet unable to be regulated efficiently – as heavily as possible was a sound one, it was difficult to see how each dish was cooking. If one was roasting, there was no room to bake, and vice versa. So this type of stove was regarded as an auxiliary of the coal range rather than as a replacement. It was something of a dead-end in design, although it enjoyed a brief renaissance in the 1920s when post-war parsimony encouraged the sales of such cookers as the Wifesjoie and the Duck Oven.

In 1850, Alfred King of Liverpool, James Sharp of Southampton, and Ebenezer Goddard of Ipswich produced gas stoves that had obvious affinities with modern cookers. Most famous was Sharp's 'Apparatus calculated to cook a Dinner for a hundred persons' which was featured on the front cover of *The Expositor*, one of the special magazines produced to publicize the inventions displayed at the Great Exhibition. Since the Royal Commission ruling prevented its being seen in action in the Crystal Palace itself, Sharp and other members of the Gasfitters Mutual Association organized an independent exhibition of gas appliances at the Royal Polytechnic Institution. Sharp's apparatus was still circular, but had a side door to the oven and a usefully broad top. Its construction sounded a little unsafe – an iron frame, with a tin-lined cylinder encased in wood. A gap was left between the cylinder and the wooden casing, which meant doubly effective insulation, using both the layer of air and the wood. The heat from the oven boiled water in the steaming-kettles placed on the top. These were fitted with taps in their sides to allow water to be drawn off, and could have pans fitted into their lids to steam vegetables and other food. There was nowhere to actually boil food, but, as the explanatory article in *The Expositor* correctly pointed out, 'Provisions cooked in this way are very superior to those boiled in water.'

It was this type of stove which Sharp used to illustrate his lecture 'Gas-tronomy', which he delivered to 800 people in Southampton in 1850. A local paper reported that:

LEONI'S

PATENT PORTABLE, ECONOMICAL

ATMOSPHERIC GAS - STOVES,

FOR HEATING, COOKING, BROILING, GRILLING, &c. ;

Also Automatic, for Roasting, Baking, &c.

One gallon of water boiled in 15 minutes; consumption 4 feet of gas.
One steak or chop grilled *under* the heat-reflector and one *over* it, both in ten minutes; consumption one 2-10ths foot of gas.
One chicken roasted in one hour; consumption 7½ feet of gas.
A joint of 3 lbs. roasted in one hour; consumption 12 feet of gas.
One pound of potatoes baked in 40 minutes over the heat-reflector, while broiling is going on underneath.
One complete dinner for 12 persons cooked in 2 hours; consumption 15 feet of gas.

The AUTOMATIC GAS-STOVE is made in several sizes, to roast from 5 lbs. up to several hundredweight of meat, is quite self-acting, and requires no attention whatever.

Six pounds of beef roasted in one hour; consumption 20 feet. Four quartern loaves of bread baked in one hour; consumption 20 feet. During the baking, a joint, fowl, &c., may be roasted under the gas-ring.

For Prices and Particulars, apply to S. LEONI, 34, St. Paul Street, New North Road, London, N.

Extract from the "JOURNAL OF GAS LIGHTING, WATER SUPPLY, AND SANITARY IMPROVEMENT," Feb. 16, 1869.

"Any contrivance which facilitates and economizes the use of gas for heating and cooking purposes deserves the encouragement of gas companies, and none that have come under our notice seem to effect that object *so completely* as LEONI'S PORTABLE ATMOSPHERIC HEATING AND COOKING GAS-STOVES, with which we have made some satisfactory experiments. One peculiarity of the apparatus is, that the processes of broiling and roasting are conducted by *reflection only* of the heat, which method has great advantages over the direct application of the heat of a gas-flame. The apparatus was tried with great success at the Paris Exhibition, and the economical results, as recorded, were much in favour of the use of gas, independent of its other advantages. It is stated that a complete dinner for twelve persons was cooked in two hours, with a consumption of only 15 feet of gas. These stoves have been found equally effective in heating apartments, and they produce no unpleasant sensation of closeness."

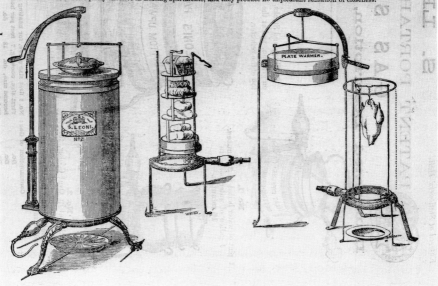

Leoni's stoves extended the gas ring into an oven with a circular metal casing
(*The Ironmonger*, 1869)

THE

EXPOSITOR:

A

WEEKLY ILLUSTRATED RECORDER

OF

Inventions, Designs, and Art-Manufactures.

No. 24.]   SATURDAY, APRIL 12, 1851.   [Price 3d.
[Stamped 4d.

APPARATUS FOR COOKING BY GAS.

[caption below illustration] SHARP'S GAS-COOKING APPARATUS, TO BE SHOWN IN OPERATION AT THE SPECIAL EXHIBITION OF THE GASFITTERS' ASSOCIATION, AT THE ROYAL POLYTECHNIC INSTITUTION.

James Sharp's wood-encased gas stove with door and room on top for steamers. Shown in London in 1851

120 people afterwards sat down to a substantial supper, cooked by gas on the lecturer's table before the audience. The bill of fare contained: – roasts: 34 lb of beef, 15 lb of mutton, 12 lb of pork. Boiled and steamed: 24 lb of mutton, a cod fish, four fowls, eight plum puddings, vegetables etc., with baked pies and tarts; the whole having been cooked with an expenditure of 156 feet of gas, the dripping collected being valued at 2s . . . The novelty of the

evening's entertainment not only excited the intellectual and digestive organs, but gratified them at the same time.

It seems likely that Sharp had more than one stove and several gas rings to provide this banquet.

Ebenezer Goddard's East Anglian, also shown at the 1851 Polytechnic Exhibition, had a much more modern look. The oven was a squared shape, with sliding shelves, and two lines of burners in the base. There were three separate burners under a hotplate on the top, and a line of gas control-taps across the front. It was even fitted with a lighter, a gas jet at the end of a long flexible tube which could be ignited by sparking a flint set in its nozzle.

At the time of the 1882 Crystal Palace Exhibition, gas cookers were still not generally in use, but several technical improvements were easing their acceptance. New gas meters ended the old reliance on measuring by feet of gas used. Since pressure could vary very dramatically – especially on 'Sundays, holidays and in very foggy weather',[4] it was much fairer to consumers to calculate by the therm, a measure of calorific value of the gas, rather than by quantity. Mixing air with gas made combustion more efficient and was a very successful selling-point on economic grounds, but one expert insisted that 'The flavour of meat roasted by plain gas was decidedly better than that of meat roasted by atmospheric gas.'[5]

The Sugg family did much to pioneer the use of gas cookers. What Samuel Hellyer was to bathroom plumbing, William Sugg was to gas. His *Domestic Uses of Coal Gas* (1884) was an excellent, well-illustrated introduction to the subject. It aimed to dispel the myths about the dangers of gas as well as exhibiting the varied and sophisticated range of appliances produced by Sugg himself – Parisian Roasters, Vienna Bread Ovens, and the backbone of his business, the Charing Cross Kitcheners. These came in all sizes, the biggest of which could cook for twenty people. The oven converted from roasting-oven, with a clockwork turnspit set in its side, to a baking-oven, lined with a close-fitting inner oven with sliding shelves. The top had four burners and a grill, and pilot-lights at each outlet. These represented, explained Sugg, 'a great saving of labour and matches, at the cost of a mere penny a day'. Moreover, they reduced the danger of explosion, 'which, if it does nothing worse, considerably destroys the equanimity of the cook'.

William Sugg's daughter, Marie Jenny, produced her *Art of Cooking by Gas* in 1890. It gave menus for each month of the year, illustrated Sugg cooking appliances, and emphasized how much better were the results of gas-cooking. 'The advantages of gas properly applied to the work of the kitchen are not known to the general public as they deserve to be', she lamented. 'Many people suffer from dyspepsia in consequence of

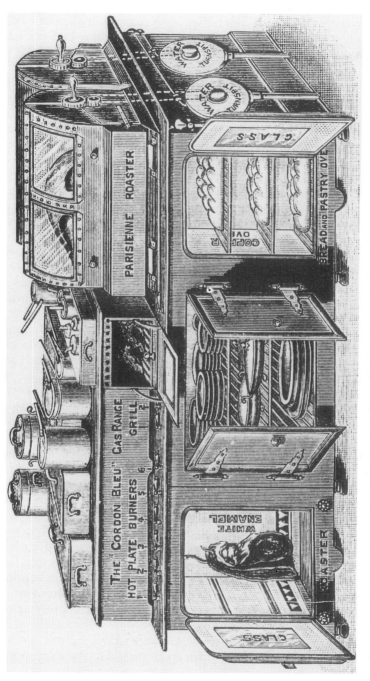

William Sugg's massive 1884 Cordon Bleu gas kitchener used water-motors to power its turnspits

the defective way food is prepared. Meat comes to the table under the name of roast meat which has never been roasted at all, but baked to a dull-brown colour – so much for appearance – and a half-boiled, half-burnt flavour – so much for taste. The question is occasionally heard: "Is it beef or mutton, or might it be pork?".'

A study of the different editions of Mrs Beeton's *Household Management* reveals the growing acceptability of gas-cooking. In the 1883 edition, which acknowledged the advantages of gas in cleanliness, labour-saving and 'the reduction of cooking operations to something of a certainty', the author is a little doubtful – so few cooks know how to handle 'the ingenious machinery necessary'. In the 1893 edition, the account of gas cookery was much more enthusiastic and evidently many gas cookers were in use by that time. But they were still auxiliaries rather than replacements for solid-fuel ranges, and frequent references were still made in women's serials and cartoons to their explosive potential.

In the 1890s, electricity began to challenge gas lighting, and far-sighted manufacturers realized that they would have to diversify to protect their own interests. Their efforts to improve, cheapen and advertise their cooking and heating appliances led to a growth of confidence in gas cooking and heating appliances at a time when interest in labour-saving appliances was increasing. Gas companies began to hire out stoves equipped with slot-meters, and so allowed customers to experiment cheaply with what was still a slightly suspect purchase.

W. Parkinson and Company of Birmingham, gas engineers since 1816, began to make gas cookers in 1890, and the records of the company give a useful survey of the development of the twentieth-century gas cooker. Their first model was closely related to the old ranges. It was cast iron, and so had to be blackleaded and polished. Topped by a handsome 'Japanned Hood and Platewarmer' and flanked by a gleaming copper boiler, it was as imposing as its coal-fired predecessors. The cook had to estimate oven temperatures, turning down the burners when she felt that they were hot enough.

By 1914, the gas cooker was an accepted part of the kitchen. Plate-racks, browning-sheets, splashbacks, spillage-trays and grills were added, and the companies began to work on more attractive finishes. The white-tiled sides and doors of the Parkinson Suburbia heralded the all-enamelled cookers of the 1920s. R. & A. Main, another firm with a great future in gas ahead of them, introduced a completely enamelled cooker in 1927, and by 1932 their Mainservor was available in several mottled colours. The structure of cookers grew lighter as fears of explosion lessened, and concern for hygiene led to the development of stumpy legs on many models. Parkinson's Kennington was an early example of an oven set high, beside the hotplates instead of below them, but until the advent of modular units such cookers took up too much space to be integrated into the average kitchen. In 1924 *Ideal Home* magazine reflected on the transformation of the gas cooker:

> From an under-sized, drab, cast-iron excrescence, which seemed specially designed to collect rust, dirt and grease, the gas-cooker of today has become a thing of beauty, with its nickel-fittings and its white enamel surround, its lofty plate-rack and easily accessible oven and hot-plate. The new automatic burners solve the problem of the domestic help who is 'frit to death' of the stove, and says 'I daren't light the thing, mum', having perchance turned the gas on in one of the old-fashioned abominations, and then run off to get the matches with the result that when she finally opened the oven door and struck the match, she was blown backwards by the explosion.

The Regulo oven thermostat was first introduced in the 1923 New World cooker made by Wrights (a firm later incorporated into Radiation). This cooker also had spreading-flame hotplate burners under a disc-bar hotplate, and its flue led from the oven instead of the cooker-top. Insulation of the ovens improved – slag wool replaced the bricks and straw used in the first attempts at heat conservation. Gas-cooking was now so widely accepted that firms such as Main, Radiation and Parkinson concentrated their energies on producing very large numbers of small cheap cookers, such as the GLC 1. This was designed as a hire cooker for the Gas, Light and Coke Company in 1934. It was small, with a three-burner hotplate and grill, a wide shallow oven with a burner down each side, and a thermostat. It had some parts made in sheet steel, and was finished in grey, mottled vitreous enamel with a white door-panl. This was the average gas cooker of the 1930s.

But the home-making magazines show that much more sophisticated appliances were available. The modern straight-down look was first seen remarkably early in the Parkinson Renown. Made in the same year as the gawky GLC 1, it was originally meant as a one-off, part of the furnishings of the complete house presented to George V on the occasion of his Silver Jubilee by the Royal Warrantholders, those companies fortunate enough to carry the 'By Appointment' crest on their stationery. When it was displayed at the Ideal Home Exhibition it aroused such interest that Parkinson made a few commercial modifications to the design and began to market it in 1937. It looked dramatically different from its rivals, sleek, white and squared-off to fit into the ranks of cupboards that were beginning to line the more up-to-date kitchens.

By the 1930s homes were being piped for gas to cook and heat by rather than to use for lighting. Safety regulations and standards institutions allied with custom and use to lay the old fears to rest, and by 1939 there were some 9 million gas cookers in use in Britain.

Cooking by Electricity

Limited networks and high costs held back the development of electric cooking, although experiments had been made almost as soon as electric light was introduced domestically. The earliest surviving electric oven, now in the London Science Museum, is a rickety affair improvized from a biscuit tin, coils of wire, and a large light-bulb. A chicken could apparently be fitted over the bulb and cooked, inside to out, by electricity. History does not relate the popularity of this contraption, but it was not a main-line invention although the same inside-out principle is now used in microwave ovens, the newest of all experiments in electric cookery.

An 1891 American patent granted to a Mr Carpenter envisaged an electric heating-unit made by enamelling insulated wires onto cast-iron plates, but the inadequacy of contemporary enamelling techniques meant that the enamel cracked and oxidation destroyed the wires. This was improved on by Rookes Evelyn Bell Crompton (1845–1940) who used nickel alloys, a crimped ribbon of wire and a double layer of enamel. He issued a catalogue in the mid-1890s, offering a good range of electric hotplates, frying-pans and saucepans. Power reached the appliances through their handles, a slow method but a safe one, and it took a Crompton saucepan eighteen minutes to boil a pint of water, at a cost of just over a farthing.

Crompton described his electric ovens in a paper that he gave to the Society of Arts in 1895. They were simple metal boxes with double sides, the inner of which had wires attached to radiate heat. The layer of air between the sides helped to insulate the oven and ensure that no heat was wasted. 'The electrically worked kitchen may be kept as cool as a dairy', he declared, and went on to deplore the slowness with which electricity was being adopted into homes. The deluge of questions that followed his speech, full of references to burnt-out appliances and electric shocks, give a clue to the reasons for the nation's hesitation. A Mr Dowsing said how difficult it was to explain to cooks the use of the separate switches for each side of the oven. Cooks tended to switch only one on, and to turn the joint round as if it was being roasted in front of an old-fashioned fire. To cool the oven off they left the door open instead of switching off the power. Clearly at this time there was little or no British market for Crompton's products, and his most elaborate designs, such as the electric kettle sold to a Russian Grand Duke for £40, were only offered in his Paris agency.

In a publicity stunt reminiscent of the early days of gas, a banquet cooked entirely by electricity was given to the Lord Mayor of London in 1894. The menus were impressive, but there was something a little half-hearted about Sir David Salomon's after-dinner speech, reported the next day: 'There was no taste of gas or coal in anything which had been placed before them, although he did not contend that the cooking was everything that could be desired, which was doubtless due to the chef being unused to the system.'

The early electric kitchen featured a great number of separate appliances. The show kitchen at the Chicago Electrical Fair in 1893 had about ten sockets, each feeding a different saucepan, frying-pan, grill or oven. This sort of kitchen was illustrated in the magazine *Black and White* in 1895, in an article about 'The School with Trained Lightning', a cookery school in London's Gloucester Road run by a Miss Fairclough:

A few hundred years ago she would have been burnt at the stake . . . due to a certain table and a few ovens which look like safes . . . Miss Fairclough stood behind the table rolling pastry, while in front in a neat row were six cooking utensils. All were bright and shining copper and steel, from the kettle to the fluted griller, and they simply stood on the table, without any fire or

A 1908 demonstration all-electric kitchen

apparent sign of heat. Yet there on the griller was a chop gaily cooking away, 'with an independent air'; in the kettle, water was boiling; on the 'hot-plate' scones were toasting; in a frying-pan potatoes were frying, while two little pots were occupied by a stewing bird and simmering jam.

Such classes as Mrs Fairclough's were evidently necessary in the early days of electric cookery. Adam Gowans Whyte, in his *The All-Electric Age* (1922) was concerned at the slowness with which servants mastered the use of electricity: 'The inertia of the domestic mind shows itself in a general hostility towards anything new, even when it saves work.' Moving pots off the heat and opening oven doors instead of turning switches off were the least of their crimes. 'Perhaps the most outrageous misuse of electrical cooking apparatus is when the cook has the habit of switching everything on full to warm the kitchen.' In defense of the erring domestics, quick reductions in heat and constant temperatures were niceties not then mastered by the electricians, and it must have been very cold in basement kitchens without the old 'tropical heat' of the coal-fired ranges.

In 1899 Mrs Beeton's manual did not mention electric cookers, but in the 1907 edition they were declared 'quite practicable, although for the present decidedly expensive'. She gave a brief explanation of how electricity worked, and added that 'It may be mentioned that the King's yacht (constructed for her late Majesty Queen Victoria) is fitted with a complete electric cooking outfit, including soup and coffee boilers, hot-plates, ovens, grills and hot closets.'

Many of the early electricians had experimented by converting gas cookers, and the originality of the 'Trained Lighting Table' vision of appliances arranged around the kitchen in a way convenient to the cook was lost. When electric cookers were purpose-built, their frames resembled the heavy iron bodies of the gas cookers. Only their accessories maintained an air of wizardry. Gleaming brass switches, white porcelain fuses, scarlet lights and fat metal cables swirling down from its control panel into the nether regions of the stove gave such an Edwardian electric stove as the Carron, now in the Science Museum, an unrivalled appearance of power and efficiency. It has roomy roasting- and simmering-ovens with glass doors, a grill and four hotplates. A pull-out shelf provided space for any other electrical aids the cook might want to plug into the mahogany switchboard set above the cooker.

The First World War distracted manufacturers from the domestic front, but the expertise gained in making heating and cooking equipment for submarines, large baking and steaming ovens for canteens and electric glue-pots for factories, could later be applied to kitchen equipment. The well-known Belling company was set up by an ex-Crompton's electrician in 1912, and by 1919 it was making fires, hotplates, breakfast cookers, immersion heaters, water-urns, irons, steamers, grillers and kettles. In the same year, its first purpose-built cooker, the sheet-metal Modernette, appeared. A split-level cooker followed in 1924, its oven beside the hob to save stooping, and the popular Baby Belling bachelor stove was introduced in 1929 at the competitive price of £4 19s 6d.

Substantial electric cookers were still too expensive for most people to afford, and so, like the gas companies, electric companies hired out their appliances. Records that remain for Manchester show the dramatic increase in popularity of electric cookers in the 1920s.

The first Baby Belling (1929) has continued in production with only minor alterations up to the present day

Year	Hired cookers	Showroom sales
1924	277	–
1925	401	–
1926	818	–
1927	1533	–
1928	1285	1061
1929	868	1052
1930	932	2089

The increased demand for electric cookers was partly a result of the extension of the electricity networks and the building of new houses wired for electricity, and partly due to improvements in the cookers themselves. The metal-sheathed element, which could be bent into any shape, to suit oven, grill or hotplate, had been introduced in the United States in 1926, and appeared in Belling cookers in 1935. A thermostat was first used in the Creda cooker in 1931, and in the Belling in 1935. Black iron and rust-prone steel disappeared behind a coating of pastel enamel on lightweight sheet-metal casings, and soon the converted could and did emphasize the cleanliness and quality of the new 'electric heat'.

Interestingly, in the battle between the respective merits of gas and electric cookery which continue to this day, one can hear the echoes of the old debate over open and close ranges. Gas is particularly good for roasting; electricity for baking. Increasingly often, kitchens have both: gas hobs, grills and rotissomats, and electric ovens for baking.

The newest addition to the cook's armoury is the microwave oven. This invention, which uses extremely short radio waves to penetrate to the heart of the food, stirring up its molecules and so creating heat, was a spin-off from Second World War radar technology. Inside the oven, a rotating fan scatters microwaves and polished metal surfaces reflect and so concentrate the heat. Although cooking times are startlingly fast – a 4lb frozen chicken takes only minutes to cook, foods cannot be browned, and some cannot be cooked at all satisfactorily. It was developed first in the United States, and introduced into Britain in 1959, but it has taken nearly 20 years to be accepted as a useful tool. The slowness with which it has been adopted reflects partly its high price, and partly consumer suspicion of the startlingly space-age process which leaves the oven cool and clean, and the food almost dangerously hot. Enthusiasm for microwave cookery is increasing, however, and the initial hesitations may soon seem as absurd as the reactions of those long-ago maids who were 'frit to death' of the first gas-stoves. Microwave ovens, more than any other domestic appliances, are significant pointers to a future when households want instant fast food with the minimum of preparation – when there is simply no-one at home to sweat over a hot stove.

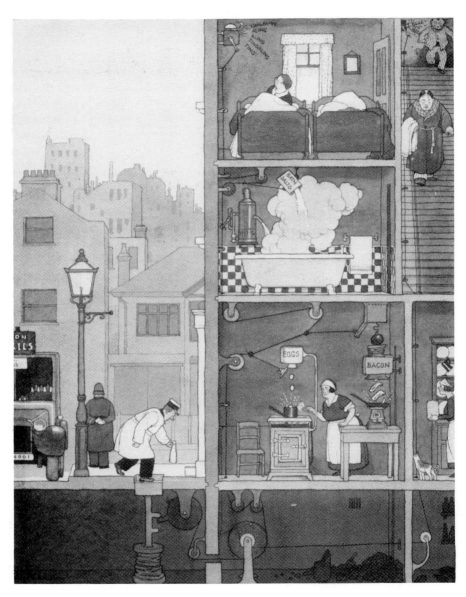

Mechanical housework envisaged by W. Heath Robinson

8

Essential Kitchen Technology

The modern housewife is no longer a cook – she is a can-opener.

Christine Frederick, Selling Mrs Consumer, 1929

Completely new approaches to food preservation and preparation were just as significant potential labour-savers as the revolution in cooking methods. The replacement of the larder by a combination of refrigerator, deep-freeze and tinned or processed food has meant the elimination of time-consuming methods of food storage and a great improvement in the variety and quantity of food available. Improved kitchen plumbing, dishwashers and small kitchen machinery means that preparing meals can be a swift, undemanding task. In theory at least, the family need no longer be dominated by the old and essential chore of feeding itself. The changing shape of kitchens over the last hundred years illustrates the development of a whole new philosophy of kitchen management.

Cold Storage

The first refrigerators were insulated ice-chests, lined with zinc, slate or 'odorless, tasteless lumber'. Some cabinets had a separate locker for ice, in which wine could be cooled, but for the best results the ice had to be in the same compartment as the food that it was supposed to be preserving. Ash's 1881 Patent Filtering Refrigerator filtered the melted ice to provide iced drinking water. The 1890 model, a cannibalistic Self-feeding Cabinet, improved on this with a metal lining which was supposed to recirculate the cold around the cabinet. Made of deal painted and grained to look like oak, it came in a variety of sizes. The smallest was 3-feet high and 2-feet wide and cost £11.10s. At the other end of the scale was the £41.10s model, 6-feet high and wide.

In England such refrigerators were a luxury, more often intended for hotels and food shops than private homes. In May 1891, *The Cowkeeper and Dairyman's Journal* advertised 'a magnificent Showcase refrigerator, available in Walnut, Mahogany or Oak, or Black and Gold'. It could be made to measure, and with its glass or marble shelves and handsome surround of decorated tiles was certainly a 'very elegant piece of cabinet furniture'. The makers were 'anticipating an increased demand for Private Houses, as much for its novelty as its refrigerating service'. It would not only be a happy addition to the furniture of a dining-room, which it could be made to match, but 'would offer an appetising attraction, that iced wines and other delicacies could be served from it to the table direct'. Preserving the low temperature of the ice-chest meant not opening it very often – Mrs C. S. Peel recalls in her memoirs of the 1890s that 'In the meat larder stood a refrigerator, only opened

Willow's patent refrigerator, for commercial or private use
(*Cowkeeper and Dairyman's Journal*, 1891)

once a day, so that the kitchen people had to bethink themselves in good time of the required meat.'[1]

Less grand ice-chests had appeared in the Great Exhibition catalogues, and continued to be sold until refrigerators proper, capable of manufacturing their own ice, were developed. The Alaska Cold Dry Air Cabinet, porcelain-lined, water-cooled, with tap and ice-well for wine, stood 3-feet high and cost £6 in 1895. The narrow, conveniently corner-shaped Ice Cabinette sold for £3 in 1907, and was recommended as 'suitable for flats'. The 1909 edition of Mrs Beeton described refrigerators as 'very necessary to a household, since they ensure both comfort and economy, and indeed promote good health in summer'. However, in her specifications of kitchen requirements for different sorts of households, a refrigerator is included only in the lists of 'any mansion' and 'a good class home'. The 'middle class home' and 'only the smallest home' managed without by wrapping their ice in a blanket and keeping it in a dark place.

In the United States on the other hand, the ice-chest was a standard item of equipment, a necessity of civilized life in the long hot summers. Mail-order catalogues offered a much wider range of chests at approximately a quarter of the cost of those on sale in Britain. Many of them seem intended to double as furniture. Sears Roebuck models were 'made from the very best selected kiln-dried ash, finished antique, highly-polished, beautifully carved, trimmed with fancy heavy bronze trimmings throughout and solid brass locks. The top also makes a useful sideboard'. It was natural, considering the climate, that the majority of patents for domestic refrigerating machines should have been taken out in the United States – nearly 3000 by 1880, none domestically successful.

Mechanical cooling systems were established in commercial use well before they were available to individual homes. The principles involved had been familiar to scientists even earlier, but not applied – for example, Michael Faraday had experimented with heating an ammonia mixture, but his aim had been to stabilize liquid ammonia rather than exploit the cooling properties involved. So the credit for inventing the refrigerator is difficult to ascribe. The freezing process involves circulating a substance with a very low boiling-point, such as ammonia, ether or carbonic acid, round a cabinet. When it evaporates it draws out latent heat, and so cools the contents. To recycle the coolant it has to be made liquid again. This can be done by compressing it, which increases the intensity of the heat to that of room temperature, and so causes the vapour to condense, or by the absorption method: mixing it with first hydrogen and then water, heating the water to separate the ammonia from it, and passing the warmed water through a condenser.

One of the first compression machines was made by Jacob Perkins, an American engineer living in London. He was granted a patent in 1834, and his machine proved quite successful in breweries and meat-packing plants. Ferdinand Carré showed a French absorption machine at the 1862 Exhibition. His process was intermittent, producing half a pound of ice every half-hour. Driven by steam-power, it was not really a domestic proposition, although Carré did design a small coal-fired model intended for use in the home. Compression machines were established in commercial use by the work of Karl von Linde, German professor of thermodynamics, who introduced his vapour-compression system in 1876.

Domestic refrigerating machines were a much later development. Gas would have been a simple domestic source of refrigerating energy, but although it was piped and available it was surprisingly late to be applied to cooling systems. Only in 1922 was a successful gas absorption machine developed in Sweden. It was the small electric motor developed at the turn of the century, that was the turning-point in the domestication of refrigerators. Again, it was the Americans who quickly developed the possibilities revealed by the European inventors. The Domelre (Domestic Electric Refrigerator) was marketed in Chicago in 1913. Kelvinator made their first machines in 1916, and Frigidaire moved into business when General Motors took over a machine invented in 1917 called The Guardian. Prices were originally very high, at about $900, but as popularity increased, mass production cut costs dramatically. A refrigerator costing $400 in 1926, when 200,000 were sold, could be bought for $170 in 1935, when 1.5 million were sold.

Just as ice-chests had been more unusual in Britain, so the refrigerator proper was regarded as an unnecessary luxury at a time when tens of thousands a year were being sold in the United States. An article in *House and Garden* in August 1923 showed the state of the market: 'Refrigerators, which are a commonplace in American house-holds, are not sufficiently known or used over here.' The writer went on to describe various ice-chests, including a particularly convenient model which was built into the outside wall of the kitchen on a similar principle to a coal-store so that the iceman could fill it without disturbing the housewife at all. The only true refrigerator it mentioned was the Staines Mannesmann,

a refrigerating machine which produces its own ice. Worked by electricity, gas or oil, this type includes a small absorption refrigeration plant consisting of pipes and boilers, and a safe in which provisions are kept. So simple is the mechanism that it is only necessary to press down a lever once a day to the position 'on', leaving it in that position for a couple of hours, during which time the plant is heated, evaporation takes place, and a temperature created low enough to cool the safe and produce about five pounds of ice.

The Mannesmann inspired confidence, with its solid wooden cabinet and huge controls, but it was clearly a luxury item. Such costly

Half the bulk of the early Frigidaire was taken up by its refrigerating unit
(*Vogue*, 1928)

novelties were ignored by *House and Garden*'s rival magazine *Ideal Home*.
Not until 1926 did a refrigerator rate a mention in its pages: then it
recommended the Swedish Electrolux, finished in dark oak or white
enamel, and complete with ice-cube trays for the cocktails of the Jazz
Age.

Frigidaire records that Britain was regarded as something of a
challenge. 'The hard sell was probably essential in a Britain which
regarded ice as only an inconvenience of winter-time and cold drinks as
an American mistake.' The first British Frigidaire was sold in 1924, and
by 1927 the number of household and commercial models had risen to
twenty. Government action banning the use of certain preservatives in
food gave the company a useful springboard for their 1928 advertising
campaign:

> When Pure Food is NOT!
> Preservatives used to retard the natural processes of decay. Most
> women think it is perfectly easy to detect decay in time. The truth
> is far different. It is there 36 hours before you can detect it. Would
> you let your family eat such food, *mouldy* food, DECAYING food?[2]

By the 1930s, the clumsy early cabinets were transformed by the
fashionable trend to 'streamlining' which moved from ships and boats
and trains to infect everything from clocks to sideboards, irrespective of
any actual motion. The new Kelvinators of 1932 set the pattern, with
bulbous round tops and bow-legs, and the zenith was reached with the
1934 Prestcold, complete with racy ventilation fins and an automobile-
style foot-pedal to open its door. They were still very large machines on
the whole, partly because of the size of their engines, and partly
because they were still thought of as replacements for larders.
Electrolux did sell a Baby model, moderately priced at £29.10s, which
foreshadowed later British trends in fitting in with waist-high units
around the kitchen. In the United States, the climate and the rapid
growth of the frozen food market made large 'ice-boxes' second only to
washing-machines in popularity.

What follows is something of a red herring; the story of the brief rise
and fall of an attractively simple little machine which gave much delight
but was overtaken by history – the mechanical ice-cream maker, one of
the few domestic appliances to be invented by a woman. 'Sightly and
palatable compôtes in water-ice borders', ice-creams and sorbets of all
sorts were an important part of the high-class cook's repertoire well
before the introduction of refrigerators. Generous quantities of cream
were used – few recipes suggested less than a pint, and most dealt in
quarts. The mixture was originally placed in a mould in a wooden pail
full of ice and salt, and stirred vigorously with a wooden spoon until it

froze – work for two hours at least, and no improvement on the sixteenth-century instructions given to Indian cooks in the *Institutes of Akbar*. In 1846, American Nancy Johnson is said to have invented a 'Freezing machine' but no details of her patent (entered in the name of William Young in 1848) remain. A freezing-machine appeared in the 1851 Great Exhibition catalogue, and a similar model was better illustrated in the 1862 Exhibition as 'Ash's Piston Freezing Machine and Wine Cooler'. By 1883, Mrs Beeton's manual declared:

> Ice is now so much in use at English tables that it has become a necessity of household economy, and dessert ices follow summer dinners as a matter of course. Dessert ices are by modern invention and ingenuity placed within the reach of most house-keepers, and it is a pleasant and easy amusement|for ladies to make ices by Mr Ash's Patent Piston Freezing Machine.[3]

Ash's machine was a hand-worked version of the compression principle of freezing water, much more complicated than the simple elaborations on wooden buckets such as the Frezo. These had a crank-handle attached to agitate the inner cylinder, and took about twenty minutes handle-turning to make an ice. English versions were the Star ('strong Tin cylinder, Whitewood Pail, 17s. 6d') and the Paragon ('Pewter cylinder, Oak Pail, £4.14s.6d'), both 6-quart machines.

Spong, king of London hardware-makers, improved on this with a cylindrical tin freezing-machine which was supposed to make an ice in only five minutes. It could be used with one of the new freezing compounds instead of merely salt and ice. So too could the American Freezer, shown in catalogues in the 1890s. Using a vacuum and a tin of 'inexhaustible freezing crystals', it only had to be inverted once. The ices it made were not as soft and fluffy as those made by the stirring method, but it was highly recommended for chilling champagne and making mousses. By 1922 a compromise machine had been developed, which needed only five minutes of handle-turning after leaving the cream in the machine for ten minutes. A freezing attachment was sold with electric food-mixers in 1931, and they are still available today, although since refrigerators with frozen food compartments are now standard kitchen equipment, and Mr Walls has come into his own, they have become much less widely used.

Domestic deep-freezes are descendants of commercial freezing processes. Meat had travelled in ships with crude refrigeration plants since the mid-nineteenth century. A pump circulated cold air from a hold filled with ice to the hold filled with meat. It was Clarence Birdseye who began using the known preservative properties of ice for the retail market. While wintering in Labrador in the early 1920s, he

PUNCH'S ALMANACK FOR 1882.   [December 8 1881.

JACK FROST; OR, THE FUTURE UNIVERSAL PROVIDER.

Punch apparently foresaw the potential of deep-frozen food
as early as 1882, although at that time only long-distance cargo ships
were equipped with freezing-plants

noticed that the flesh of fish and reindeer congealed rapidly in the
Arctic air. The Eskimos made use of this, returning months later to
caches of food which remained remarkably fresh. Birdseye copied the
process artificially by freezing food very rapidly between metal plates, a
process which he patented in 1925. By 1928 frozen foods had begun to
be marketed in the United States; 39 million lbs were sold in 1934, and
600 million lbs in 1944. Up-to-date apartment blocks in New York
provided basement ice-lockers for each tenant by 1945.

Deep-freezes could be put to use in two ways – to enlarge the scope
for preparing food in the home, increasing time spent in kitchen
management, or to make it easier to store ready-prepared food. In 1943
Life magazine showed an open-plan kitchen with a butcher's block and
a deep-freeze cabinet, emphasizing the prestige of buying fresh
ingredients, treating them and freezing them in the home. In 1944, by
contrast, *Science Digest* made a prediction much nearer the truth, even
forecasting correctly the advent of microwave ovens thirty years later:

Meat will be cooked in ton-size batches under the directions of world famous chefs, and packed into containers. Then, one minute before dinner time, the housewife will place the pre-cooked frozen meat into a special electronic oven. This oven will employ high frequency waves which will penetrate all food equally . . . in a few seconds a bell will ring, and the whole dinner will pop up like a piece of toast.

Canned Food

As essential as freezers to saving time on food preparation was the development of the tin can. Cans originated as a response to the blockade of France during the Napoleonic Wars. Cut off from its colonial sugar supplies, and with a far-flung army, France needed a new way of provisioning its forces. Napoleon offered a prize of 12,000 francs for a solution, and it was won in 1808 by Nicholas Appert, a skilled chef. He used bottles tightly sealed with corks. An Englishman, Peter Durrand, first mentioned the possibility of using tin containers in an 1810 patent, which otherwise followed Appert's specification

Assembly-line techniques in a French canning factory
(Louis Figuier, *Les Merveilles de l'Industrie*, 1873–7)

virtually word for word. He sold the patent to Donkin, Hall and Gamble in 1811, and in 1812 they set up their Extensive Preservatory in Bermondsey, and set up as 'general provision preservers'. By 1817, Donkin had sold £3,000 worth of canned food in six months, mainly to the navy. When the Admiralty sent Sir Edward Parry to explore the Arctic in 1824, Donkin helped to provision the expedition. Some of the stores were dumped and picked up five years later by Captain John Ross's expedition. Ross recorded that 'A round of beef, which had been in the stores eight years, was as good as on the day which it was first cooked.' His family kept another unopened can as a doorstop. When analysts opened it in 1958, they found the 134-year-old meat 'not palatable, but edible'.

Although such cans were popular with sailors vulnerable to scurvy and other diseases caused by dietary deficiencies, they were hardly suited to the home. Empty cans weighed 1lb, full ones 7lb, and the opening instructions recommended a hammer and chisel. They were expensive, because of the slow way in which cans were made – a tinsmith could only turn out about ten a day. Food in the centre of the cans was sometimes not properly sterilized. Smaller cans and mass production soon improved matters, and after Louis Pasteur's work on bacteria in the 1850s and 1860s scientific preservation was better understood. In the United States, scattered communities, the expansion westwards and the needs of the Civil War armies, made canned food very attractive. It was there that food was first canned on assembly lines and that factories produced cans cheaply, stamping them out by machine and using double seams instead of solder. The Chicago meat canning industry started in 1872, and the first Hawaian pineapple cannery opened in 1892. In the 1920s and 1930s canning became a home industry: many country housewives canned their own produce, using small machines to crimp on lids.

Along with cans came can-openers, now an essential little tool in even the smallest kitchen. Donkin's chisel-and-hammer technique was soon superseded. Ironmongery catalogues of the 1870s show a stubby blade set into a heavy handle, with a prong above it which is levered along the edge of the can. The prong was often decorated, usually with the head of an appropriate animal or fish. Bull's heads were the commonest, a punning reference to the 'bully beef' that was one of the most usual methods of canning meat. The 'bully' was bouillon, or gravy, added to fill the gaps between the shredded beef. The first rotary can-opener seems to have been made by the American firm of Baumgarten in the 1890s. A table-mounted version, the Blue Streak, was patented in 1922, made by Turner and Seymour of Connecticut. Seven years later a wall-mounted version not dissimilar to those used in kitchens today was being sold. There are hundreds of different patent can-openers available today, the most sophisticated of which holds the tin lid magnetically and is electrically powered.

Water in the Kitchen

The first permanent kitchen sink was a shallow stone rectangle, usually placed beside the back door as water had to be carried in from a well or pump outside. Earthenware moulded sinks, still very shallow, were a slight improvement. Galvanized iron was also used. As techniques of porcelain enamelling improved in the 1880s, the more practical and hygienic glazed fireclay sink appeared. It could be much deeper, and was fitted with more efficient waste-pipe connections. In his *The Plumber and Sanitary Houses* (1877) Samuel Hellyer shows a design for a double sink-unit, perhaps the first of its type. One side was intended for the cook's use, the other for the housemaid's slops.

Great advances had been made by 1924, when an *Ideal Home* article gave a useful summary of 'approved types of sinks'. It stressed the convenience of a separate sink for preparing vegetables, and assumed there would be a third sink in the pantry for the use of the butler or parlourmaid. Various materials were available. 'Stone is strong, but too absorbent unless the surface is glazed. Slate is also good, but costly, and apt to crack when hot and cold water are used in quick succession. Glazed earthenware commends itself as being inexpensive, strong and cleanly.' The faults of all these materials were 'their hard unyielding surfaces, often responsible for much calamitous breaking of glass during washing-up'. Most highly recommended were wooden sinks: American beech, teak, or sycamore, well-oiled and preferably lined with lead.

1934 saw the first advertisement for sinks made from light alloys such as Monel and Savestane, very similar indeed to standard stainless-steel sinks today, but of thicker metal and more costly. Cheaper but less durable enamelled sinks and deep, glazed earthenware bowls were more typical of the 1930s and 40s.

Getting rid of rubbish was a problem exacerbated by the growth of cities and food packaging and the decline in the use of solid-fuel kitcheners or open fires. 'Never on any pretext allow that a dustbin is needed. There is nothing that a kitchener cannot burn', Mrs Panton had instructed in 1898. By the 1930s most people had to use at least one galvanized-iron dustbin, emptied by the city corporation at more or less regular intervals – one of the rare instances of a domestic chore being taken out of the home.

Waste-disposal units were developed surprisingly early – the General Electric Company experimented with 'grinding units' to fit under a

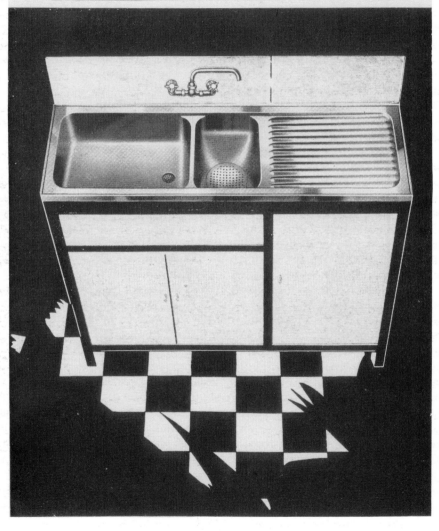

Advertisement for Savestane Stainless Steel Synkunit from the 1930s

small auxiliary sink in 1929, and they were produced commercially from 1935. Unlike most domestic appliances, they were first designed for the home, only later reaching their most successful niche, hotel, ship and institutional use. Families rejected them wholesale as unpleasantly noisy and a decided risk to households with small experimentally inclined children.

The best use of waste is of course to recycle it as heat. As early as 1911 an article in *The Architect* suggested that 'The horrid dustbin should be replaced by a refuse destructor in the scullery, which would heat the hot-water system in summer and winter alike and never require to be relighted.' A few houses were actually equipped in this way. 'The Homestead' featured in *Ideal Home* in 1924, had a rubbish chute under the sink through which waste slid straight down to a basement boiler. It was surprising that the enthusiastic flat-builders of the 1920s did not incorporate such systems in the 'homes for heroes' promised by the Government. Perhaps cheap coal meant there was little incentive to do so; it is only the energy crisis of the 1970s and 1980s which has led to serious consideration of recycling waste in the Western world.

Running water was piped to the ground floor of most comfortable homes by the second half of the nineteenth century, although it was much later in being supplied to city tenements. The quality of the supply was very variable, hence the popularity of the water filter between about 1860 and 1910. How effective it was is uncertain. The filtering medium was at first only charcoal between layers of sand and gravel, or even bundles of rushes. These could clear only the most visible impurities from the water, but by the 1860s *The Ironmonger* was recommending 'silicated carbon filters' as safeguards against cholera.

Whether they worked or not, the filters themselves were one of the most attractive of household appliances, much collected today and offering excellent examples of the art of the Doulton, Minton and Battersea potteries. An Etruscan vase studded with classical figures looked well in drawing-room or hall. The marbled china column design suited dining-room sideboards; a plain cream-coloured earthenware, stamped with the maker's crest, was good enough for the kitchen. For the bedroom, a decanter-like model was supplied, and for travelling a compact siphon in a padded case. The picnic filter, encased in wicker and with a silver tap, matched the best sort of picnic set. In 1881, the *Journal of Domestic Appliances* thought the subject merited an editorial:

> The filter is gradually but surely gaining a home for itself in every household, and soon we hope to see it become as general as tables and chairs . . . Its sale is now and then augmented by the many startling accounts of death and illness which follow the use of impure water. Then many resolve to use the filter, firmly

convinced of its value, and no longer regarding it as a molly-coddling invention and fit for only the whims of fidgetty old maids. It is the old system of shutting the stable door after the steed has taken its departure.

More permanent installations could be hired, according to the *Girl's Own Paper's* fictionalized housekeeping series of 1881–2, 'Margaret Trent and How She Kept House'. Her husband Wilfred had a filter fitted into the cistern, 'so no water could be used in the house without passing through it. This filter was hired by the year from one of the best makers, who cleaned it when necessary and kept it in good order'. As a further precaution against 'the thousands of tiny creatures which inhabit a single drop of water', Margaret used to refilter water used at table.

In 1883, Mrs Beeton's manual recommended filters, and the 1893 edition described several interesting types. Most approved were Maignan's French Patent Filtre Rapide, and a silicated carbon filter for which its inventor made extravagant claims: 'Professor Wanklyn assures us that he has passed a solution of strychnine through a silicated carbon filter and then drunk it.' Aggressively up-to-date was Judson's Aqua Pura,

> fitted with Galvano-Electric filtering medium, a powdered or granulated material prepared from mineral substances only, which by its action imparts oxygen to the water that it is brought into contact with, and completely destroys the vitality of the most minute organisms and neutralises all lead and other metallic poisons and gaseous impurities arising from the decay of animal or vegetable life, or from sewer or cesspool gases with which it may have become imbued.

In the 1890s Harrods offered riotously decorated Art Nouveau filters, the mysterious Wittmann 'animal charcoal filter' and the refreshingly simple Nibestos, with an easily replaceable filtering film. Another variation fitted on the sink tap, allowing mains pressure to force all water through its bed of charcoal. But around the turn of the century doubts about the efficacy of filters was growing. Unless cleaned regularly, filters could actually contaminate water. The 1909 edition of Mrs Beeton expressed scepticism as to their value, and suggested boiling water to purify it. After the First World War, improvements in public water-supplies led to an almost complete decline in their use, except for softening hard water. Recently, however, doubts as to the content of heavily treated water has led to a small resurgence in the filtering of drinking water.

Dishwashers

The first dishwashers reversed the principle of the water turbine invented in 1855. Metal blades turned by a hand-crank forced water against plates stacked at angles in a wire frame. An American patent of 1865 showed a machine similar to some still manufactured today. Dishes in a static frame, the principle of the most modern machines, appeared in Benjamin Howe's 1880 machine. He had complete faith in his invention, claiming that it completed operations in five minutes, and could be made of 'any size, form or material, to hold from 50 to 1,000 dishes if desired'. Such machines had limited domestic success. The hand-cranking was laborious, and the machine's efficiency limited, so few housewives were interested in them. Hotels and restaurants had more incentive to experiment. In 1885, one of the largest restaurants in Paris was using a spectacular machine, invented by Eugene Daquin. The large circular tank had two central compartments, one for hot and one for cold running water. Eight artificial hands gripped the plates and revolved around a central shaft. After passing through the hot water 'with an undulating movement' to wash off the grease, the dishes were vigorously brushed by two rotating brushes and dipped into the cold tub. Finally they were removed – by human hands – and placed in a draining-rack to dry. 'The use of the machine constitutes no danger whatsoever to either man or dish', reported the *Scientific American* approvingly.

Mrs Cockran of Indiana invented a dishwasher in the 1890s. It was a wooden tub with a hand-cranked set of plungers which drove water over the dishes. It had to be filled by hand and drained by a stopcock, but had some success, particularly when fitted with a small electric motor. In 1906 *La Nature* magazine showed an electrically powered machine of fascinating complexity. Wire baskets rolled round an overhead track to plunge into the tubs. Another machine, hand-cranked, was exhibited by a Mr Walker at the New York State Fair in 1910. Clothes-washers were also occasionally offered with a wire basket for dishes.

In the 1920s, Randall Phillips, an enthusiast for single-handed domestic efficiency, reviewed the scene a little despondently. 'Many washing-up machines have been devised, but the difficulties of working on a small scale are generally insuperable.' He hoped that the Polliwashup would solve the problem. Water was added from a boiling-kettle, a tablet of soap used to make a lather, then a handle was turned six times in each direction. In 1923 a *House and Garden* article described what was available in 'Overcoming the Drudgery of the Dishcloth'. The simplest aid was a short length of hose attached to the hot tap, with a spray nozzle at the end. This contained a soap

**Electrically powered dishwasher, for hotel use, with overhead railway
to deliver dishes** (*La Nature*, 1906)

dispenser, controlled by a thumb lever, so that the user could direct hot soapy or clear water over the dishes. It was hardly a machine, but at least one could see what was happening. The Blick was described as 'one of the simplest and best of the hand-cranked machines'. In fact it was very similar to the 1865 type, except that the dishes stood above the water and were sprayed by a central propellor. One electric machine, an unusual novelty in Britain at the time, was available from Harrods. It too was filled with a kettle, and converted to a small table when its lid was closed. An extremely sensible feature of the early dishwashers was spare plate-racks, which could be slid out of the washer and mounted on a convenient trolley when full of clean plates, so dispensing with the need to unload the dishwasher.

Electric power was an improvement on hand-cranking, but it wasn't enough to make a successful dishwasher. Users of the early dishwashers will recall how every plate had to be scanned afterwards for baked-on egg, smears of grease and cracks, not to mention the occasions when the machine broke down full of boiling-hot water and all the household china. *House and Garden* warned against 'those machines of doubtful value beyond the fascination of their clever machinery, which is more likely to appeal to the man who may have mended them than the woman who must cope with their intricacies'. Ruth Binnie and Julia E. Boxall dismissed them tersely in their 1926 manual, *Housecraft*, as 'a useless investment'. In his 1928 *How to Plan Your Home*, Martin Briggs advised that the 'bogy of washing-up' was 'more likely to be dispelled by increased simplicity in the nature of our meals than by any mechanical invention applicable to the needs of small homes'.

The 1930s saw some improvements, but more white elephants. The

OVERCOMING THE DRUDGERY OF THE DISHCLOTH

Machines Wisely Chosen and Used Supplement Good Method in
Reducing the Tyranny of the Kitchen Sink

ACTIVE muscles which seldom get out of order or cost money to repair are, after all, the most economical and efficient of household equipment, and intelligence applied to house management saves more labour than many ingenious machines. The elimination of waste movement which has been studied with such valuable results in factories is nowhere more valuable than in the house. When the routine of work has been well planned much of it can be done almost automatically, so that it is well worth while to give this careful consideration in the first place rather than to follow a different, haphazard method every day calling for fresh and unnecessary concentration and energy.

But when everything has been simplified as far as possible there remains an irreducible minimum of work which must be done. While there are still great numbers of people who really enjoy cooking, and others who find various forms of housework a not unpleasant exercise, there are very few who look upon dish washing with anything but distaste. Even in nursery rhymes it is classed with pig feeding as one of the most menial of tasks, and a

The simplest form of dishwasher consists of a stream of hot water from a washing nozzle attached to the hot water tap and directed by hand. The nozzle contains a soap mixer, operated by a thumb lever, so that soapy water is delivered for washing and clear for rinsing. This is only suitable when the supply of hot water is plentiful

promise of freedom from its drudgery held out as a lure to marriage.

An increasing number of machines to help with this task is becoming available, some of which really fulfil their makers' claims, others of doubtful value beyond the mere fascination of their clever mechanism, which is more likely to appeal to the man who may have to mend them than to the woman who must cope with their intricacies.

The points to consider in choosing one of these machines are (1) the dishwasher must be smooth inside with no corners to harbour scraps. (2) It must be self-cleansing. (3) The racks for holding dishes, etc., must be easy to handle and must hold the dishes immovable and not touching. (4) The water must reach the dishes from all sides. (5) The capacity must be equal to the needs of the family. (6) The running cost if worked by electricity, must be low. (7) It must be easy to fill and empty.

Intelligently used, these machines not only save time, labour, and that contact with hot greasy water which is to many the chief cause of objection, but the risk of breakage is greatly reduced.

(Left and above) Where electric current is available this dishwasher is a great convenience. Water is supplied by hand or from a fitted pipe. Finished in white enamel, the flat top makes an excellent kitchen table. Harrods

The "Blick" is one of the simplest and best of the machines worked by hand. It can also be used for washing clothes if desired. The plates stand in a special rack above the water, which is thrown over them by a revolving propeller

This 1923 *House and Garden* feature on dishwashers showed the
three basic types then available

first squared-off body with single-knob control appeared in 1932. An eye-level machine – in effect an enclosed plate-rack above the sink – had a short-lived success, despite the inspired addition of spare plate-racks to make loading and unloading simpler. Dishwashers were still so much of a suspect luxury that they did not appear in American mail-order catalogues until the 1950s, and by 1951 only one million had been sold in the United States. Improvements in detergents and rinsing-aids were needed, as well as electronic programming, before the machines could become efficient enough to be popular.

Opinion on their usefulness is still a matter of dispute. Personally I find them more indispensable than a washing-machine; neighbours with three small children and two busy careers to organize tried one out and got rid of it within weeks. They do make a large store of dishwasher-proof china and cutlery necessary, and inevitably seem to be full of clean dishes from breakfast when lunch ends, or, worse, full of forgotten dirty dishes just as one is trying to lay up supper. They also take away one of the tasks with which other members of the household traditionally help. If a dishwasher means the rest of the family sitting around doing nothing, then it may actually increase work for whoever is preparing a meal.

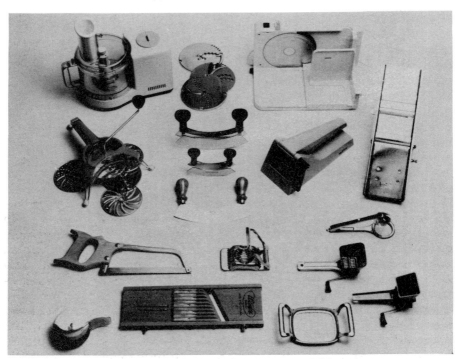

A selection of the kitchen gadgets available today
(David Mellor, *Cook's Catalogue*, 1987)

9

Kitchen Gadgetry

Women are tired of labour-saving devices. They would rather go
back to the Stone Age than be bothered with these innumerable
labour-saving machines.

Journal of Domestic Appliances, 1934

Almost all the machines described in this chapter, except perhaps for
the corkscrew, are not essential to the daily running of a home. The
nineteenth-century passion for mechanization was often inappropriately
applied to tasks that were more easily done by hand. In the panic at the
disappearance of servants, such machines were clutched at with
misplaced enthusiasm, although some did make certain jobs such as
mincing meat or cleaning knives much easier. But at least in their early
development, many of the small kitchen machines were attractive,
ingenious and of fascinating complexity. Although not relevant to the
mainstream of domestic appliance history, they do illustrate the fertility
of the inventors' minds, and the receptive attitude to the idea of labour-
saving in the home.

Preparing and preserving meat, and the use of left-overs, were very
important tasks in the old-fashioned thrift-conscious household.
Household manuals of the 1880s were full of enthusiasm for mincers. 'I
have just invested in a mincing machine', exclaimed Margaret Trent,
'and cannot imagine how I ever managed without it. All scraps of meat
of all kinds, and bacon and ham and everything of that sort, are minced
together and seasoned with pepper and salt, then pressed into
glasspots, a very little liquified butter poured on top, and it is a capital
dish for breakfast or luncheon.' 'What is a home', mused Bloom in
James Joyce's *Ulysses*, 'without Plumrose potted meat? Incomplete.
With it, an Abode of Bliss.'

Among the earliest inventors of the invaluable domestic meat
mincer, Nye and Lyon in Britain and Enterprise in the United States are

the outstanding names. Dozens of other makers soon started production, for the mincer quickly became a widely accepted kitchen tool.

Nye began making machines in 1853. By 1859, when the first issue of *The Ironmonger* appeared, he was advertising several. The 'sausage-making and general mincing machine' was 'a very little thing every husband ought to carry home to his wife'. It came in three sizes, at 1, 2, or 3 guineas. Popular at this time of the infancy of dentistry was the tiny 'food masticator', a miniature mincer, 'very neatly got up', which was intended to be screwed to the dining-table 'to assist digestion, loss of teeth, etc.'

Nye lacked the inventive flair of Arthur Lyon of Finsbury. In 1859 Lyon was offering a steamed-root and vegetable-pulper, a suet- and parsley-chopper and a cucumber- and potato-slicer as well as meat-mincing machines. His sausage-machine was described by the *Journal oj Domestic Appliances* in 1862 as an excellent invention for those people who wisely preferred to know what went into their sausages. Sausages were made by fitting an extension nozzle over the mincer and covering it with sausage skin. As the tube of minced meat came out, suitable lengths of skin were twisted over it. Lyon's mincers came in various sizes. The largest, the No. 4. had a flywheel and could cut 57lbs of meat in twenty-five minutes. The smallest were the food masticators, now improved with hot-water compartments at each side so that 'a piece of meat cut off the joint and put into the machine is cut up and laid on the plate as hot as when taken from the fire.'

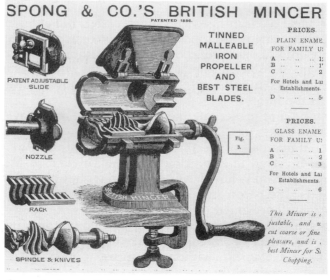

**Spong's classic British Mincer, 1886: its accessories
converted it to cut, chop, mash or make sausages**

Both Nye and Lyon lost ground in the 1880s to the London firm of Spong and Company, who are still in business today. By the 1890s Spong had sold 200,000 mincers and branched out into almost every type of small kitchen appliance. With different attachments, their mincer could do the work of a vegetable-chopper, meat-cutter and sausage-maker. One up on Nye's food masticator was the Spong Dinner Mincer, silver-plated and glass-lined. The Enterprise tinned meat-chopper was recommended by the 1893 Mrs Beeton. 'When cut', she enthused, 'the meat is forced out in a perfect cascade of shreds.' This type of mincer, with blades at the end against which a screw forced the meat, is the same as those in use today. (Tinned, incidentally, referred to the finish inside the machine, not the meat used.) Enterprise, an American firm, lived up to its name. It offered beef-shavers, fruit-presses, sausage-stuffers, graters, lawn-sprinklers, tongue-presses, ice-shredders, cheese-knives (guillotine style), coffee-mills, bone-mills, cork-pullers, vegetable-slicers, barrel-jacks, lawn-mowers, meat-juice extractors, potato-chip cutters and raisin-seeders, besides meat choppers of all sizes.

Many of the mincing- and chopping-machines had very dubious metal finishes, others had complicated interlocking blades that were difficult to clean. An alternative to the screw principle was attempted by the 1879 'American Meat Chopper'. It used a gearing system related to both the beam-engine and the sewing-machine to power a heavy blade that rose and fell on a round wooden board inside a tin. Although it was different in many basic ways, it foreshadowed the ultimate kitchen tool, the electric mixer.

Closer to the mincer in theory but much simpler was the coffee-mill. Made of wood or iron, these first appeared in their modern form in the eighteenth century, and have changed only in superficial design and materials of construction. A handle rotates a sharp screw against which beans fall from a conical hopper; the ground coffee falls into a drawer beneath. Some were exceptionally flamboyant. An Enterprise mill of the 1890s was flanked by two large gilded wheels and topped by an urn from which a bronze eagle stretched its wings for take-off. The basic coffee-mill design was so simple and successful that Spong are still selling the machines advertised in their nineteenth-century catalogues.

Egg-beaters, cream-whippers and food-mixers all aimed to make a peculiarly tiring hand movement easier. The most primitive egg-beaters are the bunches of stripped birch twigs still favoured by Scandinavians, spatulas with a long slot in the blade, and looped wire whisks. The 1850s and 1860s saw many improvements on these. Most basic was the Gothic drill. Wire loops at the base of a shaft revolved as the beater was pressed down against a screw thread. More efficient was the Dover rotary beater, patented in 1876, and, with its two whisks linked by a

"ENTERPRISE"
COFFEE MILLS

NO. 12 AND 212

No.	Capacity of Hoppers	Hoppers	Height	Diameter of Wheels	Weight	Each.
12	5 lbs	Iron	32 in	25 in	141 lbs	$24.00
212	6½ "	"	43 "	31 "	211 "	35.00

Fifty turns will Grind one Pound of Coffee.
No. 12, One in a Crate; No 212, in Two Crates and One Box.

1890s Enterprise coffee-mill with eagle perched on the lid
(Biddle Hardware Company catalogue, 1910)

small cog at the handle, the ancestor of modern hand-powered beaters. It became a byword for this type, although the original Dover was soon rivalled by dozens of competitors.

The next step was to encase the blades in a bowl. A Spong machine of the 1890s came in sizes to beat from 5 to 150 eggs, and its bowl was flanked by hot-water chambers. Such machines developed into the domestic food-mixer, strong enough to stir cakes and knead bread as well as beat eggs and cream. Food-mixers were first used commercially in such trades as baking. An imposing bread-making machine was shown in the *Illustrated London News* in 1858. The long trough had a shaft of steam-powered beaters running along it. A domestic, hand-powered parallel appeared in an American mail-order catalogue forty years later – the Van Heusen egg- and cream-beater. This catalogue also showed a mayonnaise-mixer and a bread-kneader; the interchangeable parts which make a modern food-mixer so adaptable had not yet been developed.

Developers of food-mixers wandered up some strange dead-ends before heading down the royal Kenwood road. Goodall's machine, shown at the 1862 Exhibition, was inspired by industrial grinding-machines, and it aimed to mechanize the technique of pestle and mortar. The American Meat Chopper already referred to was paralleled by a mixer of the 1870s. It had the same crank and beam, but mixing-whisks instead of chopping-blades. All such hand-powered machines could be as tiring to use as an ordinary egg-whisk unless very well geared, and they were difficult to clean thoroughly. The attachment of the small electric motors and the development of streamlined casings brought the food-mixer into its own. The London Science Museum has a 1918 electric machine made by Landers, Fray and Clark, an American company which made various domestic appliances under the name of Universal. In 1931, *Ideal Home* magazine described 'a new electrical appliance which has recently made its appearance and which auto-matically deals with practically every aspect of the preparation of food.' It cost £24, or £31 complete with enamel-topped cabinet. As well as mixing flour, milk, eggs and dough, it had a chopper attachment to cut up meat, vegetables and fruit. It even had an ice-cream-making attachment. The expense of such a machine – as much as a refrigerator – put it beyond most households' reach, although it would have been invaluable at the time, when most food preparation was done in the home.

The most popular food mixer marketed in the 1950s and 1960s was the Kenwood Chef, a machine so solid and well made that the earliest models are still beating away in long-established kitchens today. In the 1970s, mixers were transformed into food-processors, and, ironically enough, just as their functions have been made much less essential by the wide-spread availability of ready-prepared foods, they are cheaper, more adaptable and more efficient than ever before. Their lifespan, however, is a fraction of that of their ancestors.

Corkscrews became necessary tools when corks changed shape – before the late seventeenth century they were tapered and easily extractable by hand. The simple screw was given much elaborate decoration in the eighteenth century, and the most prized were the finely chased specimens produced by the steel- and silver-masters of

Italy. Silver, pewter, wood, mother-of-pearl and ivory were typical materials for handles, while the screw itself was of thick bevelled steel. Jonathan Swift valued his enough to will it to his friend the Earl of Orrery when he died in 1745. In the nineteenth century, a great deal of largely unnecessary ingenuity was applied to conquer the basically simple problem of getting corks from bottle-necks. Besides complicated travelling screws, a plethora of attachments was offered: brushes to clean out bottle-necks, blades to cut foils, knobs to push down the marbles at the top of soda bottles, and once crown seals were invented in 1892, bottle-cap openers.

Double-thread screws such as the King's screw were among the earliest mechanical corkscrews. They were thought to have been patented in 1795 by Samuel Henshall, but a modern expert, Dr Bernard Watney, has pointed out that although Henshall did make openers of the King's screw type, his 1795 patent was for a much simpler screw. Robert Stuart, writing in 1829, attributed the invention to a hostess called Mrs O'Rourke, but was uncertain as to its exact date. The king's screw had a double-action winder, down to pierce the cork and engage in a locking device, then up to remove it. The handle was of bone or ivory, and a thick brush, rather like an old fashioned shaving brush, was set in one end of it. Barrels could be decorated with a personal crest, regimental insignia, or trade marks, and cheaper versions with cut-away barrels were made later in the century. In Stuart's opinion, the type 'can receive no addition either to its beauty or convenience, unless it be probably some little steam appendage to make it self-acting'.[1] Such screws were widely produced by manufacturers such as Henshall, Cope and Cutler, or Twigg and Dowler.

Weir's Concertina, patented in 1884, was another attractive design. It worked like concertina tongs, with eight steel hinges, a short wire screw and a ring to pull on. Another mechanism was the rack and pinion with side handle. Double-lever corkscrews, such as Heely's A1 were very effective. The butterfly-shaped handle made insertion easy, and the levers at each side pushed down to draw out the cork smoothly and quickly. An alternative design was the tangent-lever screw, patented by W. Lund in 1855. This came in two parts: a simple screw with a hole in its handle, and a levering device, like a nutcracker in reverse, which was hooked round the screw and levered against the neck of the bottle. For public house or mansion use, substantial cork-drawers could be screwed onto a wall or counter, and at the other end of the scale dainty travelling corkscrews were made which could be taken to pieces and fitted into a lady's escritoire.

Less necessary than corkscrews, but interestingly ambitious technically, were the early tea-making machines. The first attempt at complete automation was probably the teamaker patented in 1902 by a

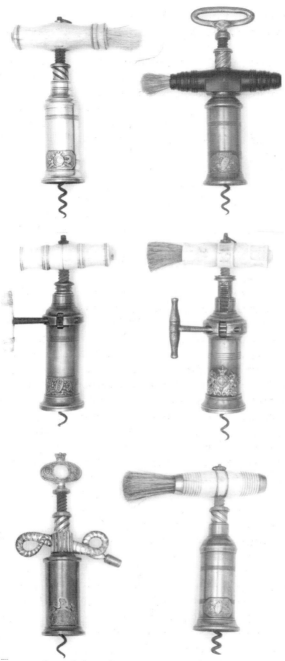

Six examples of the King's screw, probably the most popular nineteenth-century corkscrew design

Birmingham gunsmith. Of all the many beautiful domestic appliances displayed in the basement of the London Science Museum, this attracts the most admiration. Its activating mechanism is a brass alarm clock. At the required hour this rings, and the alarm winder revolves, as is usual in any alarm clock. The winder hits a lever once. This releases a metal base-plate which slides across. On the plate is a strip of sandpaper, to

A CLOCK THAT MAKES TEA!

Calls the sleeper at a given hour, automatically lights spirit lamp, boils a pint of water for tea, shaving, and other purposes, pours it into a pot, extinguishes lamp, and finally rings second bell to signify all is ready. Invaluable to Ladies, Nurses, Professional and Business Men. It is strong, simple, and in no sense a toy. Prices 25s. to 70s. Postage in United Kingdom 1s. extra. With Foreign orders sufficient postage to cover 11 lb. Weight should be sent.

Please send for Illustrated Booklet, post free from

AUTOMATIC WATER BOILER CO.,
26a, Corporation St., Birmingham,
LONDON OFFICE AND SHOWROOM—
31, George Street, Hanover Square.

Tea-maker patented in 1902 by a Birmingham gunsmith and advertised as 'A clock that makes tea!' (*Madame*, 1904)

which a match is held under spring pressure. The movement of the plate strikes the match, which lights a bowl of methylated spirits beneath a wide-bottomed copper kettle. When the water boils, a flap within the kettle vibrates, and trips the short supporting arm, tilting the kettle. At the same time it activates another lever, which pushes the metal base-plate further across, extinguishing the flame, and causing a final blow on the clock's alarm bell to announce the tea as ready.

R. Grumble of Eltham made a gas-heated tea-maker in 1930, using a solenoid in a glass box to operate a gas valve when the time-clock went off. Although the machine looks beautifully engineered and reliable, with a Crown Derby teapot as the finishing touch, it seems to have been a one-off model. Goblin started production of their very successful 'Teasmades' a few years later. The first versions were gawky and hesitant, but by 1933 a grand streamlined model appeared. It featured Aztec pillars and glowing pearlized lights flanked its square chromed clock-face, not unlike a miniature Art Deco cinema. Kettle and teapot fitted neatly behind the facade, and a tray swelled around the base to provide a space for crockery.

Cleaning knives and shoes was traditionally the work of the 'boots', a man- or boy-servant. Since men were the first to disappear from domestic service, and were generally regarded as more difficult to employ than women, mechanization was applied early and with enthusiasm to their tasks. Early trade journals and catalogues offered a mind-boggling variety of more or less useful machines for these purposes. Although again a backwater of domestic life, the variations on the two themes have left a highly collectable range of attractive gadgets.

Before the introduction of stainless steel in the 1920s, cleaning the household knives was an arduous task. Anne Cobbett's 1835 manual gave some idea of the work involved:

> When it can be done, knives and forks should be cleaned immediately after they have been used; but when they are not they ought, if possible, to be dipped in warm (not hot) water, wiped dry, and laid by until the time of cleaning comes. After bath-brick has been used, dip the handles into luke-warm water, or wipe them with soaped flannel, and then a dry cloth. Inexperienced menservants seldom *wipe* knives and forks sufficiently, but it is next to impossible for a woman to clean them well, and it is a *masculine* occupation. To preserve those not in daily use from rust, rub with mutton fat, roll each one in brown paper and keep in a dry place. A good knife-board is indispensable; covered with leather saves the steel, but the knives are not so sharp as if cleaned on a board with bathbrick. Both knives and forks are the better for

being occasionally plunged in fresh, fine earth for a few minutes.
It sweetens them.[2]

The simplest and cheapest knife-cleaner was the American, shown in
the *Journal of Domestic Appliances* in 1884. It was a small adjustable press
which could be clamped onto the blade of a knife and pulled up and
down it. More complex was Knight's machine, sold at the same time. It
came in four sizes and could clean from four to eight knives in one
minute. It looked like a miniature mangle, inside which leather or felt
pads and brushes were rotated, with two rollers between which the
knife was held while the handle was turned. Emery powder was
dispensed through a hole in the side, and an extension to the upper
roller made it possible to clean the shoulder of the knife as well. It cost
from 17s 6d to 30s – the largest size stood on a very attractive cast-iron
stand, rich in Gothic curves. The Uneek was a cheaper version of the
same principle, with india-rubber rollers and a screw to attach it to a
table.

More elegant, but without any moving parts, was Wells's knife-
cleaner. The *Journal of Domestic Appliances* gave a ponderous eulogy of it
in 1885:

> The frame is of the most primitive kind, and is made of cast-iron,
> neatly japanned and varnished, and with some ingeniously
> designed cork-pads and a couple of thumb screws effects
> everything that the most fastidious housewife could possibly
> desire. We have seen this knife cleaner, and can testify that it does
> not belie the expectation or experience of its makers. If required as
> a fixture, the machine can be screwed onto the table. With these
> desiderata so fully secured in a domestic article, it should meet
> with a good sale, especially as the price is purely nominal and
> there is literally nothing to get out of order.

The Sun machine appeared in the same year, and, at 21s, was
grander still. Made of tempered steel, leather and iron, it was cast in the
shape of a radiant sun. It would be screwed permanently to a sideboard
or table, but appears from the illustration to clean only one knife at a
time.

Exactly how worthwhile such machines were is difficult to establish.
Cassell's Household Guide implied that many had flaws when it declared
that 'Some people are under the impression that knife machines must
be destructive', but went on to insist that 'The experience of many years
convinces us that such is not the case. Knives cleaned with good
machines wear evenly, and keep a fine edge . . . The saving of time by
their use is very considerable.'

Fast, simple and durable: the Sun knife-cleaner
(*Journal of Domestic Appliances*, 1885)

The classic knife-cleaner, the most efficient as well as the most expensive, was the type shown at the Great Exhibition by William Kent. It was still being recommended as 'exceptionally good' in 1902. The knives were stuck into the sides of a broad wooden canister, inside which emery-boards and brushes were rotated by a handle to give the steel a mirror-like finish. The machine also sharpened the knives slightly, but a grindstone had to be used occasionally. Unfortunately for Kent, he did not patent his machine effectively, and soon many versions were being marketed. Gollop's cleaner cost between £3 and £7 in 1859. It could clean between six and twelve knives at a time and was available on dwarf or high stand. In 1895 Spong were producing a cut-price version, a guinea less than Kent's machine which could be screwed to a table or wall. The largest models, standing on generously curved stands with sweeping S-shaped handles, were the most beautiful of all.

By Edwardian times, further improvements had been made. Spong offered an 'oscillating rest', which adapted itself to the position of the knife, and Kent produced a cheap colonial model for 29s. The breadth of the spectrum spanned by these interesting machines was summed up in the contrast between the Victoria and the Acme, which both appeared in the Army and Navy Stores catalogue in 1907. The Victoria was a miniature version of the Kent machine, working on a horizontal plane, and only cleaning one knife at once. It was described as 'neat in appearance and not likely to go out of order', and cost 10s 6d. The Acme, at £33, was powered by a bulky electric motor, weighed 140lbs, and had a capacity of 1500 blades an hour.

Mechanization was less effective than social change in reducing the labour of cleaning boots and shoes. A spate of machines was heralded in 1873 by Southall's patent, and in the next eight years twelve more patents were filed. Several appear to have been considerably more complicated than was necessary. 'How many more machines are we to have for "japanning our trotter cases?" Is not a baker's dozen sufficient?' asked the *Journal of Domestic Appliances* suspiciously in June 1881. Not many of them impressed Mrs Beeton's manual which warned that 'Much delicacy of treatment is required in cleaning ladies' boots, so as to make the leather look well-polished, and the upper part retain a fresh appearance, with the lining free from handmarks, which are very offensive to a lady of refined tastes.'

Unfortunately, few details or illustrations of these thirteen or so machines survive. Some of them hardly deserved the name of machine. Spong's Boot-cleaning Assistant was no more than a footrest, with a hook to hang the brush on, and a small cup for blacking hanging from its central stalk. An American invention, it was surely not worth its relatively high price of 15s. More impressive, and using the rotary

The 1882 Universal boot-cleaner revolved against the shoe to offer maximum brushing power (*Journal of Domestic Appliances*)

motion which was the key to success in so many household machines, was the Universal. This cost only one guinea in 1882, and definitely made brushing easier. It consisted of two wheels on a central shaft, fastened to a table or bench-top, with clamps or screws. The upper wheel was edged with hard bristles and the lower with soft ones. Every rotation gave nearly four feet of brush surface to the boot.

A rotating hand-brush was about the limit in mechanizing the boot-cleaning process, and enthusiasm for such machines died away rapidly, to judge by the decline in advertisements. The small electric motor and its ever-adaptable spindle was eventually put to this use as well as dozens of others, and hotels today often have a more or less crude machine for polishing their guests' shoes. What made the adoption of such machines into ordinary homes unnecessary were social changes rather than mechanical ones. Shoe styles simplified, and boots for both ladies and gentlemen were no longer *de rigueur*. The improvements of streets and pavements made obsolete the wooden-soled overshoes, or pattens, on which the ladies of Mrs Gaskell's *Cranford* tripped about, and with them went the mud-splashes on clothes and dresses. Motorized transport made walking outdoors in all weathers less necessary, so both the numbers and the dirtiness of shoes were reduced. Finally, proprietary polishes were introduced in the

1890s. As chemical expertise increased, they became easy to apply and quick to wipe off. The glutinous home-made concoctions once brewed up by the Boots from gall and wormwood were replaced by resplendently named shop-bought polishes like Simpson's Royal Dragoon, Brown's Parisian de Guiche, Halsey's Enamel Lustre, or Day and Martins' Japanese Waterproof.

Apple-parers were always more popular in the United States than in Britain, perhaps because of domestic labour shortages in rural areas, perhaps because individual households could not afford to buy a machine only relevant to one short season of the year. One sensible way round the cost of the machine was to employ a travelling apple-parer – not dissimilar to the itinerant knife-cleaners who still hopefully haunt prosperous back doors today. A Vermont housewife of 1820 described a 'paring-bee' during the cider season: 'One man came with his paring machine and would pare two or three bushels in an evening. The rest of the company quartered, cored and hung the apples on strings ready for drying.'

The first apple-peeling patent was filed in 1802, and by 1836 six others had been added. The simplest just pinioned the apple on a rotating wooden fork; the knife had to be held against the fruit manually. The next development was a hanging knife, which still had to be held against the fruit. By 1856 a metal corer was patented, which featured a knife moving along a rack beside the apple. An improved version of this reached England in the 1880s. It had a second blade which sliced after the first had pared. 'It answers every expectation,' commented the *Journal of Domestic Appliances* a little ambiguously, 'and need not be despised because the price is exceedingly low.' Despite the enormous numbers of apples consumed, and therefore the great potential saving in labour, none of the best-known English books on domestic management ever referred to this invention.

Its reintroduction ten years later in the form of a potato-peeler was similarly unappreciated. Perhaps the difficulty of dealing with unexpected maggots and other imperfections was its downfall. Other approaches to the notorious potato problem had been attempted. The first was a washing and scraping machine patented in 1823. This worked on the same principle as the rubbing-board type of washing-machine. Two concave ribbed boards agitated the potatoes between them when a lever was worked back and forth. In 1882, a more grandiose machine claimed to peel fifty potatoes at once: 'Curved fillets rub rather than cut the peel from the potato. Thus there is no waste. The peels pass into the underside of the machine while the potatoes, divested of their skins, drop into a trough of water at the side.' No great enthusiasm greeted this new dimension in labour-saving, but its scraping principle would eventually be resurrected in a business-like khaki-green rotary machine made by Mouli from the 1950s, and in attachments for electric food-mixers like the French Mouli and the Kenwood Chef.

Bread-slicers were popular when the price of flour was high and a careless maid could make a loaf unfit for table use with a few jagged cuts. The 1851 Great Exhibition contained one made by the imaginative Mr Lyon of Finsbury. It gripped the loaf firmly, then a razor-sharp semicircular blade was lowered through it by hand. It was still being sold in 1882, so must have been found effective. *The Ironmonger* showed another type in 1879, and Mrs Beeton's manual respected it enough to include a full-colour illustration in the 1909 edition. This held the bread in a frame; then a sliding case with a diagonal blade was pushed forward to make the slice. In effect it was a small guillotine laid on its side.

Squeezing lemons clearly seized inventors' imaginations, and an extraordinary variety of approaches to the task were attempted. The nutcracker principle was used in a satisfying simple machine now in the Reading Museum of Rural Life. The Holborn, an iron version of this on a graceful curly stand and with a china bowl, was perhaps the aristocrat of the type, although a luxury squeezer illustrated in *The Ironmonger* in 1889 had a mahogany case and a white porcelain lining. Inside a toothed wheel mashed the lemon against the sides. But the familiar grooved glass cone was the ordinary domestic solution for most families – mechanical lemon-squeezers, like the cherry-stoners, raisin-seeders and potato-chip cutters, were only relevant for the large-scale labour-saving which such tools represented in restaurants or canteens.

The list of these specialized curiosities is endless: a biscuit-breaker on the lines of a mangle, an automatic mustard-dispenser, tongue-presses, peanut-roasters, horseradish-scrapers, ivory-bladed cucumber-slicers, milk-shake machines – they deserve a book to themselves. By the 1930s matters were clearly out-of-hand, and even the magazines were wearying of trumpeting novelties. A reaction related to the dour economic climate set in, and again and again readers were warned not to clutter up their kitchens with too many useless gadgets. The machines too lessened in charm. Rehashed versions of old ideas appeared in brittle Bakelite and tinny alloys instead of the old finely-finished hardwood and solid cast iron. The age of helpful invention was being succeeded by that of frivolous planned obsolescence.

Ultimately the increase in commercial food preservation made such machines less necesary, and it was this trend too which led to a transformation of kitchen-planning theory. More will be said about trends in 'scientific management' of housework in the final chapter, but in the course of the change from large storeroom, larder and dresser for crockery to the fitted kitchens of today, a curious dromedary of an appliance, part furniture, part machine, made its appearance: the kitchen cabinet. In its ultimate complexity, just before its complete demise, it reflected all the optimism of the would-be labour-saving 1920s and 1930s. Like so many of the best gadgets, it originated in the United States; it was also very much a fruit of women's own thinking about what they needed in the kitchen. An article on 'Household Helps and New Ideas' in the *Ladies' Home Journal* for November 1899 explained the theory behind it:

> In the preparation of the daily meals there may be a great saving of time and strength if utensils and materials be grouped together in such a manner that the worker may sit or stand in one place and have them all within reach. A kitchen cabinet, properly arranged, makes this possible. One may now buy, for ten dollars upwards, a cabinet containing closets for groceries, drawers and shelves for utensils, and a flour chest, moulding board, etc.

Two enthusiastic correspondents, Lizzie M. Lindsey of Kentucky and Bertha Marty of Indiana, described how they improvised their own cabinets from converted boxes, wash-stands and chests of drawers.

In 1900, full-page advertisements were being run for the Hoosier Kitchen Cabinet – 'saves health, good looks, strength, time and standing' – and half a million had been sold. The Hoosier contained a sanitary, steel-lined flour-bin equipped with handy sifter, metal sugar-bin, metal topped and airtight crystal jars for tea, coffee and spices, and metal-lined bread- and cake-drawer. But that was not all.

> Table-top is pure aluminium 40 inches square; there is a roomy cupboard for dishes and supplies, and another for pots and kettles, equipped with a sliding shelf so that you needn't stoop and reach. Cutlery and lined drawers, rolling pin, utensil hooks, pan racks, bread and cutting board and a clockface wants-list complete the convenience. Finish is beautiful in golden oak, water and steam-proof.

Cabinets did not reach the British housewife until the 1920s. In 1922 *House and Garden* magazine printed an article on 'The Coming of the Kitchen Cabinet'. It is a marvellous sketch in a nutshell of how attitudes to housework were changing and why.

> The American woman learnt long ago that although domestic labour became rarer and the cost of living higher, it was possible for her to do her own work and yet have time for the more

An ambitiously fitted 1920s kitchen cabinet
(Sears, Roebuck and Company catalogue, 1925)

Hoosier kitchen cabinet (*Ladies' Home Journal*, 1909)

gracious side of life, if she followed the old maxim and 'used her head to save her heels'. Women in this country have learnt much from the last few years. Domestic labour became very scarce during the war, sometimes it was unobtainable, and besides this many women found war work leading them to perform housework tasks which hitherto they had only experienced from the spectator's standpoint. They learnt how wearisome such tasks can be both to body and mind, and began to realise some of the things which make domestic labour distasteful.

The principle of the kitchen cabinet was to save time by saving steps. Everything to hand, in one well-arranged cupboard with pull-out table-top meant that the cook had to leave it only to put dishes in oven or sink. Competition between manufacturers led to more and more features: cookery-book holders on zigzag metal stalks, shelves which shot forward as one opened the cupboards, a dozen storage jars covered by a single long lid which rose up as the swing-down door-cum-tabletop was lowered, hoppers dispensing flour and sugar in measured and sieved quantities. Some manufacturers decided there was no need for any other appliance in the kitchen and fitted their cabinets with hotplates and ice-boxes as well. Quicksey and Hoosier were soon challenged by patriotic British firms such as Easiwork. The latter was ahead of its time in extending its range from cabinets to completely fitted kitchens as early as 1922. 'Wembling housewives', as visitors to the first Ideal Home Exhibition were called, were invited to inspect 'a completely arranged combined kitchen and scullery in 7' by 7' . . . entirely British, even the hardwood grown in the Empire.'

Arguably the kitchen cabinet went too far. It is impossible, or to say the least, inconvenient to put everything in the same place. One can imagine the muttered curses as cooks wrestled with stuck drawers, bruised their shins on dangling doors, dropped ice-cubes on the hotplate, stemmed an avalanche from a faulty flour-hopper and stabbed themselves in the eye with the recipe-stalk while groping among the 'seventy dishes, forty-one packages and more than a hundred articles' which were proudly housed by the Hoosier. As Randall Phillips remarked in 1920, 'Although an extremely handy contrivance, how far it would be successful in the hands of the average servant seems rather doubtful to me. One is inclined to think that dirty habits might reduce it to an unsatisfactory condition.'

The cabinet was the forerunner of attempts to give logical, time-saving shape to the kitchen, and it had enormous appeal in the tiny kitchens being built in smaller houses and flats. If kitchen development had taken a different turn, if families had decided to pool their efforts in community kitchens instead of making individual homes more self-sufficient than they had ever been, such cabinets would have been all that was needed for the few occasions that cooking was carried on.

Has the mechanization of household work really made life more simple?

10

The Domestic Mystique

The greatest Labour-Saving Apparatus which we possess is the Brain; it has not been worn out by too much use.

Mrs C. S. Peel, The Labour-Saving House, 1917

The bulk of this book has dealt with machines invented and developed between 1850 and 1950. Since the Second World War, mass-production techniques have slashed the prices of household machinery and increased their availability. Thanks to such machines, the average home is far cleaner and more comfortable than it was at the time of the Great Exhibition. Together with the mains services of water, gas and electricity, machines have reduced the problems of vermin, dirt and damp to insignificant proportions. The health of the family has improved enormously as a result. Moreover, one person can now run a house furnished with luxuries as well as necessities, and still have time to spare. Living-in domestic staff are unusual – the home is now the province of the family and the family alone.

The other side of the coin is that mass production requires mass markets. Sophisticated advertising campaigns exaggerate the attractions of domestic appliances and argue their 'necessity'; hire-purchase selling schemes make them apparently affordable even to households surviving on social security. 'Ten years ago the ordinary working woman – nearly one-half of the nation – was a slave in an antiquated kitchen; today mechanical slaves on the h.p. have sprung up around her as she works in non-telly hours', declared *The Economist* optimistically on Boxing Day, 1959. Or so the story goes. The darker side of debt and default is carefully concealed behind the slick presentation of the up-to-date life-style that we all owe ourselves now that credit cards 'take the waiting out of wanting'. But why do time-use surveys show remarkably little lessening of the hours worked by full-time housewives? How necessary is the huge current expenditure of households on domestic appliances? What effect have such machines had on liberating women from the

ancient shackles of domesticity? The answers to these crucial questions
can only be arrived at by looking more closely at the apparently rosy
picture of technological progress and improved domestic conditions for
working women that is most people's image of twentieth-century life.

Louise Peet and Lenore Salter's textbook *Household Equipment* was
first published in 1934 and its successive editions up to 1979 offer a
useful guide to the trends affecting domestic equipment since the
1930s. The huge post-war demand for appliances meant that there were
few style changes in the late 1940s – attention to design only occurs in a
buyers' market. The extension of electricity supplies to rural areas
increased the interest of country housewives in automatic washing-
machines, freezers and dishwashers: with heavy calls on their time
from farm and garden, such women could easily justify their need for
machines still considered luxuries by urban women.

By 1961, there had been a rapid succession of new models of the
familiar old appliances. They were easier to operate, and emphasized
energy-saving automatic features. Safety became an issue after a United
States survey revealed that there were more than a million accidents in
the kitchen every year. A final chapter of advice on saving motion and
energy was directed to handicapped housewives and, significant
pointer to the future, the increasing number of mothers who had jobs
outside the home.

The 1970 edition declared that 'modern space-age living has invaded
the kitchen', and added an introductory chapter on the 'wide and
greatly increased use of household appliances in the last thirty or forty
years'. There was a section about machines with electronic solid-state
controls, and another on the growing market for 'personal care
appliances' such as razors, hair-dryers and electric toothbrushes. A new
emphasis on reliability and longevity was supposed to be producing a
reduction in the need for service calls, but less starry-eyed accounts of
the market admitted that industrial machines were consistently longer-
lasting and more reliable than domestic models.[1] It remains true that
the exteriors of machines designed to suit current kitchens fashions are
often more less durable than the machines themselves: dated colours,
broken handles and hinges, chips and cracks in casings, encourage
replacement sooner than necessary.

By 1979 the general saturation of the market for the most popular
appliances, and a slower than estimated replacement rate, led to frantic
style wars among manufacturers. 'Changes take place in equipment
from month to month, sometimes almost from week to week.' Much
more attention was being paid to what the elusive consumers wanted.
New models emphasized savings on energy and water, and anti-
pollution devices. In their later editions, Peet and Salter also added a
chapter on 'maximising the satisfaction of work in the home', a

reflection of the growing demoralization of the woman who was still 'just a housewife', and her need for the same recognition and reward as that earned by the dashing 'superwoman' who seemed to bound effortlessly between home and workplace.

It is worth noting the profound conservatism of these recent trends. The main thrust and direction of the domestic appliance market as a whole has apparently changed very little since the introduction of the small electric motor in the 1920s set it on course as aiming to replace servants in the home with machines in every home. It encourages an essentially private pattern of housekeeping and home-making rather than one of community co-operation and specialization of labour. In this pattern the typical unit of consumption is a small family living in a self-sufficient household organized by a lone woman who has the time to do all the housework herself. For example, she needs to be at home to put the washing into a machine and take it out later on; in the evening she will take food out of a refrigerator, prepare it with the aid of a range of gadgets, and cook it on a stove of some sort. She will put the dishes in a dishwasher and empty it when it is clean. She will clear up the family's mess with a small portable vacuum cleaner. As currently structured, modern manufacturers aim to furnish every home with a complete range of specialized tools and appliances; the job of their marketing divisions is to sell the idea of such a life-style as well as the machines to fit it.

But the boom days are over. As table 10.1 shows, the current virtual saturation of the market means that there is very little scope for anything more dramatic than gradual sales to new households and the occasional 'mini-boom' as some essential and rapidly introduced item comes up for replacement.

Are the manufacturers wise to remain so blinkered by tradition? Yeandle's table also reflects the fact that women who work outside the

Table 10.1 Percentage ownership of domestic appliances in 1981 and 1984

Appliance	1981	1984
Vacuum cleaner	93	98
Refrigerator	93	100
Deep-freeze	49	76
Washing-machine	78	96
Tumble-drier	23	35
Dishwasher	4	11

Sources: 1981 data is taken from the General Household Survey, 1981; the 1984 data is taken from Susan Yeandle's interviews with 64 employed women, *Women's Working Lives*, (London, Tavistock, 1984).

home are likely to have more domestic appliances than those who stay in the home. What it does not show is whether such appliances are actually the best way of saving time and labour in the home, or merely the best on offer at the moment.

It is worth looking more closely at that turn-of-the-century decision to create mechanical servants. At that time there was another fairly well-canvassed option: to professionalize domestic service and to remove it completely from the home. This fitted in with the long-term trends identified by Barbara Ehrenreich and Deirdre English. The household, 'once a tiny manufacturing centre' where women made bread, butter, cloth, clothing, candles, medicines and other things essential to their families' survival became, they believe, 'a domestic void'.[2] 'Four-fifths of the industrial processes carried on in the average American home in 1850 have departed, never to return.' Given this pattern, it made sense to look to outside services to relieve the remaining chores of daily household life – cooking, cleaning and laundry.

The leading advocate of such a course was the radical feminist thinker and economist, Charlotte Perkins Gilman. While welcoming the exodus of the underprivileged and oppressed domestic servant from the home, she could see more clearly than many of her contemporaries the danger of taking on the housework herself.

> The increasing cost and decreasing efficiency of domestic service teaches most women nothing. They simply revert to the more ancient custom of 'doing their own work'. But the double pressure goes on. More and more professional women who will marry and have families and will not be house servants for nothing, and less and less obtainable service, with the sacrifice of the wife and mother to that primal altar, the cook stove.[3]

Applying Adam Smith's doctrine of specialization of labour to the home, she felt that some women ought to take up careers in cleaning in order that most were freed from housework. She suggested that each community could have a central kitchen, so that on evenings when a family did not feel like preparing its own supper it could either eat in a central restaurant or have a meal sent over to be eaten in relaxed privacy. Babycare and kindergartens for everybody's children could be run by those whose bent lay in that particular direction. Gilman never saw 'womankind' in the mass – her basic assumption was that different women would have different ambitions and talents – just as different men had.

The Women's Building at the 1893 Chicago Columbian Exposition was a remarkable illustration of the seriousness with which thinking

Charlotte Perkins Gilman (1860–1935)

women were treating the question of household management. It contained portable sinks, dish-heaters, typewriters, bath-tubs and mechanical dusters, all invented by women. Women exhibited patented transportation systems and community waterworks projects. Participants built a model hospital and kindergarten. Next door, in the Children's Building, model childcare facilities were available, featuring the latest gymnastic equipment and progressive education techniques.

As Gwendolyn Wright points out in her fascinating study of the rise and fall of the community households movement, 'The emphasis was on home, but a different kind of home':

> Mrs Coleman Stuckert showed the plans and models for her co-operative housekeeping project for Denver, which included a co-operative kindergarten and trade school, as well as a community kitchen and dining-room for 44 middle-class families . . . Nearby was a Rumford kitchen, organised by Ellen Richards for the State of Massachusetts. It consisted of a tiny woodframe model of a workingman's house containing the prototype of an inexpensive collective kitchen from which nutritionists could feed the poor.[4]

In 1914 Robert Ellis Thompson called for centralized services that would take cooking, cleaning and childcare outside the home and leave individual dwellings 'to harbour only the emotional and social aspects of domestic life'. He advocated the standardization of architecture on the grounds that it would cut construction expenses, and promote 'a sense of community likeness rather than individual differences'.[5]

In her book published in 1921 Mrs Havelock Ellis asserted the essential unfairness of the lot of domestic servants, and accepted as inevitable their disappearance from the home. Her solution to the 'servant question' which was being so hotly debated at the time, was first to put domestic service completely on a trade basis and secondly to organize community co-operation:

> If every woman could have a minimum instead of a maximum of domestic spider-threads tugging at her brain year in year out through the municipalization of laundries, bake-houses and kitchens, and restaurants worked under well-trained and methodical civil servants, just imagine what a new life would be on earth. Woman's equality would be established almost as much by this as by her economic independence, as it would open up the way in many cases for that very independence; for many women would find their real life-work in the municipal domestic factory, and be paid their true earnings as citizens . . . The professional woman, with special gifts and special hereditary equipment,

would also have a fair chance under such a system: the work of a Jane Welsh Carlyle was practically lost to us because there was no common kitchen for the wants of dyspeptics.[6]

There were practical experiments as well as Utopian theories. Mansion flats in both New York and London were built with communal heating, waste-disposal and water facilities. Some offered deep-freezes and laundries in the basements, and a piped vacuum-cleaner service. 'Dainty dinners' could be sent up from the Mansion's central kitchens, according to Lilly Frazer[7], and when the famous novelist Countess 'Elizabeth' von Arnim lived in London's Whitehall Court in the 1900s, a visitor was impressed to see a menu slipped under the door each morning.[8] But although the Countess had six children, most such apartments were seen as bachelor – male or female – affairs, a useful way for single professionals to live, but not particularly suited to families.

As earlier chapters in this book have pointed out, many domestic services are amenable to professionalization. Today only commemorated by the old-fashioned packs of Happy Families, a small army of tradesmen once called at houses to offer their services. The coalman and the sweep, the ice-man and the baker, the knife-grinder and the fishmonger all tapped at the back-door and offered their wares and services in the most convenient manner possible. In this context, it was quite natural for Lilly Frazer to suggest that 'In time, no doubt, a front doorstep cleaning brigade will form in the style of window-cleaning companies, and we will thus by payment escape the rather heavy drudgery of doorstep cleaning.'

If the only reason for servants leaving the homes had been the democratic justice case argued by Edith Havelock Ellis and her like, such a pattern of professionalization would have been extremely logical, because the labour for such services would have been available. Hoewver, the primary reason for the exodus of domestic servants was a labour shortage caused by the attraction of quite new job options for women: jobs in offices, in schools and in factories mechanized adequately enough to make work light and pleasant in comparison with domestic service. Such jobs offered reasonable terms for employment and far more promising opportunities for social intercourse.

There was a second element too – one which remains crucial to the whole domestic issue today – that prevented private servants transferring to the 'Civil Servant trades' envisaged by feminist thinkers. Professional services require payment. When domestic servants became hard to find or ideologically unacceptable, middle-class women rolled up their sleeves and declared marriage a trade. They found it an attractively economical solution to simplify their life-style and use

The tradesmen featured in this pack of 'Happy Families' playing-cards no longer ease the housewife's day

machines in the home rather than to call on outside services. Until the housewife both believes that working outside the home herself is a feasible option and also costs her time at the same rate as that of her husband or partner, professional services will seem prohibitively expensive.

At the turn of the century Gilman and her like, who called for freedom from the domestic tyranny of housework, were outnumbered. In the opposite corner to that articulate middle-class minority of feminists, and a small band of the 'better-off sort' of married working-class women – Clementina Black's 'radical suffragists' who worked from choice[9] – stood the great mass of women, of all classes, who accepted the view that 'A woman's place was in the home'. The foremost ideal of most working-class women was to get married and to quit paid work. A good husband felt it irresponsible to get married without a 'family wage' that he and his family could live on. Although there were a substantial number of married women who were workers from necessity, their ambition was to stop working. The prevailing climate of middle-class opinion was similarly hearth-based. The home as haven from the heartless world was a commonplace of nineteenth century writing. 'Pray for me', wrote William Wilberforce to his wife. 'It will be a comfort to know that you all who are, as it were, on the top of the mountain, withdrawn above the storm, are thus interceding for me who am scuffling in the vale below.' All the professional achievements and belated educational recognition that women had achieved by the end of the century could still be dismissed as uncompromisingly as this by a doyen of the domesticity school like Marion Harland:

> The chief end of woman is home-making. After all the study of her capacities and capabilities, after all the proofs she had given of her power to rule the wide empire, master the abstruse sciences and write the great book, the final conclusion of the thinker is synonymous with the earlier judgement of nature. Her first duty is to be a wife and mother and make a house. Other walks are open to her if for any reason she is unable to fulfil the purpose of her being, but in so far as the opportunity to do this is denied her, she is, in a sense, a FAILURE.[10]

Although the number of women in paid employment had increased steadily through the nineteenth century, the percentage of married women in the labour force reached an all-time low in the first few decades of the twentieth century. Fed by recruits from above and below, the typical female role in the amorphous CB middle-class mass became that of the lone housewife. By 1947, 94 per cent of women had no help of any sort in the home. Just under 2 per cent had help for 4 hours or less, just over 2 per cent had from 5–12 hours a week and just under 2 per cent had over 12 hours a week.[11] Although popularly accepted as typical, it needs to be emphasized that in historical perspective this 'classic' housewife – an unwaged woman spending rather longer hours than her husband spends at work solely responsible for the organization and maintenance of a home and family, with no children, kin, servants or outside services to help her – is an extremely short-lived cultural phenomenon, flourishing (or rather floundering) only between 1920 and 1970. Such a life resembled nothing so much as that of a garage attendant; providing services in the shape of food, clean clothes and a neatly made bed to her passing family instead of oil and petrol to passing cars.

A crumb of comfort at the failure to professionalize domestic service was offered by the movement to professionalize the status of the unpaid housewife, headed by such passionate advocates of the 'science of domesticity' as Ellen Richards, Christine Frederick and Lilian Gilbreth (see chapter 2). The new cookery schools, domestic science colleges, diplomas in home economics and manuals on 'scientific housekeeping' put an attractively businesslike gloss on the mundane matter of housework, and aimed to distract would-be professional women from avant-garde dreams of municipal organization and community co-operation. On the actual matter of applying industrial-style time-and-motion studies to the household they were on shaky ground (see also chapter 2), but they seized on a powerful theoretical tool when they took up the highly sensitive issue of home-making.

'Home-making is house-keeping plus,' wrote Lilian Gilbreth. 'The plus is the act, the individual variation, the creative work. The house-keeping is the science, the universal likenesses, the necessary activities which must be carried out in order that one may have time for the rest.' By declaring that household organization was necessarily allied with the 'creative work', they condemned women who took their respon-sibility as home-makers seriously to accept the role of domestic servants. It is bizarre in retrospect to read of the enthusiasm with which middle-class women, Hoovers hopefully in hand, planned to take up where their housemaids, cooks and nursery-maids had so thankfully left off.

> There is a great discipline in the performance of manifold modest daily tasks, cheered by the idea of procuring much happiness with small means for her family; to prepare food and raiment for the household, like the virtuous woman in the book of proverbs, sharpens the intelligence and warms the heart. Health too will gain by this system; we shall hear less of breakdowns and neurasthenia and of rest cures, and the nerve specialist may have

to put up his shutters. Simple pleasures will in time be revived and artificiality may be doomed; the higher a woman's education, the better housewife she is sure to be.[12]

Between 1900 and 1920 most feminists had abandoned the domestic arena and taken up arms on the political front. In the excitement of the campaign for women's suffrage they accepted too easily a domestic role which made true equality impossible. Gilman was one of the few who grasped the point that 'Women whose industrial position is that of a house servant, or who do not work at all, who are fed and clothed and given pocket money by men, do not reach freedom and equality by the use of the ballot.'[13] Most women were more concerned to emphasize that winning the vote was no challenge to men's domestic comfort. 'When you visit Wyoming', wrote a correspondent to *Woman's Journal* after the passing of the suffrage laws, 'you will be impressed by the happy smile of the breadwinners as they return from the cares of the day to a bright fireside and a well-ordered dinner, presided over by a home-loving, neatly gowned, womanly wife.'[14]

Another effect of the domestic science movement is pinpointed by Gwendolyn Wright:

> The domestic scientists wanted to produce trained workers who would operate smooth-running machines according to the precise instructions of the managers. Their expectations necessarily meant that housework would consume more and more of the woman's time and effort, as she struggled to keep up to the ever-rising standards. The semblance of modern functional planning became an end in itself. Few people stopped to inquire whose needs were actually being met in this arrangement.[15]

This matter of rising standards is a critically important element in making sense of the multifaceted nature of twentieth-century domesticity. The link between housework and home-making was reinforced when women accepted the argument that more efficient methods of housework could give the housewife more time to raise her standards and so improve the quality of the home. It also established the implacably endless nature of her task, and made it very hard to combine an ambition to work outside the home with a feeling of satisfaction in one's role as a good home-maker. 'Washing machines permit you to do daily, instead of weekly, laundries. Vacuum cleaners and rug shampooers remind you that you do not have to live with dust or countenance a stain on the carpet. Each of them – the dishwasher, the roll warmer, the freezer, the blender – is the material embodiment of the task, a silent imperative to *work*.'[16]

Erik Arnold agrees that many appliances were marketed not just as labour-saving devices – an approach that would most logically have led to taking such tasks right outside the home – but as ways to improve standards, thus ensuring an ever-increasing domestic market.[17] 'The interests of appliance manufacturers in mass markets co-incided exactly with the ideological assumptions of their domestic science advisers, whose belief that women's place was in the home led them to think that appropriate appliances would be designed for the individual woman user rather than for communal or shared use'.

Because of the exigencies of the mass market-place, the simple life envisaged by the optimistic 'servant-free' manuals of the 1920s was overtaken by a flood of gimcrack gadgetry and sales-talk that put a new emphasis on hygiene and efficiency. The old spiritual values of home as nest, mother as educator, father as guide and protector retreated. The new world was a material one, the new woman had to be, in Christine Frederick's telling phrase, Mrs Consumer. 'Consumptionism is the name given to the new doctrine; and it is admitted today to be the greatest idea that America has to give the world; the idea that workmen and masses be looked on not simply as workers and producers, but as consumers . . . Pay them more, sell them more, prosper more is the equation.'[18]

In Stuart Ewen's words, 'excessiveness replaced thrift as a social value. It became imperative to invest the labourer with a financial power and psychic desire to consume.'[19] The imperative was imposed by the nature of mass production. It was no economy to produce millions of vacuum cleaners for the price of thousands if only thousands could be sold. Advertising came into its own in the 1920s. It was quickly recognized as the most efficient way of creating what the psychologists in firms such as J. Walter Thompson called 'fancied needs'. As George Phelps, an advertising executive, succinctly put it, 'Advertising is a sharp and swiftly acting tool of business, and the only one by which a lone individual can engrave his message on the minds of the masses.' While intelligent women flocked into domestic science colleges to improve their housekeeping, intelligent men were signing on for marketing courses. Walter Pitkin, Professor of Marketing in the Columbia School of Journalism, advised his pupils to 'Go beyond institutional advertising to some new kind of philosophy of life advertising.' Edward Bernays, a nephew of Sigmund Freud and founder of the modern science of public relations, hoped to establish a 'mass psychology' by which public opinion might be controlled. 'If we understand the mechanism and motives of the group mind, is it now possible to control and regiment the masses according to our will without them knowing it?'

The techniques of the 'Hidden Persuaders' are too generally known to be worth rehearsing in detail here. But one aspect seems particularly important in establishing what was happening to women's picture of themselves in the domestic context. Robert Lynd commented in *Middletown*, a brilliant vignette of suburban Middle America in the 1920s, that 'Advertising . . . sends the housewife peering anxiously into the mirror to see if her wrinkles look like those that made Mrs X "look old at 35" because she did not have a Leisure Hour electric washer'. This appeal to feminine vanity was a typical ingredient in advertisements; so too was a more explicit sexual message. Domestic appliances should not only give you more time to raise your standards of housekeeping: they should give you more time to be an enticing sex object.

Popular interpretations of Freud's revelation that sex was destiny meant that women became divided and men once again ruled. Psychoanalysts dismissed feminists as 'neurotics who in some instances are compensating for masculine trends, in others are more or less successfully sublimating sadistic and homosexual ones'.[20] Glossy *Ideal Home*-type magazines conveyed an imagery of frilly lingerie and candle-lit suppers that was perfectly suited to the new ideals of 'healthy' sexual fulfilment and romantic togetherness. Woman's sexual role was an essentially passive one. 'It is not as easy as falling off a log. It is easier. It is as easy as being the log itself. She cannot fail to achieve a masterly performance by doing nothing whatsoever except being duly apprecia-tive and allowing nature to take its course.'[21] An article in *Woman's Life* in 1920 declared that 'The tide of progress which leaves woman with the vote in her hand and scarcely any clothes on her back is ebbing, and the sex is returning to the deep, very deep sea of femininity from which her newly acquired power can be more effectively wielded'. In other words, it was back to the kitchen sink. As recently as 1960, Dr Marie Robinson, author of *The Power of Sexual Surrender*, boasted that she advised her 'neurotic' professional female patients to go back to the home and 'recapture their femininity'.

After the Second World War, ideal housewives were also expected to be phenomenally attentive mothers. Children were no longer expected to do anything much to help in the house. While they were babies, they were tended and played with; as soon as they were old enough to lend a hand, they went off to school and so moved into the same off-stage bracket as the breadwinner. The prevailing ethos of childcare became that of motherhood (not parenthood) as a 'twenty-four-hour-a-day job'. Quite why children should have suddenly become so shielded from domestic responsibilities is unclear. Once a positive labour asset, both in the home and outside it, they began to live as small regal cuckoos, nourished and waited on unquestioningly. The position was as unprecedented historically (except for the odd dauphin) as the lonely and menial status of their mothers. Even in the 1920s and 1930s they were briskly treated, expected to be seen and not heard, and left to tumble up in wire netting pens healthily situated at the bottom of the garden. During the two World Wars, when labour was desperately scarce, it was quite acceptable for babies and small children to be put into nurseries, and for mothers to work in considerable numbers. It is hard to escape the conclusion that there is something a little pathological in the devoted full-time attention that has suddenly become necessary to children's mental health. It is also tempting to reflect that it could only become 'necessary' in the 1950s, when increasingly efficient domestic appliances relieved mothers of some of their housework and made extra time for childcare available.

Perhaps most interesting of twentieth-century changes in the nature of household work is the time now spent by housewives on shopping. Calculated to take up as much as one-fifth of their working hours, it is regarded by non-employed women as the most enjoyable aspect of their work next to cooking.[23] It makes them feel less isolated, and also gives them an illusion of importance. As spenders, they are also decision-makers: discriminating spending is the twentieth-century version of the nineteenth-century virtue of thrift. The growth of supermarkets has encouraged the housewife to take over work previously done by tradesmen, and so intensified the independence of the domestic unit from any other labour but that of the housewife herself.

Nothing in history is neat. For all the intricate tangle of femininity, motherhood and home-making in the well-publicized foreground of domestic bliss, what has actually been happening in the twentieth century is a steady trend towards women taking as much of a part in the labour force as men. Efficient birth control and increased life expectancy have changed the world for women dramatically, as figure 10.1 shows.

Women have literally been given a second lease of life by their liberation from the old tyranny of childbirth and its attendant dangers. It is unrealistic not to accept that this revolutionary change in the conditions of their existence will affect the pattern of their lives profoundly. In 1975–80, the birthrate in the United States sank to the 'historic low' of 1.8 per cent.[24] At the same time, women's workplace participation reached the all-time high of 51.2 per cent. 'For the first time in American history, more women are in the labour force than out of it, and women are likely to continue to stream into the workplace in the coming years', comments Gerson, in her lucid account of women's career decisions, *Hard Choices* (1986). 'Recent predictions suggest that by 1990 around 70% of all women of working age will be employed or looking for a job.' British trends echo those of the United States,

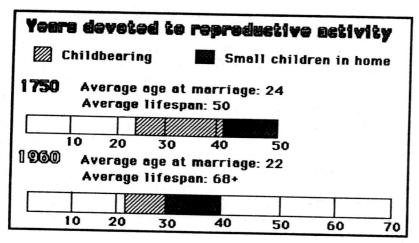

Figure 10.1 Changes in women's life patterns: 1750 compared to 1960 (from L. Tilly and J. Scott, *Women, Work and Family*, Holt Reinhart, New York, 1978)

although Britain's current unemployment problem makes a conservative backlash against women seeking employment highly likely.

What makes the statistics even more powerful indicators of far-reaching change is that it is younger women who are tipping the scales most dramatically in favour of women's employment: they no longer stop working when they marry, postpone child-bearing or renounce it altogether, and continue to work while their children are small. 'Since the 1950s, the non-domestic woman has emerged to challenge the predominance of the home-maker mother. The traditional household composed of a breadwinning husband and home-making wife dropped from 59.4 per cent of all American households in 1950 to only 30.3 per cent in 1980.'[25]

Women use their newly acquired time in a number of ways. Some still opt for traditional nurturing roles and community support. For an increasing number the massive campaign to encourage the sale of consumer goods has been too persuasive. Many households feel that one wage is no longer enough to keep a family in the style to which a wage-earning couple get accustomed before they marry and have children. The housewife is beginning at last to cost the time she spends pottering around the home unpaid, and to look for ways of cutting away the 'domestic spider-threads tugging at her brain year in year out'.

The current development of domestic technology is much complicated by such variations in the labour-saving needs of households and such different attitudes to home management. As Kathleen Gerson points out, there is a deep ideological schism between women who stay at home and women who go out to work. Women with no other occupation than housework and motherhood find it attractive to have machines in the home which enable them to raise the standards of their work, but do not dispense with the need for someone to be in the home. Their demands are for ever more sophisticated machines – zigzag sewing-machines on which to perform wonders of embroidery, food-mixers with all the appliances they need to emulate a Cordon Bleu cook. As Betty Friedan's succinct variation on Parkinson's Law has it: 'Housewifery expands to fill the time available.' The views of such women on child-rearing are strongly coloured by the fact that they are at home. They stress a small child's need for its mother's constant presence, and the irreconcilable conflicts of the demands of a career and the demands of bringing up a family 'properly'. These are the women who clock up extraordinarily long hours in the time-use surveys: Joann Vanek estimated that they worked on average 55 hours a week in 1960, several hours longer than their grandmothers in the 1920s.

New-style 'dual-career' households, in which no-one is available to do housework all day have quite different attitudes. The women in them spend only half as much time on housework as non-working women, and find it quite acceptable to let somebody else look after the children, arguing that it is in the best interest of both mother and child to do so. Such a split in domestic points of view is nothing new, but until the 1980s the first category has always outnumbered the second, and substantial profits have been made by manufacturers who supply strictly domestic technology. Once the second category outnumbers the first – and estimates suggest that this will be so by the 1990s – we can expect much more entrepreneurial interest in the provision of extra-domestic aids to household management.

At the moment, in a society where half the women work outside the home and half do not, we are in a state of flux. The shops are still overflowing with seductively designed domestic technology, sophisticated advertising techniques link marital success to microwave ovens, and books on cooking and gardening outsell any other category of literature. Domestic appliance manufacturers want to hold on to their dominant market position, and they promote the woman-as-home-manager ideology in order to do so. There will continue to be advertisements featuring trim'n frilly homebodies salivating over the latest multi-programmed washing-machine.

All this has contributed to the pressure on working women to be all things to all men – or at least to both their boss and their husband or partner. The textbook of this position is Shirley Conran's best-selling housekeeping manual, *Superwoman*. Light-hearted, witty and full of useful short-cuts, *Superwoman* is also an ideological disaster. Besides serving up imaginative suppers to an unexpected invasion of her husband's most influential work associates, changing the tyre on her car and redecorating the drawing-room on a shoe-string, Superwoman somehow holds down a full-time job, brings up the children and handles her (almost inevitable) divorce alone.

Expediency has now made working women more practical. Superwoman's juggling act is generally admitted to be untenable, and assistance of some sort is accepted as necessary. But there remain two broad areas where not nearly enough has changed, and where without change women can never take up the position in society that they now claim as their right. They are interrelated. One is the level of women's wages in comparison with those of men. The other is the matter of men sharing housework fairly and participating in parenthood.

Until women earn as much as men, there will always be a severely practical reason why it will be the mother rather than the father who breaks her career to look after their children. The most depressing aspect of the massive increase in the number of married women with children working in the last twenty years is that it is almost entirely an increase in part-time working. There is nothing inherently wrong with part-time working, especially in the context of family life, but there is something wrong in it being predominantly a woman's option, and in it offering low pay and poor-quality fringe benefits.

John Nicholson recently published an exhaustive examination of the myths surrounding human sex differences and the ascertainable facts. He came to the conclusion that the most obvious explanations for a woman's disadvantaged position in the workplace were that she took a chunk out of her career in order to look after children, and that she carried the major responsibility for household affairs, even when working as many paid hours a day as her husband. It was not just the actual time involved in such matters as good-enough motherhood and reasonable household management, but the whole attitude of mind which such an approach implied. Sights were pitched lower at the very opening of a girl's career, since she always had the mental reservation that she would be dropping it all sooner or later to be a wife and mother. Employers have treated women less well in the market-place because they felt that, given a choice between domestic and work commitments, home would often come first (in fact, statistics on absenteeism show that this is simply not so).

Kathleen Gerson has broadened Nicolson's picture by taking a survey of women with different baseline commitments to careers, and examining the reason why some fulfilled their ambitions and others changed their plans. One of the most interesting of her revelations is the difference that chance opportunities made to the women. Unexpected appreciation in the workplace led several women who had planned to give up their jobs to persevere with working; more typically, dead-end low-status jobs led women who had originally hoped for permanent employment to take the 'domestic option' that many still look on as a woman's privilege. Privilege it may be, but until as many men as women find it an attractive option, it will have a suspect tinge of exploitation.

So to the vexed matter of men's participation in housework and parenthood – still staggeringly low according to surveys, for all the TV sit-coms about house-husbands and boy nannies that suggest otherwise. The evidence is that it is a mistake to attempt to solve the problem of one woman doing two jobs (three if you count child-rearing) by asking two people to do one and a half (or two) each. Modern domestic labour-saving appliances do make daily life far easier, cleaner and more comfortable – but they do not save enough time and effort in the home to allow both adults to be fully employed, to bring up a family and to enjoy some leisure and recreation. If Nicholson is right in claiming that housework and childcare disadvantage women in the workplace, then for men to take on more of the chores of a family will simply lead to heavy discrimination at work against those responsible for a family – men and women alike. It is possible that men need to be congratulated rather than nagged at for their clear-sighted refusal to fall into the trap of trying to be more than one person, of experiencing their children, in Bacon's classic phrase, as 'hostages to fortune . . . impediments to great enterprise'.[26]

In an ideal world, all employers will become as family-minded as some of the banks and insurance companies are becoming – they will offer several years leave to a parent of either sex, with the option of part-time work and refresher courses. Until that golden age, would-be successful dual-career families have two ways of solving their problems. Ironically, they are the same two options that were rejected by middle-class families at the turn of the century in favour of the glorious mirage of mechanical servants.

First, there has been some evidence of an unexpected increase in the numbers of domestic servants. It is unproven as yet, because Department of Employment statistics no longer aggregate domestics as a separate category, and many service jobs are unofficial. But domestic employment agencies report a significant rise in vacancies, although they say that in general there are more vacancies than suitable applicants. Many of the vacancies have been created by changes in work-permit regulations which have debarred the Filipino and Mediterranean migrants who used to fill a large proportion of domestic jobs. Jonathan Gershuny believes that the increase is 'a labour supply phenomenon – not so much the rich getting richer as the poor, especially women, desperately needing work.'[27]

Clearly, domestic service is no more popular than it ever was. Most jobs entail long hours and low pay. Most are filled by women with absolutely no alternative employment, who stay for a short a time as possible. The criticisms levied on the system by such democratic thinkers as Edith Havelock Ellis still hold good. Reviving domestic service is not a credible option today, for all the high rate of unemployment on the one hand, and the crying need of dual-career families in the other.

A distinction needs to be made between domestic service and what Gershuny has called the 'new service economy'. For the second option open to working couples is to rely more on services outside the home – the course recommended by Gilman in 1906.

There are already signs of a revived interest in removing labour from the home altogether. More and more shops are opening up in the so-called 'unsocial' hours, making it possible for working couples to shop and eat with the minimum difficulty. Much of the labour has been taken out of cooking by the unholy alliance of frozen food and the microwave oven. Trends also show far more families buying 'take-aways' or eating out at realistically priced snack-bars during the week and buying a traditional Sunday lunch at a nearby pub at weekends. Entertaining at home is dying away entirely or becoming simplified. In large cities, where the numbers demanding such services make their provision viable, dinner-parties are increasingly often supplied commercially by small teams of enterprising cooks, and the career woman who once rushed home from her office to pull on a pinny can now sink into a hot bath and wait for the doorbell to ring with an easy mind.

People who cost their own time realistically may stop buying washing-machines and tumble-driers and return to laundries or make use of service washes in laundrettes: the success of the washing-machines installed in the 'family centres' on some large London estates show that the ancient sociable traditions of the communal washing ground can be revived and are experienced as welcome breaks from family life. Perhaps one day the fantasy world of My Beautiful Launderette will become a social commonplace. Because of generally improved quality of housing, decorations and furnishings, basic house-cleaning need no longer be a daily routine. Ultimately it may become a monthly blitz just like window-cleaning – left in the capable hands of mobile cleaning firms such as The Maids Ltd., Scrubbers, or Wombat and Mop, who use industrial cleaning methods to make houses considerably cleaner than any overworked and underpaid daily-help ever did. When garden contractors mow lawns during the week on a regular basis, suburban weekends will not longer be made hideous with the cacophony of a dozen rival machines.

In the context of child-rearing, instead of stressing the baby's need

Professional cleaners in action in the 1980s

for a constantly attentive mother, developmental psychologists now allay parental guilt feelings by revealing that babies seem to enjoy company. They can distinguish between their mother and their father and their care-taker at a very early age, and survive occasional separation with equanimity – it even seems to speed up their cognitive development. Demand for work-place crèches and nursery schools is increasing; failing those, working parents shift for themselves by using child-minders or joining 'Share-a-Nanny' schemes to give their children what they see as the best of both worlds: a familiar care-taker and stimulating company. Now that so many mothers work, neighbourhood 'latchkey groups' can relieve the isolation of the after-school hours – Denmark has organised after-school clubs for the children of working mothers for many years now. What is becoming increasingly evident is that numbers solve problems. When being a working mother was not unusual but stamped with social stigma, it was hard to ask for help. Once it is unusual not to have a job, friends and neighbours can co-operate to their mutual gain. We are back to the perceptions of Lilly Frazer in 1913:

> Early rising is essential, method and order are indispensable, the use of labour-saving implements is advisable, and above all co-operation is necessary – co-operation between the diverse members of the family, between the householder and tradesmen, and between acquaintances, friends and relations; also between the municipality and the householder. Without this co-operation, all that I could suggest here would be vain.[28]

Numbers not only solve problems – they create economies of scale. It seems likely that the trend to using professional domestic service agencies could increase in a virtuous spiral: more clients will make costs fall; reduced prices will lead to more clients. Two other new trends should make more sophisticated services possible. Transport is infinitely more efficient and flexible today than it was in 1900. Combined with the huge potential of information technology – of computer terminals and modems in every home – it means that special needs can be catered for across far wider areas than before.

It is important not to underestimate the attraction of the 'domestic option' that makes so many women give up work altogether rather than change from an unsatisfactory job. The longer we all live, the more often we are likely to value variety rather than security of employment, and the tyranny of the nine-to-five treadmill has been well documented in Ehrenreich and English's highly perceptive analysis of men's position, *The Hearts of Men* (1983). Interestingly, in counterpoint to women's new and necessary self-assertion, men are reconsidering the assumed advantages of their own position. Just as women's work-patterns are changing, so are men's. In the United States, men's labour-force participation has dropped from 86.4 per cent in 1950 to 77.2 per cent in 1980. They tend to work shorter hours and change careers more often than they did thirty years ago – in fact, their work patterns 'increasingly resemble the part-time interrupted model once reserved primarily for women'.[29]

Moreover, there is some evidence that men are rediscovering a role as fathers that they lost when they were pushed outside the home by the Industrial Revolution. The gloomy prediction made by Bertrand Russell in his *Marriage and Morals* (1929), that feminism and the Welfare State would soon ensure that fathers were of no more importance in the family than cats and dogs, has not just been unfulfilled; it seems to be positively contradicted. Schaeffer and Emerson's research in the 1960s showed that nearly 60 per cent of infants were as attached to their fathers as their mothers at 12 months, even in a situation when the mother had been the primary caregiver. These days baby-care books talk of parenting rather than mothering, and dozens of 'introductions to fatherhood' lie beside the familiar manuals for mothers. Rocking the cradle and feeding the baby is no longer cissy; ten years ago heads turned in the street at the sight of a man pushing a pram. Changing nappies is not now by definition women's work. It may not be coincidence that the new trend is to buy disposable nappies and eliminate the most unpleasant aspects of the chore altogether. The huge sales of Robin Skynner's books on family therapy reflect the widespread popular agreement with his belief that the father's family role goes far beyond Russell's economic functionalism. Economic exigencies still prevent most fathers from putting into practice the 'new model fatherhood', but the mutual satisfactions inherent in balanced parenthood may become an increasingly powerful factor in influencing work-patterns and the division of responsibility for home management.

I have no intention of painting a utopian fantasy of how life could be, or of giving a prescription for how it ought to be. All the trends that I have described are measurable realities. They seem to suggest that, albeit slowly and unsteadily, our society is changing profoundly in the attitudes taken up by both women and men in their domestic relation. Making a home that lives and breathes, rather than window-dressing an empty shell, is becoming a high priority. The current boom in DIY home improvements and gardening can be seen as a sign that genuine productivity is coming back to the home; the 'domestic void' is being filled.

In this context, the part played by mechanical household appliances in liberating both men and women from boring and repititious household tasks is a vital one. The problem is, as has become evident in examining the history of their development, the contribution of such machines has also been erratic, much distorted by the commercial necessities linked with mass production. Louis Mumford asked a sobering question twenty years ago.

> What would become of mass production and its system of financial expansion if technical perfection, durability, social efficiency and human satisfaction were the guiding aims? The very condition for financial success – constantly expanding production and replacement – works against these ends. To ensure the rapid absorption of its immense productivity, mega-technics resorts to a score of different devices: consumer credit,

instalment buying, multiple packaging, non-functional designs, meretricious novelties, shoddy materials, defective workmanship, built-in fragility, or forced obsolescence through frequent arbitrary changes in fashion.[30]

Ultimately the potential of any machine should lie in the mind of its user rather than its maker. The tide is turning against isolated domesticity and the Dazzling Mums with hands that wash dishes as soft as their faces. Wives no longer want to be lonely garage attendants, however glamorous the setting of the pumps. Consumers are not indefinitely malleable nor totally undiscriminating, and hopefully the market will eventually follow their lead. Unnecessary machines – and the labour they entail – should leave the home. Instead, properly-paid professionals can take over the drudgery of domesticity, and leave men and women enough time to make their houses satisfying homes.

Notes

All references to books are in short-title form. Full details can be found in the bibliography.

Chapter 1 Homes without machines

1 Beeton, *Household Management*.
2 Rundell, *Domestic Cookery*.
3 Royal Society, *Philosophical Transactions*, 1827.
4 Beeton, *Household Management*.
5 Gaskell, *Ruth*.
6 Haweis, *The Art of Housekeeping*.
7 Beeton, *Household Management*.
8 Haweis, *Art of Housekeeping*.
9 Brockway, *Bermondsey Story, The Life of Alfred Salter*.

Chapter 2 Of pig-iron and parlourmaids

1 *Journal of Domestic Appliances*, 1 September 1882.
2 *Electricity in Daily Life*, 1891.
3 Quoted in Habbakuk, *American and British Technology in the Nineteenth Century*.
4 Beecher, *The American Woman's Home*.
5 McBride, *The Domestic Revolution*.
6 Rowntree, *Poverty: A Study of Town Life*.
7 Lanceley, *From Hall-boy to House-Steward*.
8 Quoted in Ehrenreich and English, *For Her Own Good*.

Chapter 3 The mechanical tailor

1 30 June 1860.
2 *Journal of Domestic Appliances*, 11 March 1893.
3 *Englishwoman's Domestic Magazine*, 1867.
4 *Scientific American*, 1878.

5 'Reminiscences of an Old Sewing Machine Hand', *Journal of Domestic Appliances*, June 1888.
6 *Journal of Domestic Appliances*, September 1882.

Chapter 4 Laundry work

1 Beecher, *The American Woman's Home*.
2 *Journal of Domestic Appliances*, October 1908.
3 *Girl's Own Paper*, 1881–2.
4 Gowans Whyte, *The All-Electric Age*.
5 Frederick, *Housekeeping with Efficiency*.
6 Giedion, *Mechanization Takes Command*.
7 Clark, 'Report on Gas Appliances'.

Chapter 5 House-cleaning

1 Booth, 'The Origin of the Vacuum Cleaner.
2 *Der Vacuumreigiger, ein Apparel zür staubfreien Reiniging die Wohnraüme*, Munich 1905.

Chapter 6 The bathroom

1 Webster and Parkes, *Encyclopaedia of Domestic Economy*.
2 Gerhard, *On Baths and Different Forms of Bathing*.
3 Hellyer, *The Plumber and Sanitary Houses*.
4 Grossmith, *The Diary of a Nobody*.
5 *Journal of Domestic Appliances*, March 1902.
6 *Illustrated London News*, September 1853.
7 Panton, *From Kitchen to Garret*.

Chapter 7 From roasting-spit to trained lightning

1 Oakley, *The Sociology of Housework*.
2 Cobbett, *The English Housekeeper*.
3 Beecher, *The American Woman's Home*.
4 Sugg, *The Domestic Uses of Coal Gas*.
5 Clark 'Report on Gas Appliances'.

Chapter 8 Essential kitchen technology

1 Peel, *A Hundred Wonderful Years*.
2 *Good Housekeeping*, March 1928.
3 Beeton, *Household Management*.

Chapter 9 Kitchen gadgetry

1 *Historical and Descriptive Anecdotes of Steam Engines*, 1829.
2 Cobbett, *The English Housekeeper*.

Chapter 10 The domestic mystique

1 Corley, *Domestic Electrical Appliances*.
2 Ehrenreich and English, *For Her Own Good*.
3 Gilman, *The Home: Its Work and Influence*.
4 Wright, *Moralism and the New Model Home*.
5 Thompson, *The History of the Dwelling house*.
6 Ellis, *Democracy in the Kitchen*.
7 Frazer, *First Aid to the Servantless*.
8 Usborne, 'Elizabeth', *The Author of Elizabeth and Her German Garden*.
9 Black, *Married Women's Work*.
10 Harland, *Modern Home Life*.
11 Davidson, *A Woman's Work is Never Done*.
12 Frazer, *First Aid to the Servantless*.
13 Gilman, *The Living of Charlotte Gilman: An Autobiography*.
14 Quoted in Ehrenreich and English, *For Her Own Good*.
15 Wright, *Moralism and the New Model Home*.
16 Quoted in Ehrenreich and English, *For Her Own Good*.
17 Erik Arnold, *New Scientist*, 18 April 1985, see also his excellent book with Wendy Faulkner of edited papers on this subject, *Smothered By Invention*, 1985.
18 Frederick, *Selling Mrs Consumer*.
19 Ewen, *Captains of Consciousness*. I am indebted to this book for most of the following references.
20 Quoted in Ryan, *Womanhood in America*.
21 Lyndberg and Farnham, quoted in Ryan, *Womenhood in America*.
22 Quoted in Beauman, *A Very Great Profession*.
23 Oakley, *The Sociology of Housework*.
24 Gerson, *Hard Choices*, 1985.
25 Ibid.
26 Bacon, 'Parents and Children'.
27 *The Listener*, 4 December 1986.
28 Frazer, *First Aid to the Servantless*.
29 Gerson, *Hard Choices*, 1985.
30 Mumford, *The Myth of the Machine*.

Bibliography

General works

Adamson, Gareth, *Machines at Home*, Lutterworth Press, London, 1969.

Anthony, Sylvia, *Women's Place in Industry and Home*, G. Routledge and Sons, London, 1932.

Bacon, Francis, 'Parents and Children', *Essays*, 1625; republished by World's Classics, Oxford, 1937.

Bayne-Powell, Rosamond, *Housekeeping in the Eighteenth Century*, John Murray, London, 1956.

Beauman, Nicola, *A Very Great Profession*, Virago, London, 1983.

Bennett, Enoch Arnold, *Riceyman Steps*, Cassell and Co., London, 1923.

Bentley, Nicolas, *The Victorian Scene*, George Weidenfield and Nicolson, London, 1968.

Black, Clementina, *Married Women's Work: A report for the Women's Industrial Council*, London, 1915.

Booth, H. Cecil, 'The Origin of the Vacuum Cleaner', *Transactions of the Newcomn Society* (London), vol. 15, p.63, 1935.

Branca, Patricia, *Silent Sisterhood: Middle Class Women in the Victorian Home*, Croom Helm, London, 1975.

Briggs, Martin Shaw, *How to Plan Your House*, English Universities Press, London, 1928, 1937.

Brockway, Archibald Fenner, *Bermondsey Story. The Life of Alfred Salter*, Allen and Unwin, London, 1949.

Browne, Geoffrey, *Patterns of British Life*, Hulton, London, 1950.

Buchanan, Robert Angus, *Industrial Archaeology in Britain*, Allen Lane, London, 1974.

Burman, Sandra (ed.), *Fit Work for Women*, Croom Helm, London, 1979.

Chadwick, Edwin, *Report on the Sanitary Conditions of the Labouring Population of Great Britain*, House of Lords Sessional Papers, London, 1842.

Clapham, Sir John Harold, *Concise Economic History of Britain*, vols 1–2, Cambridge University Press, Cambridge, 1949.

Clark, Daniel Kinnear, 'Report on Gas Appliances', in *The Exhibited Machinery of 1862*, Day and Son, London, 1864.

Coppersmith, Frederick, and Lynx, Joachim Joe, *Patent Applied For*, Co-ordination Press and Publicity, London, 1949.

Cooper, Grace Rogers, *The Invention of the Sewing Machine*, Bulletins of the Smithsonian Institute no.254, Washington DC, 1968.

Corley, Thomas Anthony Buchanan, *Domestic Electrical Appliances*, Jonathan Cape, London, 1966.

Dana, Richard Henry, *Hospitable England in the Seventies*, John Murray, London; Cambridge, Mass., 1921.

Davidson, Caroline, *A Woman's Work is Never Done: A Social History of Housework 1630–1950*, Chatto and Windus, London, 1982.

Dawes, Frank, *Not in Front of the Servants*, Wayland, London, 1973.

Denby, Elizabeth, *Europe Rehoused*, Allen and Unwin, London, 1938.

Derry, Thomas Kingston and Williams, Trevor Illtyd, *A Short History of Technology*, Clarendon Press, Oxford, 1960.

Deane, Phyllis and Mitchell, B.R., *Abstract of British Historical Statistics*, Cambridge University Press, Cambridge, 1971.

'The Demand for Domestic Appliances', *National Economic Review*, London, 1980.

Eastlake, Sir Charles Lock, *Hints on Household Taste*, London, 1968; revised 1878.

Edwards, Frederick, *Our Domestic Fire-Places*, London, 1865.

Ehrenreich, Barbara, and English, Deirdre, *For Her Own Good: 150 Years of the Experts' Advice to Women*, Pluto, London, 1979.

Ehrenreich, Barbara, and English, Deidre, *The Hearts of Men: American Dreams and the Flight from Commitment*, Plut, London, 1983.

Ellis, Edith Lees (Mrs Havelock), *Democracy in the Kitchen*, Haslemere, London, 1894.

Emerson, Ralph Waldo, *English Traits*, Routledge and Kegan Paul, London, 1856.

Ewen, Stuart, *Captain of Consciousness*, McGraw Hill, New York, 1976.

Farr, Michael, *Design in British Industry: A Mid-Century Survey*, Cambridge University Press, London, 1955.

Faulkner, Wendy, and Arnold, Erik, *Smothered by Invention: Technology in Women's Lives*, Pluto, London, 1985.

Franklin, Linda Campbell, *From Hearth to Cookstove*, House of Collectibles, Florence, Ala.

Frederick, Christine, *Selling Mrs Consumer*, The Business Bourse, New York, 1929.

Gaskell, Elizabeth Cleghorn, *Cranford*, Chapman and Hall, London, 1853.

Gaskell, Elizabeth Cleghorn, *Ruth*, Chapman and Hall, London, 1855.

Gerhard, W.P., *On Baths and Different Forms of Bathing*, New York, 1895.

Gershuny, Jonathan, *The New Service Economy: The Transformation of Employment in Industrial Societies*, Macmillan, London, 1978.

Gerson, Kathleen, *Hard Choices: How Women Decide about Work, Career, and Motherhood*, University of California, Los Angeles, 1985.

Giedion, Siegfried, *Mechanisation Takes Command*, Oxford University Press, New York, 1948.

Gilbreth, Lilian, *The Homemaker and Her Job*, Appleton, New York, 1927.

Gilman, Charlotte Perkins, *The Home: Its Work and Influence*, McClure Phillips, New York, 1903.

Gilman, Charlotte Perkins, *The Living of Charlotte Perkins Gilman: An Autobiography*, Appleton, New York, 1935.

Girouard, Mark, *Victorian Country Houses*, Oxford University Press, Oxford, 1971.

Glissman, A.H., *Evolution of the Sad-Iron*, M B Printing Photolithography, Oceanside, California, 1970.

Government Statistical Service, *Annual Abstract of Statistics*, H M S O, London, 1971.

Gowans Whyte, Adam, *Forty Years of Electrical Progress. The Story of G.E.C.*, Ernest Benn, London, 1930.

Guwans Whyte, Adam, *The All-Electric Age*, Constable and Co., London, 1922.

Greer, Germaine, *The Female Eunuch*, MacGibbon and Kee, London, 1970.

Grossmith, George and Weedon, *The Diary of a Nobody*, J.W. Arrowsmith, Bristol, 1892.

de Haan, David, *Antique Household Gadgets and Appliances*, Blandford, Poole 1977.

Habakkuk, Hrothgar John, *American and British Technology in the Nineteenth Century*, Cambridge University Press, Cambridge, 1962.

Harrington, Sir John, *Metamorphosis of Ajax*, London, 1596.

Harrison, Molly, *Home Inventions*, Usborne Publishing, London, 1975.

Hartley, Dorothy Rosaman, *Food in England*, Macdonald, London, 1954.

Haslett, Caroline, *Electrical Handbook for Women*, Electrical Association, London, 1965.

Hellyer, Samuel Stevens, *The Plumber and Sanitary Houses*, London, 1877.

Hetherington, John Rowland, *Selina's Aunt*, John R. Hetherington, Birmingham, 1965.

Hillier, Bevis, *Art Deco*, Studio Vista, London, 1968.

Jekyll, Gertrude and Jones, Sydney Robert, *Old English Household Life*, B.T. Batsford, London, 1939.

Jewell, Brian, *Veteran Sewing Machines*, David & Charles, Newton Abbott, 1975.

Lanceley, William, *From Hall-Boy to House-Steward*, E. Arnold and Co., London, 1925.

Lantz, Louise K., *Old American Kitchenware 1725–1925*, Nelson and Everybody's Press, Camden, NJ, and Hanover Penn., 1970.

Laslett, Peter, *The World We Have Lost*, Methuen, London, 1965.

Laslett, Peter and Wall, Richard, *Household and Family in Past Time*, Cambridge University Press, Cambridge, 1972.

Lewis, Jane, *Women in England 1870–1950: Sexual Divisions and Social Change*, Wheatsheaf, Sussex, 1984.

Lewis, Jane, (ed.), *Labour and Love: Women's Experience of Home and Family 1850–1940*, Blackwell, Oxford, 1986.

Lewton, Frederick, L., *The Servant in the House: A Brief History of the Sewing Machine*, Smithsonian Institution Report, Washington DC, 1929.

Lister, Raymond George, *Decorative Cast Ironwork in Great Britain*, G. Bell and Sons, London, 1960.

Lochhead, Marion Cleland, *The Victorian Household*, John Murray, London, 1964.

Lynd, Robert Staughton and Helen Merrell, *Middletown: A Study in Contemporary American Culture*, Harcourt, Brace and World, NY; Constable and Co, London, 1929.

Lynd, Robert Staughton and Helen Merrell, *Middletown in Transition: A Study in Cultural Conflicts*, Harcourt, Brace and World, NY; Constable and Co., London, 1937.

Lyon, P. 'Isaac Singer', *American Heritage Magazine*, October, 1958.

McBride, Theresa M., *The Domestic Revolution: The Modernisation of Household Service in England and France 1820–1920*, Croom Helm, London, 1976.

Malos, Ellen (ed.), *The Politics of Housework*, Allison and Busby, London, 1980.

Mumford, Lewis, *The Myth of the Machine Vol. II, The Pentagon of Power*, Secker and Warburg, London, 1967.

Nicholson, John, *Men and Women: How Different Are They?* Oxford University Press, Oxford, 1984.

Norwak, Mary, *Kitchen Antiques*, Ward Lock, London, 1975.

Nowell, Smith, S., *Edwardian England*, Oxford University Press, Oxford, 1964.

Oakley, Ann, *The Sociology of Housework*, Martin Robertson, London, 1974.

Oakley, Ann, *Housewife*, Penguin, London, 1976.

O'Dea, William Thomas, *The Social History of Lighting*, Routledge and Kegan Paul, London, 1958.

Palmer, Ray, *The Water Closet*, David and Charles, 1973.

Peel, Dorothy Constance, *A Hundred Wonderful Years: Social and Domestic Life of a Century, 1820–1920*, John Lane, London, 1926.

Phillips, R. Randall, *The Servantless Home*, Country Life, London, 1920.

Randall, Wilfrid L., *The Romance of Electricity*, Sampson Low and Co., London, 1931.

Robinson, Marie, *The Power of Sexual Surrender*, W.H. Allen, London, 1950.

Rowntree, Benjamin Seebohm, *Poverty: A Study of Town-Life*, Macmillan, London, 1902.

Rumford, Sir Benjamin Thompson, Count, *The Complete Works of Count Rumford*, vol.4, Harvard University Press, Cambridge, Mass.; Oxford University Press, Oxford, 1968–70.

Russell, Bertrand, *Marriage and Morals*, Allen and Unwin, London, 1929.

Russell, Dr, *The Uses of Sea Water in Diseases of the Glands*, London, 1753.

Ryan, Mary, *Womanhood in America: From Colonial Times to the Present*, New Viewpoints, New York, 1975.

Schumacher, E.F., *Small is Beautiful: A Study of Economics as if People Mattered*, Blond and Briggs, London, 1978.

Skynner, Robin, and Cleese, John, *Families, and How to Survive Them*, Methuen, London, 1983.

Stiegler, G.J., *Trends in Employment in the Service Industries*, Princeton University Press, Princeton, 1956.

Sinclair, Andrew, *The Better Half: The Emancipation of the American Woman*, Jonathan Cape, London, 1966.

Stuart, Robert, *Historical and Descriptive Anecdotes of Steam Engines*, London, 1829.

Sugg, William T., *The Domestic Uses of Coal Gas*, Walter King, London, 1884.

Summerton, Arthur, *Treatise on Vacuum-cleaning*, London, 1912.

Surtees, Robert Smith, *Mr Sponge's Sporting Tour*, Bradbury and Evans, London, 1853.

Szalai, Alexander, *Use of Time*, Pergamon, Oxford, 1977.

Taine, Hippolyte Adolphe, *Notes sur L'Angleterre*, trans. Edward Hyams, Paris, 1872; Thames and Hudson, London, 1957.

Thackeray, William Makepeace, *The History of Pendennis*, Bradbury and Evans, London, 1849–50.

Thompson, Robert, *The History of the Dwelling-house, and its Future*, Lippincott, New York, 1914.

Tilly, Louise, and Scott, Joan, *Women, Work and Family*, Holt Reinhart, New York, 1978.

Trollope, Anthony, *Barchester Towers*, London, 1857.

Turner, Ernest Sackville, *What the Butler Saw: Two Hundred and Fifty Years of the Servant Problem*, Michael Joseph, London, 1962.

Usborne, Karen, *'Elizabeth', The Author of Elizabeth and Her German Garden*, Bodley Head, London, 1986.

de Vries, Leonard, *Victorian Inventions*, John Murray, London, 1971.

Wilson, Elizabeth, *Only Halfway to Paradise: Women in Postwar Britain 1945–68*, Tavistock, London, 1980.

Wright, Gwendolyn, *Moralism and the New Model Home: Domestic Architecture and Cultural Conflicts in Chicago 1873–1913*, Yale University Press, Yale, 1980.

Wright, Lawrence, *Clean and Decent*, Routledge and Kegan Paul, London, 1960.

Wright, Lawrence, *Home Fires Burning. The History of Domestic Heating and Cooking.* Routledge and Kegan Paul, London, 1964.

Wright, Lawrence, *Warm and Snug. The History of the Bed*, Routledge and Kegan Paul, London, 1962.

Yarwood, Doreen, *The English Home*, B.T. Batsford, London, 1956.

Yarwood, Doreen, *The British Kitchen: Housewifery since Roman Times*, Batsford, London, 1983.

Yarwood, Doreen, *Five Hundred Years of Technology in the Home*, Batsford, London, 1983.

Yeandle, Susan, *Women's Working Lives*, Tavistock, London, 1984.

Periodicals

Black and White; Cowkeeper and Dairyman's Journal; Domestic Appliances; Domestic Life; The Englishwoman's Domestic Magazine; The Expositor; The Family Economist; The Giornale di Roma; Gentleman's Magazine; Girl's Own Paper; House and Garden; Ideal Home; Illustrated London News; The Ironmonger; Journal of Design; Journal of Domestic Appliances and Sewing Machine Gazette; Ladies Home Journal; The Ladies Treasury; Mechanics Magazine; La Nature; Philosophical Magazine; Practical Mechanics Journal; Scientific American; Vogue.

Contemporary manuals

Bateman, Robert Allen, *How to Own and Equip a House*, R. A. Bateman, London, 1925.

Beecher, Catherine Esther and Stowe, Harriet Elizabeth Beecher, *The American Woman's Home*, J.B. Ford and Co, New York, 1869.

Begbie, Harold, *Life without Servants, by a Survivor*, London, 1916, 1930.

Beeton, Isabella Mary, *Household Management*, S.O. Beeton, London, 1859–61 and later editions.

Binnie, Ruth, and Boxall, Julia E., *Housecraft*, Sir I. Pitman and Sons, London, 1926.

Cassell and Co., *Cassell's Household Guide*, London, 1869–71.

Cobbett, Anne, *The English Housekeeper*, London, 1835.

Conran, Shirley, *Superwoman*, Sidgwick and Jackson, London, 1975.

Davidson, Hugh Coleman (ed.), *The Book of the Home* (8 vols), Gresham Publishing Col., London, 1905.

Frazer, Lilly, *First Aid to the Servantless*, Heffer's, Cambridge, 1913.

Frederick, Christine, *Housekeeping with Efficiency*, London, 1913.

Harland, Marion, *Modern Home Life*, 1902.

Haweis, Mary Eliza, *The Art of Housekeeping*, Sampson Low and Co., London, 1889.

Noble, Mrs Robert, *Labour-saving in the Home*, Macmillan's Sixpenny Self-help Library, London, 1930.

Novy, Priscilla, *Housework without Tears*, Pilot Press, London, 1945.

Panton, Jane Ellen, *From Kitchen to Garret*, Ward and Downey, London, 1888.

Peel, Dorothy Constance, *How to Keep House*, A. Constable and Co., London, 1902.

Peel, Dorothy Constance, *The New Home*, A. Constable and Co., London, 1898.

Peet, Louise J., and Salter, Leonore E., *Household Equipment*, John Wiley, London and New York, 1930; and successive editions to 1979.

Rundell, Marie Eliza, *A New System of Domestic Cookery*, John Murray, London, 1808.

Smallshaw, Kay, *How to Run your Home without Help*, John Lehmann, London, 1949.

Spon, Edward and Francis N., *Spon's Household Manual*, E. and F.N. Spon, London, 1887.

Sugg, Marie Jenny, *The Act of Cooking by Gas*, Cassell and Co., London, 1890.

Webster, Thomas, and Parkes Mrs C., *Encyclopaedia of Domestic Economy*, London, Longman, 1844, 1861.

Catalogues and trade publications

General

Country Gentleman's Association, London, 1894.

Festival of Britain, London, 1951.

Montgomery Ward, USA, 1927.

Official Catalogue of the Great Exhibition, introduced by Henry Cole, London, 1851.

Sears Roebuck, Chicago, Ill., 1898.

Victorian Shopping (Harrods 1895 catalogue), London, 1895; reprinted David and Charles, Newton Abbott, 1972.

Yesterday's Shopping (Army and Navy Stores 1907 catalogue), London, 1907, reprinted David and Charles, Newton Abbott, 1969.

Bathware and kitchenware

Doulton and Co., Stoke-on-Trent, 1885–1903.

Bathware

Twyford 'Twentieth Century', London, 1900.

Electrical appliances

The Story of Belling, Enfield, 1962.

Gas appliances

Parkinson (Cowan), London, 1912.

Ironmongery

Fearncombe, London, 1866.
Spong and Co., London, 1890.

Solid fuel appliances

Smith and Wellstood, Bonnybridge, 1907.

Index

Acme knife cleaner, 168
advertising, 177, 188–9
Aetna Ironworks: gas-cooker, 122
Aga ranges, viii, 121–2
AI corkscrew, 162
Alaska Cold Dry Air Cabinet, 139
Alberta sewing-machine, 47
All-British Boudoir carpet-sweeper, 78
American Freezer, 143
American Meat Chopper, 159, 161
anthracite ranges, 120
anti-pollution devices, 178
Appert, Nicholas, 145
apple-parers, 170
Aqua Pura filter, 150
Arnold, Erik, 188
Art Deco, 90, 165
Art Nouveau, 101, 119, 150
Ash: refrigerators and freezer, 137, 143
Athena Quadrangular Lavatory, 104–5
Automatic Water Boiler Company, 164

Baby Belling electric cooker, 133
Baby carpet-sweeper, 78
Baby Daisy vacuum-cleaner, 86
Baby Electrolux refrigerator, 142
Bacon, Francis, 3, 194

Baker: mangles, 66
Banks, J. A., 34
basins, 104–6
bathrooms, 16, 90–110
    decor and fittings, 98, 99, 100–1, 102–3, 105, 110
    showers, 16, 92–3, 94, 106
    washstands and basins, 104–6
    water-closets, 18, 106–10
baths, 16–17, 91, 93–4, 97–102
    steam, 16, 92
batlets, 66
Baumgarten can-opener, 146
Beecher, Catherine, 32–3, 56, 65, 102, 116
Beeton, Isabella, 38
    on cooking stoves, 114, 120, 129, 132
    on filters, 150
    on kitchen gadgetry, 159, 168, 171
    on laundry, 11–12; washing-machines, 57, 59
    on meals, 6–7
    on refrigerators/freezers, 139, 143
    on servants, 33
    on spring-cleaning, 15
Belling electric cookers, 133–4
Bennett, Arnold, 83
Bessemer, Henry, 22
Binnie, Ruth, 152
Birdseye, Clarence, 143–4

Bissell, Melville Reuben: carpet-
    sweepers, 77–9
Black, Clementina, 185
Blick dishwasher, 152, 153
Blodgett and Lerow sewing-
    machine, 43
Blue Streak can-opener, 146
Boiling Steam Therma geyser, 94
boot-cleaners, 165, 168–9
Booth, H. Cecil: vacuum-cleaners,
    76, 80–2, 83, 84, 86, 88
Bostel, D. R.: water-closet, 110
bottle-jack, 114, 115
Boulton and Watt, 25
Bowden, Mr: mangle, 67, 68
Boxall, Julia E., 152
box-irons, 69
box-mangle, 66
Bradford, Mr
    mangle, viii
    washing-machines, 57, 59
Bradshaw sewing-machine, 42
Bramah, Ernest: water-closet, 108
Branca, Patricia, 35
bread, 8
    maker, 161
    slicer, 171
Briggs, Martin, 152
British Thompson Houston, 30
British Vacuum-Cleaner Company
    (BVC, later Goblin), 31, 82, 84, 86
British Westinghouse, 30
Brooklyn power station, 28, 29
Bryan, Donkins and Company:
    vacuum-cleaner, 81

cabinets, kitchen, 172–5
Califont geyser, 24, 96
Canadian Red Star washing-
    machine, 57
Canadian Washer, 56
canned food, 145–7
can-openers, 146
Carlyle, Jane Welsh, 183
Carpenter, Mr: electric cooker, 130
carpet-sweepers, 77–9
Carré, Ferdinand, 26
    refrigerator, 140

Carron: electric cooker, 132
cesspits, 18
Chadwick, Sir Edwin, 23
    on slums, 18–19
Champion irons, 72
charcoal
    baths heated by, 94
    filters, 150
    furnaces, 22
    iron, 71
    ranges, 115
    washing-machines powered by,
        60, 61
Charing Cross Kitcheneres, 126
Chatterton and Bennett: washing-
    machine, 59
Cherrytree Spray Washer, 59
children
    bearing, 190–1
    caring for, 20, 180, 182, 189–90,
        192, 193, 195–8
    labour by, 5, 61, 154, 189
Chubb, Stephen: mangle, 66
Clayton, Mr, 25
cleaning, 13–19, 76–89
    carpet-sweepers, 77–9
    professionalization of, 180, 182,
        183, 185, 195, 197
    spring-cleaning, 14–15, 89
    timetables, 14
    vacuum-cleaners, 27, 31, 80–9
Clegg, Samuel, 25
Clown sewing-machine, 48
coal
    for cooking, 5, 23, 113–22
    for heating, 94, 101, 117
    for smelting iron, 21–2
Cobbett, Anne, 3, 114, 165
Cockran, Mrs: dishwasher, 151
coffee-mills, 159–60
cold storage, 136–45
Cole, Henry, 94
communal
    bakeries, 113
    bathing, 91, 92, 110
    laundry activities, 10, 65, 195
community households, 182–3
Concertina corkscrew, 162

Conran, Shirley, ix, 192–3
Constantine, Mr: kitchen range, 120
consumerism, viii-ix, 177, 188–9, 191
cooking, 5–9, 113–34, 179, 195
    coal-fired ranges, 23, 112, 113–22
    by electricity, 23, 31, 128, 130–4
    by gas, 23, 122–30
Cope and Cutler: corkscrews, 162
Cordon Bleu gas cooker, 127
corkscrews, 161–3
Cort, Henry, 21
Cragside (house): electric lighting,
    28
cream-whippers, 159
Creda electric cooker, 134
crimping-machines, 69, 71
Crompton, Rookes Evelyn Bell
    electric cooker, 130, 131
    electric iron, 73
Crystal Palace
    cleaned, 84
    Exhibition (1851) *see* Great
        Exhibition
    Exhibition (1882), 126
Cummings, Alexander: water-
    closet, 108

Dalén, Gustav: Aga, 120–1
Damen: folding bath-tub, 100
Daquin, Eugene: dishwasher, 151
Darby, Abraham, 21
Daussin steam-engine, 50
Davidson, Caroline, 33
Day and Martins: shoe polish, 170
deep-freezes *see* freezers and
    freezing machines
Dinner Mincer, 159
dishwashers, 27, 31, 151–2, 178, 179,
    187
Disraeli, Benjamin, 1
dog-power, 5–6, 50
dolly, 55–6
    machines imitating, 57, 58
Dolphin water-closet, 110
Domelre refrigerator, 140
domestic mystique, 176–99
Domestic Science Convention
    (USA), 39

domestic science movement, 186–8
Donkin, Hall and Gamble: canning,
    146
Doulton filters, 149
Dover rotary beater, 159–60
'dual-career' families, 192, 194
Duck Oven gas cooker, 123
durability of machines, lack of, 178
    198–9

earth-closets, 18
Easiwork kitchen cabinet, 175
East Anglian gas cooker, 126
Edison, Thomas, 27–8
Edison: sewing-machine, 50
Edison-Swan Company, 28–9
egg-beaters, 159
Ehrenreich, Barbara, 39, 180, 197
Electric Servant washing-machine, 63
Electric Suction Sweeper, 87
Electrical Association for Women, 30
electricity, ix, 177, 178
    for cooking, 23, 31, 128, 130–4
    for dishwashers, 152–4
    for heating water, 23, 92, 94
    for irons, 73–4
    for lighting and heating, 23, 27–8
    for refrigerators, 140–2
    for sewing-machines, 51–2
    for vacuum-cleaners, 82, 86–9
    for washing-machines, 62–5
Electrolux
    refrigerator, 140, 142
    vacuum-cleaner, 88
Empire water motor, 51
enamel
    basins, 105
    baths, 100
    cookers, 120, 122, 128, 129, 130
    sinks, 147
    washing-machines, 63
Enamel Lustre shoe polish, 170
English, Deirdre, 39, 180, 197
English Electric, 31
Enterprise
    coffee mills, 160
    mincer, 157
    tinned meat chopper, 159

Entwhistle and Kenyon: carpet-sweepers, 78
Esse range, 122
Evans, Oliver: oven, 114
Ewart: geysers, 24, 94, 96
Ewbank carpet-sweeper, 78
Ewen, Stuart, 188
Excelsior sewing-machine, 47
exhibitions, 120, 123, 126, 131
    see also Great Exhibition; London Exhibition

Factotum washing-machine, 60
Fairclough, Mrs; cookery school, 131–2
family *see* domestic mystique
Family Sewing-Machine, 46
Faraday, Michael, 26, 129
Fearncombe: showers, 92–3
feminists, 185, 187, 189
55s sewing-machine, 47
Figuier, Louis, 145
filters, water, 149–50
First Aid to the Servantless, 86
Fisher, A. J.: washing-machine, 62
flat-irons, 69–70
Float Washer, 59
fluting-iron, 69
food
    preparation *see* cooking
    storage and preservation, 3, 4, 136–47
food-mixers *see* mixers
Ford, Henry, 31
Franklin, Benjamin: stove, 117
Frazer, Lily, 183, 197
Frederick, Christine, 38, 62, 137, 186, 188
free-standing ranges, 117–20
freezers and freezing-machines, 26, 142–5, 178, 179, 187
    see also ice
French Patent Filtre Rapide, 150
Freud, Sigmund, 189
Frezo ice-making machine, 143
Friedan, Betty, 192
Frigidaire refrigerators, 30, 140, 141, 142

Frister and Rossman sewing-machines, 47
Froy bathrooms, 103
Fuller, Buckminster: bathroom, 103
Furlong: ironing and polishing machine, 72

Garden Cities, bathrooms in, 102
gas, 177
    for cooking, 23, 122–30
    for irons, 71–2
    for lighting and heating, 23, 25–6, 30, 92, 101
    for refrigerators, 140
    for tea-making machines, 165
    for washing-machines, 60
    for water heating, 92, 101
Gas, Light and Coke Company, 25, 129
Gaskell, Elizabeth, 12, 169
gasoline *see* oil/paraffin/petrol
General Electric company, 30, 147
General Motors: refrigerators, 140
Gerhard, W. P., 93
Gershuny, Jonathan, 194–5
Gerson, Kathleen, 190, 191–2, 193
geysers, 23, 92, 94–6
Gibbs, James, 46
Giedion, Siegfried, 27, 62
Gilbreth, Lilian, vi, 38, 186–7
Gilman, Charlotte Perkins, 27, 180, 185, 187, 195
GLC I gas cooker, 129
Goblin (earlier BVC)
    Teasmades, 165
    vacuum-cleaner, 88
Goddard, Ebenezer: gas cooker, 123, 126
goffering iron, 71
Gold Medal carpet-sweeper, 78
Gollop: knife-cleaner, 168
Good Housekeeping vacuum-cleaner, 86
Goodall: grinding-machine, 161
Gothic Revival stove, 117
Gowans Whyte, Adam, 62, 132
Grand Rapids carpet-sweeper, 78, 79

Great Exhibition (1851), vii–viii, 177
  cooking stoves, 26, 115, 122, 123
  ice chests and freezers, 4, 139,
    143
  kitchen gadgetry, 168, 171
  sewing-machines, 41, 47
  showers and baths, 92, 94
  washing-machines, 56, 66
Griffith vacuum-cleaner, 86
Griscom Electro-motor, 51
Grossmith, George and Weedon, 35
  98
Grover and Baker sewing-machines,
  43, 45, 46
Grumble, R., 165
Guardian refrigerator, 140

Harcourt, Vernon: geyser, 94
Harland, Marion, 185
Harrington, Sir John, 106, 107
Haslett, Caroline, 30
Havelock Ellis, Edith, 27, 182, 183,
  195
Haweis, Mrs, 14–16
Heely: corkscrew, 162
Hellyer, Samuel, 97, 98, 101, 108,
  147
Henshall, Samuel, 162
Holborn lemon-squeezer, 171
Hoosier Kitchen Cabinet, 172, 174,
  175
Hoover, W. 'Boss' and Hoover
  Company
  vacuum-cleaners, 30, 31, 87, 88,
    89
  washing-machines, viii, 63
Hoskin's washing-machine, 56
Hotpoint
  BTH washing-machine, 63
  iron, 73
Housewife's Economiser washing-
  machine, 56
housewives, ix, 178, 180, 183, 185–7,
  192, 197
Howe, Benjamin: dishwasher, 151
Howe, Elias: sewing-machines, 42,
  43, 44–5, 46
Humphries, Maria Gay, 77

ice
  -chests, 137–9, 140
  harvesting 3–4
  -houses, 4–5
  -making machines, 26
  see also freezers and freezing
    machines
Ice Cabinette, 139
ice-cream maker, 142–3
Ideal Home Exhibition, 129, 175
immersion heaters, 23, 94
insulation
  of cookers, 121, 129, 130
  of ice-chests, 4
Ipswich, 123
iron
  industry, 21–2
  kitchen ranges, 113–22
irons, 11, 31, 69–74
Italian ('tally') iron, 69
Itonia water-closet, 109, 110

Jee, George: mangle, 66
Jennings: geyser, 94
Johns, Edward, 104
  water-closet, 109, 110
Jones, William: sewing-machine,
  47
Judkin, Charles: sewing-machines,
  47, 50
Judson: filter, 150
Junker and Ruh sewing-machines,
  47

Kelvin, Lord, 28
Kelvinator refrigerators, 140,
  142
Kendalls pleating machine, 71
Kenney, David T., 84
Kennington gas cooker, 128–9
Kent, William: knife-cleaner, 168
Kenwood mixers, 161, 171
Kimball and Morton sewing-
  machine, 48–9
King, Alfred: gas cooker, 123
King, J. T.: washing-machine, 60
King's screw corkscrew, 162, 163
Kinnear Clark, Daniel, 59, 67

kitchens
gadgetry, 156–75, 179, 188;
cabinets, 172–5
technology, 135–54; canned food,
145–7; cold storage, 136–45; *see
also* freezers and freezing
machines, 1, refrigerators;
dishwashers, 27, 31, 151–4;
water in kitchen, 6, 147–50
see also cooking
knife-cleaners, 165–8
Knight: knife-cleaner, 166
Knox, Susan R.: goffering-machine,
71
Kwick-Kleen carpet-sweeper, 78

Lancely, William, 34
Landers, Fray and Clark: mixer, 161
larders, 3, 138
laundry work, 8, 10–13, 54–74
daily routines, 11–12
irons, 11, 31, 69–74
mangles and wringers, 11, 23,
65–9
see also washing-machines
lavatories *see* water-closets
Leamington kitchen range, 115
Leeds Fireclay Company bathroom,
90
lemon-squeezers, 171
Leoni: gas stove, 123, 125
Liebig company, 112
Lindsey, Lizzie M.: kitchen cabinet,
172
Lion sewing-machine, 48–9
Lion water-closet, 110
Lithgow: gas iron, 72
Little Gem iron, 72
London Exhibition (1862), 57, 59, 60,
123, 140, 143, 161
Lund, W.: corkscrew, 162
Lynd, Robert, 189
Lyon, Arthur: kitchen gadgetry,
157, 158, 159, 171

McBride, Theresa, 33, 35
Magnet vacuum-cleaner, 88
Maignan: filter, 150

Main, R. & A.: gas cookers, 128, 129
Mainservor gas cooker, 128
Malos, Ellen, vi
mangles, 11, 23, 65–9
Mann, J. R.: water-closet, 110
Marty, Bertha: kitchen cabinet, 172
Marvellous Washer, 60, 61
mass production, ix, 30–2, 99, 103,
105, 140, 144, 146, 158–9, 177,
198–9
Maugham, Benjamin: geyser, 94, 95
Maytag
mangles, 67
washing-machine, 10, 63
meat, preservation of, 3
meat-cutters, 159
men
housework and childcare by, 194,
197–8
servants, decline in numbers of,
33, 36
vacuum-cleaning by, 82
work patterns, 197
microwave ovens, 134, 195
mincers, 157–9
Miniature carpet-sweeper, 78
mixers, 27, 159–61, 187, 192
Modernette electric cooker, 133
Moldacot Pocket Sewing-Machine
Company, 48
Monel sinks, 147
Money, Dr: washing-machine, 60
Morison, Mr: washing-machine, 59
Morphy Richards, 31
Mouli potato-peeler, 171
Mulparvo washing-machine, 63
Mumford, Louis, 198–9
Murdoch, William, 25

National Grid, 31, 63
Nettleton and Raymond sewing-
machines, 47
New Family sewing-machine, 46
New Home Memory Craft 6000
sewing-machine, 52
New World gas cooker, 129
New York State Fair (1910), 151
Nibestos filter, 150

Nicholson, John, 193, 194
'night-soil', 18, 106
Noble, Mr: bath, 93
Nye: mincer, 157–8, 159

Oakley, Ann vi, x, 113
oil/paraffin/petrol
    for heating, 92, 101
    for irons, 71
    for lighting, 27
    for refrigerators, 140
    for vacuum-cleaners, 82
Old Faithful Self-working Washer,
    59
open ranges, 114–15
Optimus water-closet 108
Oxenham, Hugh: mangle, 66
Oxenham, Thomas: mangle, 66

Pan-American washing-machine, 57
Panton, Jane Ellen, 104, 116, 147
paraffin *see* oil/paraffin/petrol
Paragon freezer, 143
Parkes, C., 66
Parkinson, W. and Company
    gas cookers, 128, 129
    laundry stove, 72
Parlour Queen carpet-sweeper, 78
part-time work, 193, 197
Pasteur, Louis, 146
Patent Economiser kitchen range,
    116–17
Patent Filtering Refrigerator, 137
patent pool, 45
patents, numbers registered, 21, 31
Pearson: washing-machine, 60, 61
Pedal Zephyrion sewing-machine,
    48
Peel, Constance, 97, 138, 177
Peet, Louise, 178–9
Perkins, Jacob: refrigerator, 139–40
Pfaff sewing-machines, 47
Phelps, George, 188
Phillips, Randall, 61–2, 175
Piston Freezing Machine, 143
polishers, 27
polishes, 15, 169–70
Polliwashup dishwasher, 151

posser *see* dolly
potato-peelers, 170–1
Potter, Orlando B., 45
Potts, Mary Florence: irons, 69, 70
power stations, 28–9
Prestcold refrigerator, 142
Princess sewing-machine, 48
professionalization of cleaning, 180,
    182, 183, 185, 195, 197
public facilities *see* communal
Public Health Act (1849), 23
Puffing Billy vacuum-cleaner, 76,
    82

Quicksey kitchen cabinet, 175

Radiation: gas cookers, 129
Raeburn range, 122
ranges, kitchen, 23, 112, 113–22
    closed, 115–22
    open, 114–15
Red Star washing-machine, 57
Reform Club, gas cookers in, 122
refrigerators 26, 31, 137–42, 179
    absorption, 140
    compression, 139–40
    electric, 140–2
    gas, 140
    selling techniques, 142
refuse destructors, 149
Regulo oven thermostat, 129
Renown gas cooker, 129
Richards, Ellen Swallow, 39, 182,
    186
Robson, Thomas: washing-machine,
    60
Ronuk floor-polisher, 89
Rosenthal sewing-machine, 48
rubbish disposal, 147, 149
Rumford, Count (Benjamin
    Thomson): kitchen ranges, 114,
    120, 182
Russell, Bertrand, 197, 198
Russell, Dr, 91

Saint, Thomas, 42
Salamander charcoal heater, 94
Salter, Lenore, 178–9

sausage-makers, 158–9
Savestane sinks, 147, 148
'scientific management', 38–9, 171,
    186
Scott, Baillie, 101–2
Seely, H. W.: iron, 73
Self-Feeding Cabinet refrigerator,
    137
selling techniques
    refrigerators, 142
    sewing-machines, 45–6
    vacuum-cleaners, 88
servants, 19, 32–8, 85, 88, 177, 182,
    183
    decline in numbers, ix, 33, 36, 38
    increase in numbers, 194–5
    professionalized *see under* cleaning
sewage, 18–19
sewing, hand, 12–13
sewing-machines, 27, 42–52, 192
    chain-stitch, 42, 43, 46, 48
    decorated, 48–9, 50
    lock-stitch, 47, 48
    portable, 46
    selling techniques, 45–6
    treadle-powered, 46, 48
    'war', 44–5
Shanks: bathware, 99–100, 110
Sharp, James: gas cooker, 21, 123,
    125, 126
shoe-cleaners, 165, 168–9
shopping, 190
showers, 16, 92–3, 94, 106
Siemens vacuum-cleaner, 85
Simpson: shoe polish, 170
Singer, Isaac Merritt: sewing-
    machines, 42, 43, 44–6, 47, 49,
    51
sinks, kitchen, 4, 147–50
Smith, Adam, 180
Smith, James and Wellstood,
    Stephen: stoves, 71, 117,
    119–20
Smoke Abatement Exhibition (1882),
    120
solid fuel *see* charcoal; coal
Southall: boot- and shoe-cleaner, 168
Soyer, Alexis, 122, 123

Spangler, James Murray, 86–7
spits, 5–6, 114
Spong and Company
    boot- and shoe-cleaner, 168
    beater, 160
    freezer, 143
    household manual, 30
    knife-cleaner, 168
    mincer, viii, 158–9
spring-cleaning, 14–15, 89
Staines Mannesmann refrigerator,
    140–1
Standard carpet-sweeper, 78
standards, raised, 187–8, 192
Star freezer, 143
Star vacuum-cleaner, 86
steam-baths, 16, 92
steam-engines/steam-power, 22
    sewing-machines, 50
    vacuum-cleaners, 80–1
steam-irons, 74
steel industry, 22
Steinfeld and Blasberg sewing-
    machines, 47, 48
stoves
    laundry, 71–2
    see also under cooking
Stowe, Harriet Beecher, 32
street-sweeping, 77
Strode and Company: baths, 98
Suburbia gas cooker, 128
Sugg, Marie Jenny, 126
Sugg, William, 25, 126
    on gas cookers, 126, 127
    on geysers, 94
    on steam-baths, 92
Summerscales Dashwheel washing-
    machine, 60
Sun knife-cleaner, 166, 167
Superior Bath Cabinet, 100–1
'superwoman' concept, ix, 179,
    192–3
Swan, Joseph, 27–8
Sweden: refrigerators, 140, 142
Swift, Jonathan, 162

tanks, hot water, 96–7
Tattersall: carpet-sweeper, 78

tea-making machines, 162, 164–5
Tellus vacuum-cleaner, 88
Thackeray, William M., 92
Thimmonier, Barthelemy: sewing-machines, 21, 42
Thompson, E. D., 94
Thompson and Houston, 30
Thompson, Robert Ellis, 182
Thomson, Benjamin *see* Rumford
Thor washing-machine, viii, 63
time and motion studies, 38–9,178, 186
tins and tin-openers *see* canned food
toilets *see* water-closets
Treasure kitchen range, 120
'Trent, Margaret' (fictional), 35, 36, 37, 60, 150, 157
Trolleyvac vacuum-cleaner, 86
Trollope, Anthony, 23
Tudor, Mr: ice exporter, 4
tumble drier, 60, 179
Turkish baths, 92
Turner and Seymour: can-opener, 146
turnspits, 5–6, 114
Turtleback sewing-machine, 46
Twelvetrees, Harper: washing-machine, 57
Twigg and Dowler: corkscrews, 162
Twyford water-closet, 108
Tyler, Mr: bath-heater, 94
Tyson steam-engine, 50

Uncle Sam stove, 118
Uneek: knife-cleaner, 166
Universal boot- and shoe-cleaner, 169
Universal mixer, 161
Universal vacuum-cleaner, 88
Universal washing-machine, 63–4

vacuum-cleaners, 27, 31, 80–9, 179, 187
  electric, 82, 86–9
  fixed, 84–5
  lawsuits, 81–2
  portable, 86–9
  selling, 88

'tea-parties', 82
  water-powered, 88
Van Heusen: egg-and-cream-beater, 161
Vanek, Joann, 192
vegetable-choppers, 158–9
Victoria knife-cleaner, 168
Vortex vacuum-cleaner, 85
voting rights, 187
Vowel washing-machine, 59

Wakefield, E. G., 32
Walker, Mr: dishwasher, 151
Wanklyn, Professor, 150
Warriner: bath, 94
Wars, First and Second, effects of, viii, 36, 132, 189–90
washbasins, 104–6
washboards, 56, 57
washerwoman, 10, 61–2
  machines imitating, 57, 59
Washerwoman's Assistant, 56
washhouse, 11
washing *see* bathrooms; laundry
washing-machines, viii, 27, 31, 35, 55–65, 178, 179, 187, 195
  automatic, 64
  costs of, 61–2, 64
  electric, 62–5
  hand-operated, 55–62
  rocking, 59
  rotating cylinder, 57, 59–60, 64
  vertical axis, 57, 58, 64
washstands, 104, 106
waste-disposal units, 147, 149
water, 23, 177, 178
  hot, 23–4, 92, 94, 96–7, 101
  in kitchen, 6, 147–50; filters, 149–50
  lack of, 17–18
  motors, 23, 25; for sewing-machines, 51; turbine, 28; for vacuum-cleaners, 88
  see also bathrooms; laundry
Water Witch vacuum-cleaner, 88
water-closets, 18, 106–10
Watney, Dr Bernard, 162
Webster, Robert: mangle, 66

Webster, Thomas, 66
Weir: corkscrews, 162
Weir, James: sewing-machine, 47
Wells: knife-cleaner, 166
Wenham Lake Ice Company, 4
Westinghouse, 30
    iron, 73
Wheeler: water motor, 51
Wheeler, Nathaniel and Wilson,
    Benjamin: sewing-machines,
    42–3, 45, 47, 49–50
Whight and Mann sewing-machine,
    47
White, George, 32
Whittaker Brothers: mangle, 67
Whitworth, Joseph, 77
Wifesjoie gas cooker, 123
Wilkinson, John: steel, 22
Willcox and Gibbs sewing-machine,
    46
Willow: refrigerator, 138
Wilson, Benjamin *see* Wheeler
Winzler, W. A.: gas-cooker, 122
Wittmann water filter, 150

women
    and electricity, 30
    as home-makers, 178, 180, 183,
        185–7, 192, 197
    movement and feminism, 62, 185,
        187, 189
    as servants, 34–5
    as sex objects, 189
    working, 178, 183, 185, 190–2,
        194
Wood, J. Riddall, 17
workhouse diet, 8
Wright, Gwendolyn, 182, 187
Wright, John, and Company: gas
    rings and cookers, 122, 129
wringers, 65, 67, 68–9

yacht stoves, 119–20
Yeandle, Susan, 179
Yorkshire Maiden washing-
    machine, 21, 57, 58
Young, William, 143

Index by Ann Hall